Cloud Auditing Best Practices

Perform Security and IT Audits across AWS, Azure, and GCP by building effective cloud auditing plans

Shinesa Cambric

Michael Ratemo

BIRMINGHAM—MUMBAI

Cloud Auditing Best Practices

Portfolio Manager: Mohd Riyan Khan

Publishing Product Manager: Prachi Sawant

Senior Editor: Divya Vijayan

Technical Editor: Rajat Sharma

Copy Editor: Safis Editing

Project Coordinator: Ashwin Kharwa

Proofreader: Safis Editing

Indexer: Hemangini Bari

Production Designer: Shyam Sundar Korumilli

Marketing Coordinator: Ankita Bhonsle

Senior Marketing Coordinator: Marylou De Mello

First published: January 2023

Production reference: 1151222

Published by Packt Publishing Ltd.
Livery Place
35 Livery Street
Birmingham
B3 2PB, UK.

ISBN 978-1-80324-377-1

www.packt.com

To all the women in technology that continue to press forward and do hard things – you have unknowingly served as mentors, role models, and trailblazers. To Jasmine, Nia, Shawn, and Shani for constantly encouraging me to let my little light shine and being proud of me no matter what I do.

– Shinesa Cambric

To the ones who believed in my potential and planted the seed leading me to pursue the current path. To my mentees and mentors – you helped me discover my passion for educating others. To my family, professional peers, Jacky A., James S., Steve S., and others who pushed and encouraged me to write this book.

– Michael Ratemo

Contributors

About the authors

Shinesa Cambric (CCSP, CISSP, CISA, CISM, CDPSE) is a cloud security, compliance, and identity architect with expertise in the design and implementation of security architecture and controls. Her experience includes designing IAM and governance solutions, building insider threat programs, and providing subject matter expertise on the intersection of governance, risk, and compliance with IT and application security. She is a certification content advisor for CertNexus and CompTIA, her work has been included in global forums, such as RSAC and DevOps.com, and she is a contributing author to the books *97 Things Every Information Security Professional Should Know* and *Shifting Security Left*. Shinesa volunteers, provides subject matter expertise, and mentors with several organizations, including Cloud Security Alliance, fwd:cloudsec, **Women in Cyber Security (WiCys)**, **Information Systems Security Association (ISSA)**, as a training lead with the Women's Society of Cyberjutsu, and as a board member with non-profit group Cloud Girls.

I am extremely blessed to have an opportunity to follow that voice that put a dream in my heart and then provided a pathway for me to act. In my eyes, this was nothing short of miraculous.

I want to give special thanks to Prachi Sawant at Packt for connecting with me, believing in my idea, and constant support. You are amazing!

Thank you to my co-author, Michael Ratemo, for taking this journey with me. I reached out and you didn't hesitate to come on board and make history. I know the personal sacrifices this took and it means a lot.

Huge thanks to Evan Wolfe and Mani Keerthi for your feedback and even more so for your continued friendship and support. I wish everyone were so fortunate to have people like you in their corner.

Finally, a huge thank you to my family and friends for your continued love and support!

Michael Ratemo (CISSP, CISA, CISM, GCSA, CCSK, CIA) is a cybersecurity leader and Principal Consultant at Cyber Security Simplified. He speaks security in a language businesses can understand and has built a career creating effective security strategies that are customized to protect organizations. He is skilled in elevating the effectiveness of an organization's security programs, to help drive business value and mitigate risks across large and complex environments. In addition, Michael is the author of the LinkedIn Learning Course, *Building and Auditing a Cyber Security Program*. Michael holds a BS in Computer Science and engineering from the University of Texas at Arlington, and an MBA from the University of North Texas.

I want to thank Shinesa Cambric, my amazing co-author, for sharing the vision to create this book. Having an idea and turning it into reality is not as easy as it sounds. Throughout our professional experiences, we noted a gap in how cloud audits were being performed, hence we sought to create a solution to fill this need. Even though the process of writing the book was demanding, it provided a very enriching experience.

In addition, I want to thank members of the Packt team, who provided unique insight into the content of the book. Special thanks to Prachi Sawant, Publishing Product Manager at Packt, for your encouragement and guidance every step of the way.

Finally, to everyone at the Cloud Security Alliance (CSA), and specifically, Rick Blue, Global Director, and training partners at Cloud Security Alliance. I am tremendously grateful for your support and incredible inspiration.

About the reviewers

Evan Wolfe (CISSP) is a cybersecurity professional with over 10 years of experience working in information technology, with a primary focus on cloud engineering and security. Evan has been an instructor for Dallas College, where he taught courses on AWS, developing applications in the cloud, and Kubernetes. He received his bachelor's degree in Computer Information Technology from California State University, Northridge and is currently pursuing his master's degree in cybersecurity from Georgia Institute of Technology. Currently he is focused on leading cloud security initiatives through software engineering, data analytics, automation, and security testing.

Mani Keerthi Nagothu is a cybersecurity professional with global work experience. Her expertise is in cybersecurity strategy, incident response, risk management, security awareness, and training. She has been a speaker at various conferences including (ISC)^2 Security Congress, InfoSec World, Cloud Security Alliance, and many more. She is passionate about sharing knowledge with others and spends her time in cybersecurity research and latest trends in the industry.

Table of Contents

Part 2: Cloud Security and IT Controls

3

4

5

Part 3: Executing an Effective Enterprise Cloud Audit Plan

6

7

8

9

Walk-Through – Assessing Policy Settings and Resource Controls   199

10

Walk-Through – Assessing Change Management, Logging, and Monitoring Policies   209

Preface

As many companies move to the cloud and shift business operations to hybrid, single cloud, or multi-cloud environments, it's important that enterprise IT auditors be prepared with the tools and knowledge to effectively assess risk and controls, given this a business trend that is here to stay. Using assessment procedures and frameworks based on on-premise and legacy environments doesn't fully translate to cloud environments, leaving the enterprise with potential gaps in risk control coverage. This book will guide an auditor to understand where security controls can and do exist, procedures for accessing them for review, and best practices for testing their effectiveness. By the end of the book, you will be able to build an audit plan and assess security and compliance controls for the three major enterprise cloud environments (Amazon, Google, and Microsoft).

Who this book is for

This book is primarily intended for IT and security auditors who are responsible for building audit plans and testing the effectiveness of controls within an enterprise that may be moving, or has already moved to adopting cloud services. This book provides insight for beginner to advanced IT and Security auditors looking to learn more about what exists in the cloud so that they can ask questions and leverage tools that may lead to better test coverage. Other IT professionals whose job includes assessing compliance, such as DevSecOps teams, identity, and access management analysts, cloud engineers, and cloud security architects, will also find plenty of useful information in this book. Before you get started, you'll need a basic understanding of IT systems, cloud environments, and a solid grasp of IT general computing controls and cybersecurity basics. However, past experience configuring or performing a risk assessment on cloud environments is not required.

What this book covers

Chapter 1, Cloud Architecture and Navigation, provides a fundamental understanding of what a cloud environment is, navigating through different cloud provider environments, and roles and responsibilities between the cloud service provider and an auditor.

Chapter 2, Effective Techniques for Preparing to Audit Cloud Environments, covers the standard resources available to develop an audit plan, and align controls to a cloud environment, and the tools for policy and compliance automation.

Chapter 3, Identity and Access Management Controls, walks through configuration and control options for a digital identity, including authentication and authorization and reviewing activity logs.

Chapter 4, Network, Infrastructure, and Security Controls, looks at policies and options for defining and controlling network and infrastructure access and navigating security control centers.

Chapter 5, Financial Resource and Change Management Controls, introduces features available within each of the cloud environments for resource management, including billing and cost controls, and tracking changes within the cloud environment.

Chapter 6, Tips and Techniques for Advanced Auditing, provides guidance on common pitfalls an IT auditor should look out for, tips and techniques to leverage, and ideas for preparing for more advanced audits, including a primer on other cloud environments such as Alibaba, IBM, and Oracle.

Chapter 7, Tools for Monitoring and Assessing, gives a deeper insight on tools and options that exist for auditors to monitor cloud platforms, within each of the three major cloud providers.

Chapter 8, Walk-Through – Assessing IAM Controls, covers simple assessments for hands-on experience assessing identity and access management controls within the three major cloud providers.

Chapter 9, Walk-Through – Assessing Policy Settings and Resource Controls, provides practice opportunities for assessing security and compliance settings, and reviewing resource management controls.

Chapter 10, Walk-Through – Assessing Change Management, Logging, and Monitoring Policies, offers an opportunity to practice assessing compliance for changes made within the cloud environment, as well as how to leverage cloud native tools for performing logging and monitoring in the cloud.

To get the most out of this book

To navigate through the hands-on practice chapters of the book, it's best to have a "sandbox" environment with some administrative privileges or set up your own personal cloud environment for Amazon Web Services, Microsoft Azure, and Google Cloud Platform. If you choose to set up your own personal cloud environment, at the time of this writing, each of the three major cloud providers has options for a setup that is free for at least the first 30 days and then moves to a "pay-as-you-go" model. Please carefully review the terms and agreements to understand the financial implications of long-term usage.

Software/hardware covered in the book	Operating system requirements
Any of the latest versions of Google Chrome or Microsoft Edge	Windows, macOS, or Linux (any)
Amazon Web Services	Windows, macOS, or Linux (any)
Microsoft Azure	Windows, macOS, or Linux (any)
Google Cloud Platform	Windows, macOS, or Linux (any)

Download the color images

We also provide a PDF file that has color images of the screenshots and diagrams used in this book. You can download it here: `https://packt.link/Kq3mr`.

Conventions used

There are a number of text conventions used throughout this book.

Any command-line input or output is written as follows:

```
aws iam-list users
```

Bold: Indicates a new term, an important word, or words that you see on screen. For instance, words in menus or dialog boxes appear in **bold**. Here is an example: "A **cloud service provider** (CSP) may want to provide a certification to its customers regarding its defined and operating controls through a **System and Organization Controls 2 (SOC 2)**."

> Tips or important notes
> Appear like this.

Get in touch

Feedback from our readers is always welcome.

General feedback: If you have questions about any aspect of this book, email us at customercare@ packtpub.com and mention the book title in the subject of your message.

Errata: Although we have taken every care to ensure the accuracy of our content, mistakes do happen. If you have found a mistake in this book, we would be grateful if you would report this to us. Please visit www.packtpub.com/support/errata and fill in the form.

Piracy: If you come across any illegal copies of our works in any form on the internet, we would be grateful if you would provide us with the location address or website name. Please contact us at copyright@packt.com with a link to the material.

If you are interested in becoming an author: If there is a topic that you have expertise in and you are interested in either writing or contributing to a book, please visit authors.packtpub.com.

Share your thoughts

Once you've read *Cloud Auditing Best Practices*, we'd love to hear your thoughts! Scan the QR code below to go straight to the Amazon review page for this book and share your feedback.

https://packt.link/r/1803243775

Your review is important to us and the tech community and will help us make sure we're delivering excellent quality content.

Download a free PDF copy of this book

Thanks for purchasing this book!

Do you like to read on the go but are unable to carry your print books everywhere? Is your eBook purchase not compatible with the device of your choice?

Don't worry, now with every Packt book you get a DRM-free PDF version of that book at no cost.

Read anywhere, any place, on any device. Search, copy, and paste code from your favorite technical books directly into your application.

The perks don't stop there, you can get exclusive access to discounts, newsletters, and great free content in your inbox daily

Follow these simple steps to get the benefits:

1. Scan the QR code or visit the link below

https://packt.link/free-ebook/9781803243771

2. Submit your proof of purchase
3. That's it! We'll send your free PDF and other benefits to your email directly

Part 1:
The Basics of Cloud Architecture and Navigating – Understanding Enterprise Cloud Auditing Essentials

This section will cover the essential knowledge of cloud structure and design, navigating within an enterprise cloud environment, the roles and responsibilities as they relate to security controls, and preparing to audit **IaaS (Infrastructure as a Service)** and **PaaS (Platform as a Service)** service cloud models as an enterprise IT auditor.

This part comprises the following chapters:

- *Chapter 1, Cloud Architecture and Navigation*
- *Chapter 2, Effective Techniques for Preparing to Audit Cloud Environments*

1

Cloud Architecture and Navigation

As companies become increasingly more digital and shift to the use of cloud platforms and services to meet demands for availability, flexibility, and scalability, the toolset of an IT auditor must expand to meet this shift. For many companies, many of their critical operations are being performed either partially or entirely within cloud and even multi-cloud environments. As an auditor, it's important to have the skills necessary to understand risks when using cloud services and assess the applicability and effectiveness of controls to protect company assets when using cloud services.

In our first chapter, we will focus on providing an overview of responsibilities when assessing risks and controls, as well as navigation within cloud environments.

In this chapter, we'll cover the following topics:

- Understanding cloud auditing
- Cloud architecture and service models
- Navigating cloud provider environments

By the end of this chapter, we will have a good understanding of how cloud shared responsibility impacts you as an IT auditor, what are the different cloud architectures and deployments you may encounter, and the fundamental navigation skills you need to interact with the three major cloud computing platforms.

Understanding cloud auditing

As companies look for ways to lower costs, increase efficiency, and enable remote and distributed workforces, the expansion and adoption of cloud subscription-based services continue to grow. Along with that growth, there's a need to make sure the IT controls for a company have been reviewed, adapted, and adequately applied and assessed to address the criticality of cloud services used as part of the IT ecosystem.

With cloud environments, several different types of **auditing** exist. A **cloud service provider** (**CSP**) may want to provide a certification to its customers regarding its defined and operating controls through a **System and Organization Controls 2** (**SOC 2**). Other companies may want to certify that their environments meet **International Organization for Standardization** (**ISO**) or **National Institute of Standards and Technology** (**NIST**) standards or implement controls according to a given compliance framework, such as **Payment Card Industry** (**PCI**) compliance. In this book, we will focus on auditing a CSP customer environment from a general IT computing perspective.

Whether you are performing as an internal or external auditor within a cloud customer (enterprise) environment, it's important for you to understand how an IT computing control that's traditionally been applied against an on-premise environment may still be relevant. However, it will require adjustments to your testing procedures when validating them in a cloud environment. An example of this would be **PCI Data Security Standard** (**PCI DSS**) controls requiring organizations to establish and maintain a detailed enterprise asset inventory. The dynamic nature of cloud environments and the speed and scale at which new assets can be provisioned can make this a challenge. In this instance, not only should an enterprise IT auditor be aware of whether this inventory exists and covers all enterprise assets to ensure they have effective control coverage, but they should also be aware of the processes around billing and financial management within the cloud, how change management and resource allocation are performed, and which users have administrative rights to these functions. In some cases, you may need to consider how the control has to support the effective operations of a multi-cloud environment and the ability across cloud provider platforms to satisfy a particular control. The ability to categorize and quantify risks related to the use and integration of cloud services into an organization's business processes is quickly becoming an essential skill for auditors.

Shared responsibility of IT cloud controls

When planning and executing an audit, it is critical to understand cloud shared responsibility (and in the case of **Google Cloud Platform** (**GCP**), "*shared fate*") model agreements with CSPs whose services have been integrated into the customer environment in scope to be audited. The intent of the shared responsibility model agreements is to provide clear guidance on the security, controls, and obligations to compliance that the CSP is responsible for, and what the cloud consumer/customer will need to take responsibility for. Anytime you have a cloud-based component as part of your business operations, it is important that you understand the shared responsibility model with that CSP. In general, shared responsibility simply means there are actions, tools, processes, capabilities, and controls that the CSP is responsible for and others that the cloud customer will be responsible for, and some that require joint responsibility for full control coverage. An example of this would be in the case of *NIST Cybersecurity Framework control RS.CO.1: Personnel know their role and order of operations when a response is needed.* In a traditional on-premise environment where the company owns and manages all parts of the infrastructure, understanding who has responsibility for this control and testing compliance of the control would likely be very straightforward. In cloud environments, and especially in multi-cloud or hybrid environments, assessing this control becomes much more complex.

Role of an IT auditor

Shared responsibility agreements help with understanding what information or test evidence may need to be obtained directly from the CSP, which areas the CSP expects the customer to have controls for, and which areas carry a joint responsibility for defining and implementing security controls and protections. In particular, the last two areas should be a primary focus for an IT auditor to understand which risks the customer (enterprise) has elected to accept or address, through security or configuration controls, and build an audit plan that assesses the effectiveness of those controls. In most cases, it will be helpful (and potentially required) for the IT auditor to obtain an assurance report from the CSP, with SOC 2 *Type 2* reports being a common report from the CSP that provides a "qualified opinion", based on an independent audit, of the effectiveness of the operating controls for which the CSP has taken responsibility. The report can be used to identify deficiencies in testing and control coverage that need to be addressed for the customer (enterprise) environment. A SOC 2 Type 2 report is based on "trust service principles" defined by the **American Institute of Certified Public Accountants (AICPA)**. These principles cover the categories of security, privacy, confidentiality, integrity, and availability for the CSP environment. An independent assessor determines if the CSP complies with one or more of the five trust principles and issues a report attesting to the operating effectiveness of the control over a given time period (generally 12 months). Based on the business practices of the organization undergoing a SOC 2 assessment, the content of the report may vary. Each organization can design its own control(s) to adhere to one or all of the trust service principles. As an enterprise IT auditor, you will be responsible for reviewing and understanding the "qualified opinion" on the SOC report, as well as closely reviewing the scope of which trust principles have been covered and the time period of testing. Additionally, organizations undergoing a SOC 2 compliance review may elect not to perform additional procedures to mitigate any residual risks for gaps identified in the SOC report or for trust principle areas for which they have elected to not have controls. You will need to review and support your organization in discerning if there is an effective level of coverage. You should also note that SOC 2 Type 2 reports may not be acceptable for some international companies. For example, some international companies in Europe prefer *ISO 27001*. Your auditing procedures and review of shared responsibility need to take into account the regions for which the cloud environment has been deployed, the business usage and types of applications that will be supported, and the data protections required across the regions. Consideration also needs to be taken regarding the timing of received assurance reports. Depending upon your organization's audit cycle, there may be a gap in the timing coverage of the CSP's standard assurance report made available to all of its customers, and the audit period and requirements of your organization for when control is to be tested. In this case, you will need to obtain a bridge report that provides an attestation of control effectiveness during the gap period.

When operating within a multi-cloud environment, there are likely to be many similarities in the cloud shared responsibility model across cloud providers; however, each agreement should be reviewed independently and assessed as part of an end-to-end review of control coverage for every relevant process executing through the cloud environment. Additionally, the responsibilities between the CSP and cloud customer may differ depending upon the vendors, services, and deployment models used, requiring the auditor to be aware of the complete architecture of the customer's cloud environment, the services being consumed, and how those services relate back to business and IT operations. Additional resources on shared responsibility with the three major CSPs can be found in the following list:

- **Shared Responsibility Model, Amazon Web Services (AWS) Elastic Compute Cloud (EC2)**: `https://aws.amazon.com/compliance/shared-responsibility-model/`

- **Shared Responsibility Model, Microsoft Azure**: `https://docs.microsoft.com/en-us/azure/security/fundamentals/shared-responsibility`

- **Shared Responsibility Model**, GCP: `https://cloud.google.com/blog/products/identity-security/google-cloud-security-foundations-guide`

- **Cloud Security Alliance** explains shared responsibility: `https://cloudsecurityalliance.org/blog/2020/08/26/shared-responsibility-model-explained/`

Now that we discussed the types of cloud auditing covered in this book and now understand the shared responsibility between cloud providers and the cloud customer to implement IT controls, we have begun to build our foundation for applying best practices in cloud auditing. To further build your cloud foundation, we will now review cloud architecture and service models and the impact they have on cloud auditing.

Cloud architecture and service models

As an IT auditor, it is important to be aware of the cloud architectural and deployment design changes that have been made and that influence operations within the IT environment being audited. Knowing how cloud services have been enabled and integrated with business operations is key to validating the scope of compliance testing and potential exposure related to risk.

Understanding gaps or weaknesses within the *architecture* and *design* of a cloud environment is essential to providing guidance on where there may be breakdowns of the **confidentiality**, **integrity**, or **availability** (**CIA**) business goals of an organization. Providing a technical understanding of how to identify these gaps and which technical or non-technical solutions exist for mitigation or remediation is one of the goals of this book. The cloud architecture and deployment choices may not have only impacted the technology in use, but may have also impacted which employees may be maintaining a given service on-premise versus within the cloud, and thus impact who would need to be contacted for walk-through interviews, architectural diagrams, and evidence gathering. For example, the employees responsible for managing on-premise network configuration may be different than those who manage the virtual configuration within the cloud environment.

It may have also impacted the legal and regulatory compliance an organization must meet and how those obligations should now be tested. In the previous example, where separate employees are now responsible for maintaining network infrastructure based upon where it is done, understanding this separation of responsibility may also be a factor in effectively assessing the **separation of duties (SoD)** as well as identity and access control policies throughout the environment. Determining if the business operates within a hybrid (using both *on-premise* and *cloud-based* services), single-cloud, or multi-cloud environment has direct implications on the audit program, risks to be assessed, testing steps, and testing evidence that needs to be produced. For companies that have an existing legacy environment and are migrating to the cloud, or may be operating in a hybrid landscape, identifying which service models are in use will help in validating existing controls are still applicable (given the cloud shared responsibility model), and if so, are being tested thoroughly and within the right technologies.

To prepare you to apply best practices in auditing various types of cloud configurations, we will now review cloud architectures, and next, we will look at cloud services. We will close out the chapter with information on how to navigate within the three main cloud providers.

Cloud architecture

There are an infinite number of variations on how a company may choose to implement its cloud environment, and each may have nuances to consider when performing an audit assessment; however, we will focus on the most important general concepts you will encounter and need to know to build a good foundation concerning cloud architecture. Let's find out what they are in the following sections.

Public and private cloud deployments

A company may choose to operate within either a *public* or *private* cloud environment, or even have some combination of the two, depending upon their business, operational, security, and/or compliance requirements. With a **public cloud deployment**, the company has chosen to use services from a CSP, where the CSP is managing the physical infrastructure in a location that is owned/managed by the CSP. In the case of a **private cloud deployment**, the infrastructure may be managed both on-premise at the customer's location or by a third-party CSP. A private cloud restricts the use of the infrastructure to a single company or organization.

Hybrid cloud environments

Considering there are companies that have been around much longer than the concept of *cloud computing* has been in existence, it can be expected that there are a large number of organizations operating in environments that use a combination of on-premise and cloud IT technologies. This may be due to the complexity of migrating all their legacy functionality to the cloud, or there may be legal, compliance, security, or data sensitivity reasons. Referring to the information we covered on the shared responsibility agreements between CSPs and customers, the customer may have chosen not to accept the risk related to moving certain applications or workloads into a cloud system. Having the context of why the customer is operating within a hybrid environment is highly relevant to understanding which security and data controls should be in place to maintain the separation, assessing the effectiveness of controls that have been put in place to protect boundaries, and understanding and articulating the risk if boundaries have been crossed as part of the use or integration of a particular cloud service.

Cloud-native/cloud-first environments

Some companies have chosen to adopt a technology philosophy of only using solutions that are built in the cloud and specifically for cloud environments. In this type of architecture, it comes critical to have reliance on third-party audits (such as SOC 2), the time period and cycle of such audits, and the assessment of where gaps may exist between the third-party-assessed controls of the cloud provider compared to the controls that the customer requires.

Multi-cloud environments

As companies utilize more cloud services, it is becoming increasingly common to find architectures that are based on **multi-cloud** environments. Having a multi-cloud environment means the company is leveraging one or more service models from at least two different cloud providers. In some cases, this may be to take advantage of the best-in-class features of a given CSP, or it may be to support redundancy or other business operational requirements. In assessing multi-cloud environments, the auditor should have familiarity with each of the cloud platforms as well as an understanding of any integration occurring between them. Now that we have learned about forms of cloud architecture and their impact on auditing, we will now look at the various types of cloud services.

Cloud services

In general, there are three cloud service models covered in the following list. This book will focus on the first two:

- **Infrastructure as a Service (IaaS)**: In this service model, the cloud customer manages the virtual compute, storage, and network resources through a portal (also known as a management plane), or through APIs with the CSP. The customer is not responsible for securing the underlying physical hardware but is responsible for the operating systems and software running within this service. As an auditor, some key testing and control questions to ask could include the following:

  - Who has access to the management plane to administer the infrastructure resources?

  - Who has access to the administration APIs?

  - Which images are being used, and do they adhere to company policies and standards?

  - What is the backup strategy being used for the infrastructure?

  - What is the process used for maintaining patching?

- **Platform as a Service (PaaS)**: In this service model, the CSP manages the hosting environment, services, and tools, and the customer creates, manages, and deploys the applications running within the environment. The CSP is generally responsible for both the physical and virtual infrastructure security and maintenance. As an auditor, some key testing and control questions to ask might include those previously shown, as well as the following:

- What is the process for reviewing and managing changes by the CSP as part of periodic updates and patches it may be applying?

- Who has access, and what is the process to deploy a new application?

- Is this application internal- or external-facing? What are the network controls surrounding who can get to this application?

- **Software as a Service (SaaS)**: With this service model, the customer is interacting with an application that has been built and provided by the CSP. This application may be hosted with the CSP or with another third party; however, responsibility for the security and configuration of the entire underlying infrastructure is generally the responsibility of the CSP. In this instance, some key testing and control questions an auditory may ask could include the following:

  - Which data does this application have access to?

  - How is this application integrated through APIs and other methods into other parts of the IT environment?

  - Who is responsible for managing users and the user life cycle regarding access to this application?

In the previous sections, we covered some foundational information about the architecture of cloud environments and the types of cloud services that you as an auditor may find as you begin to perform an IT general computing controls audit. As a final step in building your foundational toolkit and preparing to learn auditing best practices, we'll next look at how to perform basic navigation to a cloud environment.

Navigating cloud provider environments

To effectively audit an IaaS or PaaS deployment for any of the three major cloud providers, it is important to understand basic navigational components within those platforms. In this section, we will gain a basic understanding of fundamental navigation within **AWS EC2**, **GCP**, and **Microsoft Azure**.

Cloud platforms and services are inherently dynamic, and this is one of the benefits of leveraging a cloud service. With that in mind, the navigational components within a cloud environment do change, including the renaming of components and services. The navigation structure presented in this section is what exists as of the time of this writing. We will focus primarily on the use of the web-based console for accessing and navigating components within the cloud environments.

Note that each of the cloud providers leverages **role-based access control (RBAC)**. This means that the content you can access and view or maintains is based upon the access that has been granted to your account. To become more familiar with navigation within the cloud providers, I encourage you to set up a free account that you can use for training and development purposes to view the full breadth and depth of cloud services from an administrator's perspective.

Navigating Amazon AWS EC2

To enter the AWS management console, we will begin at the following URL: `console.aws.amazon.com`.

Depending upon your organization's **identity and access management (IAM)** integration and customizations, you may have an organization-specific URL to use and additional authentication procedures. For new and/or uncustomized AWS deployments, you will be routed to a sign-in page similar to what is shown in the following screenshot:

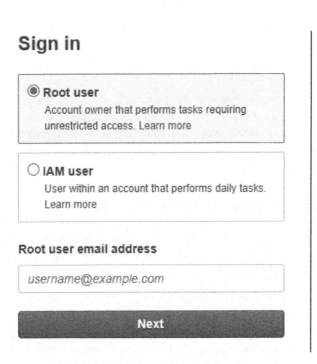

Figure 1.1 – AWS console initial sign-in

Upon successful authentication, depending upon the roles and permissions granted to your account, you will find a **Console Home** page, as shown in *Figure 1.2*. Please note that depending upon the region selected when the cloud provider relationship was established, the region that appears within your URL after sign-in may differ. The AWS Console Home page is made up of various **widgets**, and this home page is customizable, meaning the widgets may be removed and other widgets added. On the left top panel of the AWS **Console Home** page, you will see a **Services** option:

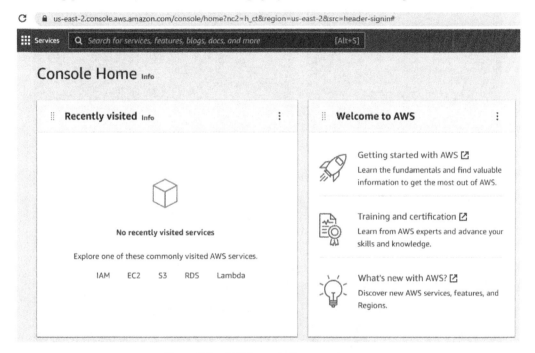

Figure 1.2 – AWS Console Home main page

Within the **Services** option, you will find a navigable list of various AWS service groupings. Clicking on hyperlinked items within the **Services** list will present an additional list of options aligned with those service groupings or categories:

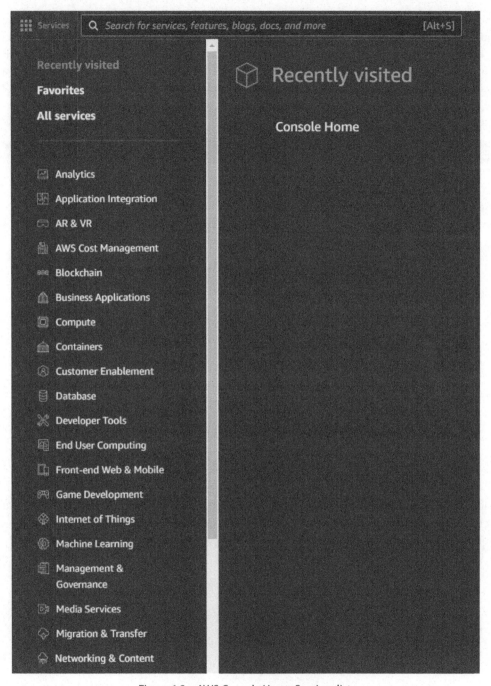

Figure 1.3 – AWS Console Home Services list

On the right side of the **Console Home** page, you will find a drop-down option available under the account login that will display **Account ID** information, as well as additional information related to the **Organization**, **Billing Dashboard**, and **Security credentials** configuration, and **Settings**. Let's see how that looks in the following screenshot:

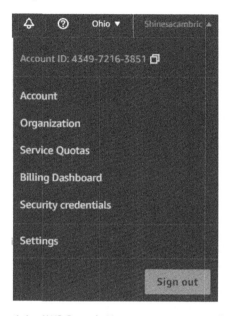

Figure 1.4 – AWS Console Home account sign-In details

Within the main body of the **Console Home** page, you will find widgets available for learning more about AWS, the health status of your AWS environment, and direct links to AWS cloud services:

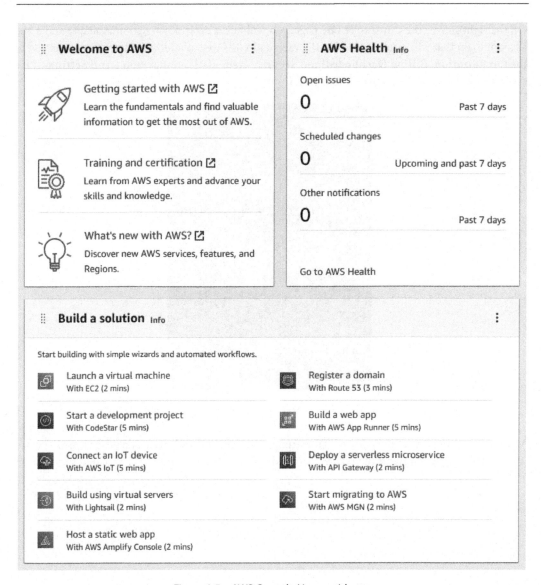

Figure 1.5 – AWS Console Home widgets

Now that you've learned how to successfully sign in to the AWS console, understand the items that you may see within the **Console Home** page, how to navigate and find a list of services within AWS, and understand that customizable sections of the home page in AWS are known as widgets, let's take a look at navigating within the Microsoft Azure portal.

Navigating the Microsoft Azure portal

To enter the **Microsoft Azure** management console, we can begin at the following URLs: `portal.azure.com` or `azure.microsoft.com`.

Depending upon your organization's IAM integration and customizations, you may have an organization-specific URL to use and additional authentication procedures. Let's take a look at what your initial sign-in experience in Azure may look like in the following screenshot:

Figure 1.6 – Microsoft Azure initial sign-in

The Azure portal home page is made up of various **blades**, and depending upon your organization's configuration, your initial entry into the portal may look similar to what's in the following screenshot, which shows a list of services along with a panel of recent resources that have been accessed:

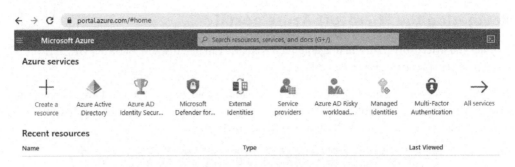

Figure 1.7 – Microsoft Azure portal home page

On the left panel, you will find a drop-down menu that will allow you to navigate to a *dashboard* or a list of *services* and *resources*:

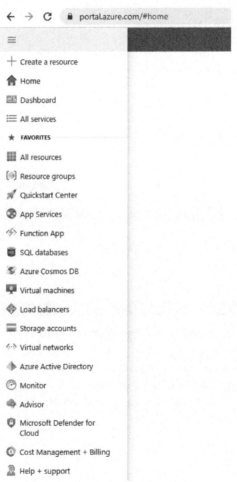

Figure 1.8 – Microsoft Azure portal home page navigation panel

Additionally, you will find options under the **Navigate** section, which are **Subscriptions**, **Resource groups**, **All resources**, and **Dashboard**, in the middle of the home page pane, as follows:

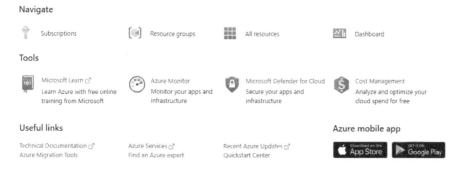

Figure 1.9 – Microsoft Azure portal dashboard Navigate section

When navigating to **Dashboard**, you may have a list of *private* or *organizational*-level dashboards that have been made available to you, and these dashboards may be customizable:

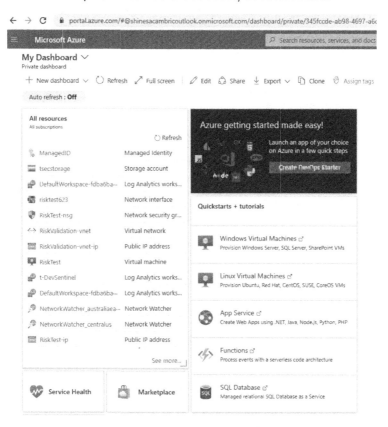

Figure 1.10 – Microsoft Azure portal personal dashboard

On the top right of the Azure portal home page, you may find additional information about your account, or you can switch the Azure portal directory you are logged in to, assuming you have additional accounts and permissions. To learn more about where these options appear, let's take a look at the following screenshot:

Figure 1.11 – Microsoft Azure portal sign-in details

Additional information you may be able to access in this section, depending upon your roles and permissions, includes permissions assigned to you, billing details for the Azure account, and contact information associated with your account:

Figure 1.12 – Microsoft Azure portal account details

You are now well on your way to a great understanding of navigating within the three major cloud providers. We've walked through how to navigate in both AWS and Azure, and now let's look at the final cloud provider we will be learning to navigate—GCP.

Navigating GCP

To enter the GCP management console, we can begin at the following URL: `console.cloud.google.com`.

Depending upon your organization's IAM integration and customizations, you may have an organization-specific URL to use and additional authentication procedures, but the home page should look something like this:

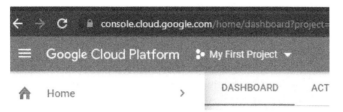

Figure 1.13 – GCP home page

The GCP home page is made up of various **cards**, and depending upon your organization's configuration, your initial entry into the portal may look like what's seen in *Figure 1.14*, with a list of cards displaying available resources and status, along with an open panel of pinned and available products and resources that have recently been accessed:

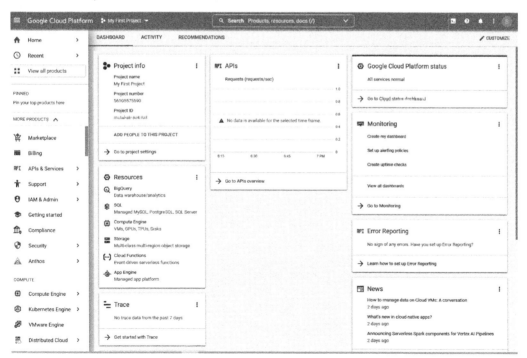

Figure 1.14 – GCP home page dashboard

We've covered a lot in this section that will help you with successfully navigating to and within each of the three major cloud provider platforms—AWS, Microsoft Azure, and GCP. For each of these providers, we've learned about starting URLs that may be used to sign in, what an initial home page or dashboard may look like, and some of the terminology associated with navigating within each of these providers. Our foundational toolkit is now complete!

Summary

In this chapter, we have reviewed the concept of cloud auditing and the importance of understanding the concept of cloud shared responsibility models and how those may differ across cloud providers, cloud deployment models, and cloud services. We have also looked at general concepts to be aware of related to cloud architecture, deployment, and service models and how this may impact the risk and compliance assessments for an organization. Finally, we reviewed fundamental concepts around the basic structure and navigation within each of the three major cloud platforms covered in this book (AWS, Azure, and GCP).

Knowing these foundational concepts will establish the primary tools you need to begin deeper learning on the best practices of cloud auditing, allowing you to define a list of cloud and IT security controls to be considered, identify IAM controls that are in place, and utilize policy and automation for your audits.

Now that we have reviewed these core concepts of cloud environments, in the next chapter, we'll begin identifying effective techniques for preparing to audit cloud environments.

2
Effective Techniques for Preparing to Audit Cloud Environments

The areas and scope for your company's audit will be dependent on your company's goals, controls, and environment setup. However, when it comes to cloud auditing, there are some key common elements that you can use to ensure you are successfully prepared to assess the cloud environment according to the defined audit scope. By understanding these elements, you can take advantage of established tools and frameworks to build confidence in the coverage and completeness of your audit.

This chapter will guide you through cloud auditing frameworks, as well as cloud vendor and open source tools available to assist with testing controls that verify management goals for compliance.

In this chapter, we'll cover the following main topics:

- Understanding the steps in preparing to audit an enterprise customer cloud environment
- Effective techniques to map controls to cloud auditing activities
- Basic tools and frameworks to build out your cloud audit program
- Opportunities to leverage automation to assess and enforce policy and compliance

By the end of this chapter, we will have the insight and resources needed to develop an audit program for your enterprise customer cloud environment that builds on established tools and frameworks for assessing and automating controls.

Preparing to perform a cloud assessment

As an auditor, you are performing a critical role in assessing cloud controls. According to several reputable organizations, most cloud security failures and breaches are due to misconfigurations. Diligent and thorough auditing can help you identify those misconfigurations so that they can be addressed and the associated risks can be remediated. Like many other IT audits, performing a cloud assessment begins with a foundation of IT general controls. A gold standard reference for IT general controls is ISACA COBIT controls. In the cloud context, you need to establish other referential and ancillary frameworks that will help with establishing an audit program that is specific to the cloud. The **Cloud Security Alliance (CSA) Cloud Controls Matrix (CCM)** is one the leading cloud-specific frameworks. More information on additional frameworks will be shared in the *Auditing frameworks and governance* section later in this chapter.

In preparing to start your enterprise cloud assessment, you must determine the management objective of this audit. The objective of the audit will be determined through discussion with the management of the cloud customer. Document the stated business purpose for which the cloud environments and services to be audited exist. Not only does this help determine the approach that should be taken with the audit, but this will also determine the most relevant frameworks to be utilized, as well as the scope of controls to be assessed as you begin to build an audit plan that effectively covers the in-scope components of the enterprise cloud environment(s).

The next step is understanding the cloud service model (IaaS, PaaS, or SaaS) and deployment model (public, private, community, or hybrid) to enhance the context and further define the scope. The cloud service model identifies to what extent resources are managed by the cloud customer in comparison to the cloud service provider (shared responsibility model). As a cloud customer moves from SaaS to PaaS to IaaS, their responsibility accumulates and so does the risk. For example, in SaaS, the cloud customer is not responsible for applying security patches to the application, but in IaaS, the cloud customer is responsible for applying patches to any application installed on the infrastructure.

In addition, the cloud deployment model defines the specific type of cloud environment based on ownership, as well as the cloud's nature and purpose.

The next essential area will involve gathering security and compliance artifacts and documentation from the cloud service provider. Each of the big three cloud service providers – AWS, Azure, and GCP – provide on-demand access to security and compliance reports for the products and services that they run.

In AWS, these reports are available in Amazon Artifact: `https://aws.amazon.com/artifact/`.

In Azure, the reports are available in Microsoft Trust Center: `https://www.microsoft.com/en-us/security`.

Finally, in GCP, the reports are available in Google Compliance Reports Manager: `https://cloud.google.com/security/compliance/compliance-reports-manager`.

Reports available include **Service Organization Control (SOC)** reports, **International Organization for Standardization (ISO)** reports, and certifications from accreditation bodies, among other documentation. For audits related to trust services criteria (security, availability, processing integrity, confidentiality, or PR), the IT auditor should review a SOC 2 type 2 report. For audits related to internal control over financial reporting, the IT auditor should review the SOC 1 type 2 report.

Confirm if there is an existing cloud-related framework in use or work with stakeholders to identify a framework that incorporates cloud-specific functions. The CSA CCM is one of the leading cloud-specific frameworks that the IT auditor can utilize. (More on industry frameworks that can be used is covered in the *Auditing frameworks and governance* section later in this chapter.) In alignment with other IT audits, you will need to review the risk register, previously assessed controls, and previous audit results. Identify if anything has changed in the risk management approach and if any previously assessed components have been newly migrated to the cloud.

If any compensating controls have been identified, are they still relevant based on any new or changed operations within the cloud environment? Determine if the controls are operated manually or automated and if that's changed since the last time a formal audit was conducted. Here, you will also want to access and review any cloud provider SLAs, compliance reports, and audit attestations, such as in a SOC 2 type 2 report and service trust reports from the cloud service provider, and contract agreements, and compare this with the customer controls list and risk register to identify coverage and ownership of controls for customer-identified risks related to cloud applications and services. For both IT and business processes now performed in a cloud system, does the current control list adequately cover the identified risks, risk classification, exposure, and plans to address? As cloud services often change, determine if the testing procedures noted are still accurate or if any updates are needed.

As the next step, get an inventory of the cloud applications in use by both business and IT individuals to fully vet which cloud applications and services are in scope for the audit. A comparison should be made of the controls within the IT network and integration architecture that includes the cloud applications and services. In addition to understanding third-party integrations, APIs, and workload identities impacting the network and integration architecture for the cloud systems, it's also key to understand the criticality of the data, what types of data flow in and out of cloud applications and services, how that data is accessed and processed, and where this data is stored either short or long term within a cloud environment. Be sure to also review the company policies and procedures for IT and cloud computing applications and services to identify any separation-of-duties requirements related to cloud infrastructure components, system access, and data processing that must be enforced at a technical controls level. You should also request information on the roles, responsibilities, and procedures related to supporting, configuring, and using cloud services, as well as responsibilities related to establishing new cloud services and performing billing operations.

As part of the initial audit interviews you would be conducting, you should ask specifically about cloud service points of contact. With the dynamic and self-serve nature of cloud applications and services, functions that were traditionally considered IT responsibilities may now be performed by someone with a traditional business role or title. An auditor should not assume an individual in IT is responsible for the configuration or operational maintenance of a cloud service.

When gathering foundational and control test items, you may have the ability to gather some of this information yourself directly from the cloud application or service through an auditor or view-only role. In some cases, an *auditor* role may provide limited privileges for you to view information for specific areas only and restrict you from others. Some *view-only* capabilities within cloud environments may require elevated rights, which means working with the appropriate administrator of that service to pull the information needed. This book is a guide to knowing what questions to ask and will provide specific guidance on which areas within the cloud environments you should expect to see evidence from based on the control area(s) you are assessing. In summary, here is the checklist for preparing to audit the cloud:

- Define audit objective

- Understand the cloud service and deployment model to define the scope

- Gather security and compliance artifacts and documents from the cloud service provider

- Adopt and tailor a cloud-specific framework

- Identify the current controls and risks

- Get an inventory of cloud applications

- Understand cloud integrations and data flows

- Obtain cloud customer policies, standards, and procedures

Now that we've covered the preparation needed to begin a cloud audit, let's look at techniques for understanding how to effectively map IT general controls to enterprise cloud environments.

Effective techniques for aligning IT controls to cloud environments

As an IT auditor performing risk and controls assessments within an enterprise cloud environment, establishing audit goals is essential to helping you develop a clear alignment between controls to be tested and the process to effectively test those controls within the cloud. As mentioned in the *Preparing to perform a cloud audit* section earlier in this chapter, the paradigm of classifying business versus IT functions has changed with the migration to the cloud, requiring a shift in how we think about and assess technical controls within an enterprise cloud. From a broad sense, in the cloud environment, we should focus on determining whether the risks and controls we are assessing for effectiveness are financially focused, operationally focused, or cybersecurity-focused to come up with a logical grouping or mapping of what should be in scope for testing. Let's look at them in detail:

- **Financially focused**:

    If the risks are determined to be financially focused, the control testing should identify who has access to modify control configurations for establishing new and extending existing resource and application capacity (including automated scripts that may perform this function), how those costs are allocated, and who receives billing and capacity related event information. From a financial standpoint, there also needs to be an awareness of any regulatory and legislative requirements that need to be adhered to (such as PII and data privacy protections) since violations of these requirements could lead to significant financial implications. In this instance, adopting controls and test procedures that focus on data security (storage, masking, encryption, and loss prevention) will be required.

- **Operationally focused**:

    When the controls being assessed are centered around operational risks, the IT auditor will want to scope in controls related to the change management of IT resources within the cloud (including VMs, databases, applications and services, automated scripts, and APIs). To effectively assess change management, an asset inventory should be maintained, and asset management tools, configuration, and automated policies should be in scope for review. There should also be robust logging in place that captures changes being performed, as well as clear procedures and separation of duties technically enabled within the enterprise cloud. The retention period for these logs should also be reviewed. Another area that falls under operational risks would be assessing the software supply chain, especially in the case of enterprises that have adopted PaaS services to support their software development life cycles.

- **Cybersecurity focused**:

    Although cybersecurity has been called out as a separate area of focus, the reality is that anything and everything that is digitally connected should be assessed for cybersecurity risks and control effectiveness. In this section, we've highlighted this separately for ease of pointing out more granular areas of cybersecurity controls. However, as part of due diligence on the part of an IT auditor, we strongly encourage the cybersecurity components to be incorporated into every enterprise cloud audit, and it may be beneficial to have the results of any recent pen testing findings while going through the controls assessment.

Your cybersecurity controls will fall into three categories that align with the acronym **CIA**, which is a well-known acronym within the cybersecurity industry. This acronym stands for **Confidentiality, Integrity, and Availability** and essentially any cybersecurity controls that protect a business should be in support of one or more of these areas:

- In the area of Confidentiality, access to applications, services, and data is limited to those who require it. With this in mind, we should focus on IAM controls that support least-privilege and just-in-time zero-trust access for all identities, logical access controls and data loss procedures, automated policies that enforce security controls on dynamically configured resources (such as VMs), and properly configured network boundary and firewall controls.

- Next in the CIA triad is Integrity. Integrity assessments and controls should validate that applications, resources, and data all exist in the form in which they were intended, and any changes have been appropriately authorized. In the cloud, controls focused on network and infrastructure resource management, default resource images and policies, and change management procedures should all be in scope for review. There should be established technical controls for how changes are approved (or rolled back), and the ability to detect any unauthorized changes in an environment, with an amount of logging configured that aligns with the ability to detect changes as well as the risk appetite of the enterprise. Technical data security policies exist and should also be part of the change management procedures.

- The last component of the CIA triad is Availability. The intent is to ensure cloud services are running and operational based on business service-level requirements. One area to have in scope here would be to assess monitoring and alerting configurations – in the event of service degradation, has monitoring and alerting been established to detect this, and does it align with business service-level requirements? Who will receive alerts and what is the technical process to review and respond? Are there preventative controls that are or can be put in place, such as failovers or automatic capacity increases? Another area to be mindful of when it comes to availability is backups and business continuity. Does the contractual agreement with the cloud service provider align with the business risk appetite and requirements? There should be a review of which resources and services are included in backups, where those backups are being stored, and for how long. And be sure to assess whether backups are being stored in the same region as the primary service and if this is an acceptable risk for the business. Additionally, it's important to understand if the enterprise environment is multi-cloud and how that would impact business continuity.

Going back to *Chapter 1*, *Cloud Architecture and Navigation*, where we discussed shared responsibility and the role of a cloud auditor, we must keep in mind that some of these controls may not be owned or configurable by the enterprise. The cloud service provider may be responsible for some portion of the controls, and it is important to review any agreements for this. Although the cloud service provider may take a level of responsibility, the enterprise still has accountability for effectively controlling risk in their IT and business operations, which may necessitate additional controls above and beyond what the cloud service provider takes responsibility for.

Auditing frameworks and governance

With the growth of enterprises using cloud services, frameworks with specific best practice cloud controls have been created by several reputable sources and are a great starting point for developing new cloud-specific controls for a business. Organizations such as CSA and ISACA have published both general controls for cloud environments, as well as some that are specific to cloud vendors. One thing to keep in mind is that these really should be used as a starting point. Depending on how your enterprise is integrated, the services they've adopted, and if it's a multi-cloud environment, you will likely need to make some adjustments to ensure all risks are covered and that the testing procedures reflect the specific environment you are testing.

The CSA is a non-profit organization that not only offers education and information on securing cloud environments but also offers certifications for individuals as well as an assurance registry of trusted cloud providers. The CCM, which can be found at `https://cloudsecurityalliance.org/research/cloud-controls-matrix/`, is focused on addressing cybersecurity controls and is periodically updated to remain relevant as cloud computing changes. In the *Effective techniques for aligning IT controls to cloud environments* section earlier in the chapter, we reviewed that as an IT auditor who is performing with due diligence within a cloud system, cybersecurity should be reflected in operational risks and fully incorporated into operating controls; referencing the CSA CCM will assist with this. Some additional pros of the CCM are that the controls that are included are mapped to other well-known and global security standards, regulations, and control frameworks, helping to reduce the number of reference resources that might be required based on your auditing goals.

ISACA is another well-known global organization focused on equipping those in the governance, risk, and security domains with best practices, education, and frameworks that support assurance and control assessment. ISACA may be best known for its COBIT Controls framework as well as several certifications related to IT risk management and IT auditing, including the **Certificate of Cloud Auditing Knowledge** (**CCAK**), which was developed in conjunction with the CSA. Like the CSA, they offer a general cloud computing audit program/framework. This program does not provide a map of other industry standards and controls but does map to controls within COBIT. Additionally, ISACA does offer more specific audit programs for some cloud service providers with general testing step information that can be referenced.

In addition to CSA and ISACA resources, traditional security frameworks continue to be extremely valuable when auditing an enterprise cloud environment, and as highlighted earlier in this section, some cloud-specific frameworks refer to other established IT general control frameworks. Another resource that IT auditors may find valuable to help in establishing enterprise cloud controls is the one made available by the **Center for Internet Security** (**CIS**). CIS offers a list of both general and cloud provider-specific controls focused on cybersecurity and hardening an IT/cloud environment. The controls, like what is offered by CSA, are mapped to other established regulatory and security frameworks.

Beyond the items listed, there are many other established frameworks that an IT auditor can certainly use and map cloud controls to. The important step with these traditional frameworks is understanding what your testing procedures will be in the cloud to address that control and for those new to cloud computing, this may be a challenge. Given the additional overhead in performing that step, it is worthwhile to leverage cloud-specific frameworks for the cloud-specific portion of your IT auditing when you are able.

In this section, we've covered helpful techniques for aligning IT general controls with enterprise cloud risk and control assessments. Now that we have an idea of how to align our controls with enterprise cloud environments, let's look at the tools available to assist with performing cloud audits across the three major cloud providers.

Basic cloud auditing tools and frameworks

Each of the three major cloud providers has some inherent capabilities that support gathering audit evidence. These capabilities are represented in cloud-native tools. In addition, open source tools exist for added coverage where cloud-native tools are limited.

Native tools for auditing Amazon AWS

The following are some tools to audit AWS:

- **AWS Security Hub**: AWS Security Hub provides a unified view of the security posture in AWS and helps benchmark the AWS environment against security industry standards and best practices.

  AWS Security Hub aggregates data from multiple AWS services and third-party partner products to enable prioritization of security issues. The following is a screenshot of the interface of AWS Security Hub:

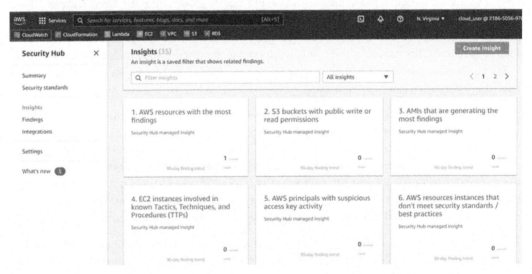

Figure 2.1 – Interface of AWS Security Hub

> **Information**
>
> You can refer to the AWS Security Hub documentation at `https://docs.aws.amazon.com/securityhub/index.html` for more information.

- **AWS Trusted Advisor**: AWS Trusted Advisor provides a set of best practice checks and guidance to provision resources following AWS best practices.

The following screenshot is from the AWS documentation that shows an example of the AWS Trusted Advisor interface:

Figure 2.2 – Trusted Advisor interface

- **AWS Config**: AWS Config is a service that facilitates the evaluation of the configurations of AWS resources. AWS Config can track configuration history and provide notifications when AWS configurations change. Additionally, AWS Config provides you with a way to view and measure compliance within the cloud account based on policies. The following is a screenshot of the interface of AWS Config:

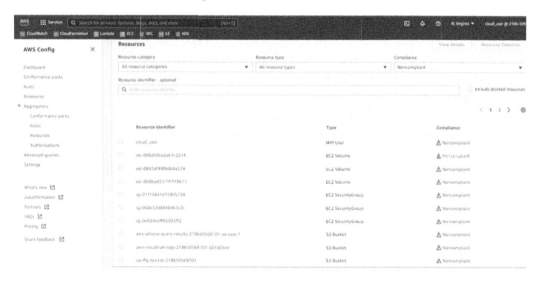

Figure 2.3 – AWS Config interface

- **Amazon Inspector**: Amazon Inspector is a security vulnerability tool used to assess the network visibility and security vulnerability posture of AWS workloads. Amazon Inspector is an automated service that examines AWS workloads for security weaknesses. The following is a screenshot of the interface of Amazon Inspector:

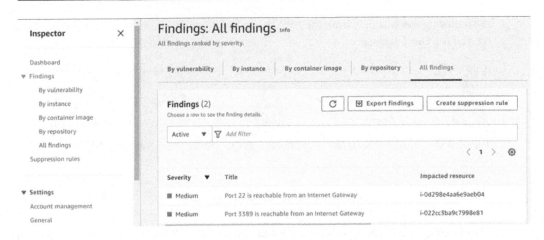

Figure 2.4 – Amazon Inspector interface

Native tools for auditing Microsoft's Azure portal

The following are some available tools within Azure for auditing assessment information:

- **Microsoft Defender for Cloud/Azure Security Center**: Microsoft Defender for Cloud (formerly known as **Azure Security Center**) is Azure's native solution. The service helps measure, maintain, and improve the level of security by continuously assessing resources and providing recommendations. The Microsoft Defender for Cloud documentation can be found at `https://docs.microsoft.com/en-us/azure/defender-for-cloud/`.

The following is a screenshot of the interface for Microsoft Defender for Cloud:

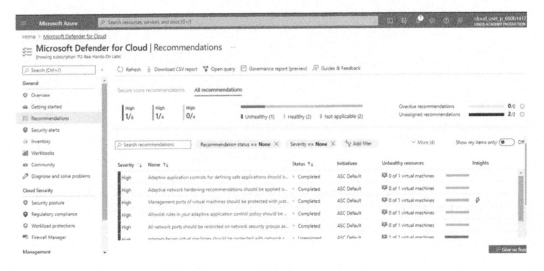

Figure 2.5 – Microsoft Defender for Cloud

- **Microsoft Purview/Azure Purview**: Microsoft Purview (formerly **Azure Purview**) is a centralized data governance and risk management service that helps manage data. The following is a screenshot of the interface of Microsoft Purview:

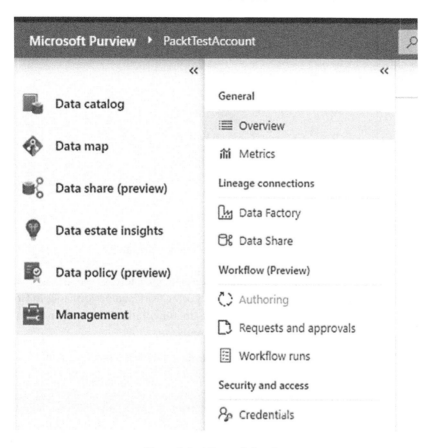

Figure 2.6 – Microsoft Purview

Native tools for auditing Google Cloud Platform

The following are some available tools to use when auditing **Google Cloud Platform** (**GCP**):

- **Google Security Command Center**: Google Security Command Center provides a centralized view of the overall security status of the workloads hosted in GCP. Google Security Command Center identifies misconfigurations and common application vulnerabilities to ensure cyber hygiene. The Google Security Command Center documentation can be found at `https://cloud.google.com/security-command-center/`.

The following is a screenshot of the interface of Google Security Command Center:

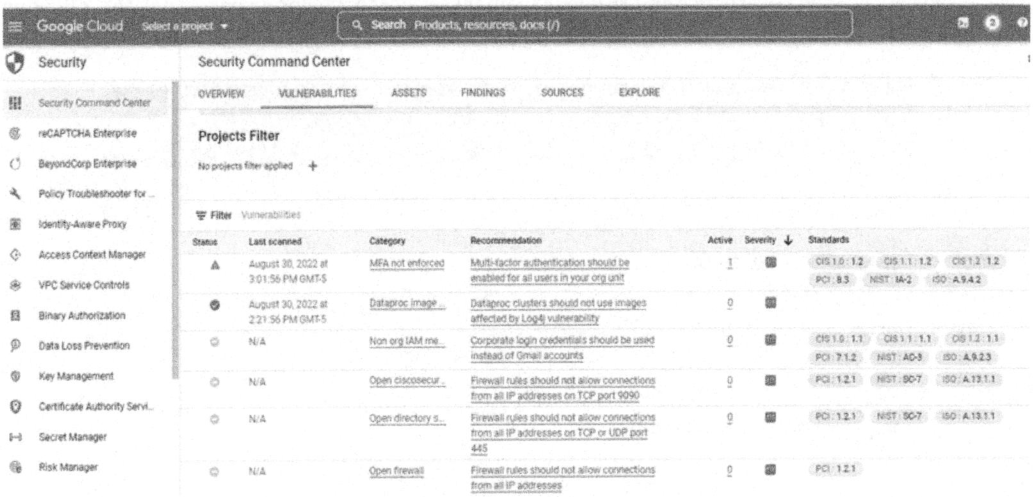

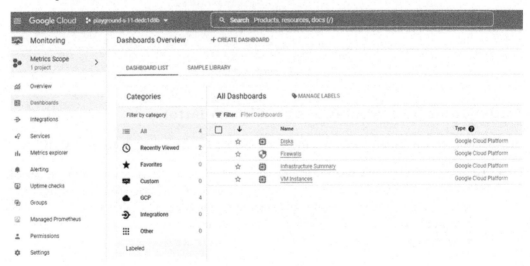

Figure 2.7 – Google Security Command Center

- **Google Cloud's Operations Suite/Stackdriver**: Google Cloud's Operations Suite (formerly **Stackdriver**) is a collection of services for monitoring workload performance in Google Cloud workloads. Google Cloud's Operations Suite documentation can be found at `https://cloud.google.com/products/operations`.

The following is a screenshot of Cloud Monitoring, which is a key feature of Google Cloud's Operation Suite:

Figure 2.8 – Cloud Monitoring

Open-source tools

In addition to the native tools offered by cloud providers, there are several open-source tools available for auditing and assessing your cloud environment. Some common open-source auditing tools are listed as follows:

- **CIS Web Services Benchmarks**: The **Center for Internet Security (CIS)** offers security and compliance assessment benchmarks for Amazon, AWS, and Google. The CIS AWS Security Benchmarks documentation can be found at `https://www.cisecurity.org/benchmark/amazon_web_services/`.

- The CIS Microsoft Azure Benchmarks documentation can be found at `https://www.cisecurity.org/benchmark/azure/`.

- The CIS GCP Benchmarks documentation can be found at `https://www.cisecurity.org/benchmark/google_cloud_computing_platform`.

- **Scout Suite**: Scout Suite is an open-source multi-cloud security audit tool that enables security posture assessment of cloud environments. By using **Application Programming Interfaces (APIs)** exposed by cloud service providers, Scout Suite can be configured to collect data from risk areas for manual inspection.

- **CloudMapper**: CloudMapper is an open-source tool developed by Duo Security for visualizing AWS cloud environments.

- **Cloud Custodian**: Cloud Custodian is an open-source tool developed by Capital One for implementing automated security, compliance, and governance.

- **DevOps Audit Defense Toolkit**: The DevOps Audit Defense Toolkit provides prescriptive guidance on how auditors should conduct audits in organizations where DevOps practices are in use.

- **Prowler**: Prowler is an open-source security tool for performing AWS security best practices assessments, audits, incident response, continuous monitoring, hardening, and forensics readiness. It contains controls covering security frameworks including ISO27001, PCI-DSS, HIPAA, GDPR, and the CIS Critical Security controls.

Native tools versus open-source tools

There are two broad categories of tools available to secure cloud services. The two categories are native tools offered by cloud service providers and open-source security tools. The AWS platform is more mature than Azure and GCP. As a result, AWS has more native tools for performing audits. With native tools, you can get better integration and performance. However, you forgo portability as native tools are tied to a specific cloud provider.

On the other hand, open-source tools provide more flexibility and less dependence on proprietary cloud platforms. However, they may be more complex to integrate. Organizations should weigh their use cases and determine what approach to take. Ultimately, the decision regarding what type of tools to use to secure your cloud services will depend on the specific cloud architecture and the nature of the cloud customer's security needs.

Now that we've reviewed a list of frameworks and tools to help with auditing, let's discuss automating compliance.

Leveraging policy and compliance automation

Cloud deployments are very dynamic for organizations to rely on manual resources. Given the complexity and scale of the platforms on the cloud, it can be a challenge for the teams to manually apply or validate security and compliance policies. As a result, there are numerous opportunities for the IT auditor to leverage automation to assess and enforce policy and compliance in the cloud. Cloud automation is the use of automated tools and processes to execute workflows in a cloud environment that would otherwise have to be performed manually.

One tool an IT auditor can utilize to monitor changes in a cloud customer's cloud is Terraform Enterprise. Terraform Enterprise has a product named Sentinel. Sentinel has the functionality to ensure an organization's code against infrastructure aligns with specific policies. This idea is called Compliance as Code or Policy as Code.

With Compliance as Code, controls and policies are agreed to and defined in a tool such as Sentinel. Sentinel will constantly monitor the applications for changes. Any change is evaluated and checked according to the compliance rules. If Sentinel detects that an application violates a compliance rule, it triggers another action or modifies the application back into a compliant state.

As an example of Compliance as Code, imagine a company that is subject to PCI regulations. Requirement 4 of PCI mandates an organization to "Protect Cardholder Data with Strong Cryptography during Transmission over Open, Public Networks." The organization has a standard to implement **Transport Layer Security** (**TLS**) 1.2 or newer for data in transit, which is a strong cryptographic standard.

The organization can then write a policy in Sentinel that evaluates whether there are any protocols older than TLS 1.2 running on the organization's systems. If a violation is found, Sentinel triggers an alert, allowing the IT auditor to monitor this control.

Further details on implementing Terraform Enterprise can be found in *Chapter 10, Walk-Through – Assessing Change Management, Logging, and Monitoring Policies*.

Summary

In this chapter, we reviewed some key common elements to know about while preparing to perform an effective audit within a cloud environment. Our goal was to ensure you have the frameworks, techniques, and tools at your disposal to build confidence in your enterprise cloud auditing. Knowing and understanding these key elements prepares you for success, provides you with information to be proficient and efficient in your evidence gathering, and potentially reduces the time it takes to complete an audit program. We learned about the preparation steps and frameworks to perform a cloud audit, the established tools that are either natively available or open-source and will help you efficiently collect testing evidence, and the opportunities that exist to automate compliance enforcement and assessment.

The information we discussed in this chapter has hopefully equipped you so that you can begin establishing an audit program playbook using widely available resources. Now that we have reviewed the techniques to get started with an enterprise customer cloud audit, in the next chapter, we will dive deeper into one of the premier areas for compliance assessment – Identity and Access Management.

Part 2:
Cloud Security and IT Controls

In *Part 1*, we covered key information needed to successfully navigate and prepare to perform an audit of customer environments within AWS, Google Cloud, and Microsoft Azure. With that foundation established, in this section we will gain a more in-depth understanding of the functional components of cloud security configuration and cloud security controls important to performing a customer (enterprise) IT audit.

This part comprises the following chapters:

- *Chapter 3, Identity and Access Management Controls*
- *Chapter 4, Network, Infrastructure, and Security Controls*
- *Chapter 5, Financial Resource and Change Management Controls*

3
Identity and Access Management Controls

Identity and access management (IAM) components are key areas to assess for risk and compliance of any system, and this holds especially true for cloud environments where there may no longer be physical controls to mitigate risk and provide a gatekeeping function to critical services and applications. Security breaches within cloud environments are widely acknowledged to be because of cloud misconfigurations, and the ability to configure (or misconfigure) cloud services requires an account with access to those services. Ensuring the appropriate accounts have access to only the resources they need and in the timeframe needed is a principle of the Zero Trust methodology that has grown in adoption as companies continue to adopt and shift services into cloud environments. Zero Trust requires that all identities be authenticated and authorized before gaining least-privilege access to resources, and each of the three major cloud providers offers functionality and configurable controls in support of this. As an IT auditor, you should review these areas to ensure the features are properly set and configured in alignment with business risk objectives.

In this chapter, we'll cover the following main topics:

- User authentication and authorization
- Permissions, roles, groups
- Device management
- Reviewing activity logs

By the end of this chapter, we will be able to identify the configuration for identity authentication, authorization, and access to assess if it meets control requirements. We will have also learned how to assess audit and activity log configuration, which is important to capture any malicious behavior and attempts to bypass risk controls.

User authentication and authorization

At the core of IAM is delivering a life-cycle process for the authentication and authorization of identities. In the past, the focus may have been on identities specifically tied to a human user. However, as companies rely more on automations, API integrations, device-to-device integrations, and other dynamic digital services, attention should be given to proper authentication and authorization of non-human identities as well. These non-human identities include things such as devices, service accounts, and workload identities, which should be considered as part of the audit, and in *Chapter 1, Cloud Architecture and Navigation*, we discussed the importance of understanding the end-to-end IT infrastructure and landscape prior to starting an audit, which should include these items.

In the case of user authentication and authorization, it's important to understand the source of identities and where those are managed. Cloud providers offer the ability to consume, share, and/or sync identity information within hybrid environments, across cloud providers, and with separate cloud-based identity stores. Additional functionality that may be configured is the ability for third-party managed identities to access your enterprise's cloud resources, such as in the case of **business-to-consumer** (known as **B2C**), **business-to-business** (known as **B2B**), or with the use of social sign-ins. These types of external identity integrations and configurations are typically separate from the configuration options for enterprise identities. Other scenarios may include cross-account identities, where the identity is part of the organization but may reside within a cloud environment linked to a separate account (AWS), separate tenant (Azure), or separate project (GCP). With this in mind, it's important to understand all identity use cases, integration points, and where the identity life cycle should begin and end for all identity types. This will help with verifying the **source of truth** for identities and assessing all the necessary components where configuration should allow, or, in some cases, preventing identities from being managed directly or accessing resources. This will also aid in determining which controls are in scope for review.

Another important item to understand is the default approach that each of the cloud providers takes to authentication and authorization. For example, in a newly created Microsoft Azure environment, the security default behavior will be to enforce MFA and user registration to MFA within 14 days, and with GCP, service accounts have permission to call Google Cloud APIs. To learn more about default authentication and authorization settings, check out the following links:

- AWS: `https://docs.aws.amazon.com/IAM/latest/UserGuide/reference_policies_evaluation-logic.html`

- Azure: `https://learn.microsoft.com/en-us/azure/active-directory/fundamentals/concept-fundamentals-security-defaults` and `https://learn.microsoft.com/en-us/azure/active-directory/fundamentals/users-default-permissions`

- GCP: `https://cloud.google.com/iam/docs/overview`

Example IAM controls

The primary focus of this book is on **IT general** controls that can be applied to IaaS and PaaS service models. In most cases, these controls will also be relevant to SaaS service models; however, the breadth and depth of fully assessing controls for SaaS are not covered in this book. As mentioned in *Chapter 2, Effective Techniques for Preparing to Audit Enterprise Cloud Environments*, there are several frameworks that can be used as guidelines for a list of controls and test procedures when defining the scope of your audit. Here, we'll highlight a few example controls from the **Center for Internet Security** (**CIS**) and the **Cloud Security Alliance** (**CSA**) that are relevant to assessing IAM features within enterprise cloud environments.

CIS control benchmarks

As mentioned in *Chapter 2, Effective Techniques for Preparing to Audit Enterprise Cloud Environments*, the CIS benchmarks not only provide a list of general IT controls (not cloud-specific) but also map them to other common security and regulatory control frameworks, as well as offer vendor-specific control frameworks. Here, we'll note a few of the applicable general controls as mentioned in CIS. Please note this is not an exhaustive list of applicable controls but is an example reference only. Determination of all applicable controls will need to be based on system architecture and integration, business risk management goals, and enterprise operational procedures:

- **CIS Control 4 Sub-Control 4.7—Manage Default Accounts on Enterprise Assets and Software**: Manage default accounts on enterprise assets and software, such as root, administrator, and other preconfigured vendor accounts.

- **CIS Control 5 Sub-Control 5.1—Establish and Maintain an Inventory of Accounts**: Establish and maintain an inventory of all accounts managed in the enterprise.

- **CIS Control 5 Sub-Control 5.2—Use Unique Passwords**: Use unique passwords for all enterprise assets. Best-practice implementation includes, at a minimum, an 8-character password for accounts using MFA and a 14-character password for accounts not using MFA.

- **CIS Control 5 Sub-Control 5.3—Disable Dormant Accounts**: Delete or disable any dormant accounts after a period of 45 days of inactivity.

- **CIS Control 6 Sub-Control 6.5—Require MFA for Administrative Access**: Require MFA for all administrative access accounts, where supported, on all enterprise assets, whether managed on-site or through a third-party provider.

- **CIS Control 6 Sub-Control 6.8—Define and Maintain Role-Based Access Control**: Define and maintain **role-based access control** (**RBAC**) by determining and documenting the access rights necessary for each role within the enterprise to successfully carry out its assigned duties.

- **CIS Control 13 Sub-Control 13.5—Manage Access Control for Remote Assets**: Manage access control for assets remotely connecting to enterprise resources.

To find a comprehensive list of CIS benchmark controls, go to `https://www.cisecurity.org/benchmark`.

Now that we've taken a look at some example controls from CIS that could be applicable to both on-premise and cloud environments, let's take a look at controls from the **Cloud Security Alliance (CSA) Cloud Controls Matrix (CCM)**.

CCM

Within the CSA CCM v4.0 framework, controls that would be relevant to the technical assessment of IAM functions mentioned in the remaining sections would primarily fall under the control domain of IAM; however, there are also applicable controls under other control domains. Examples of CCM controls an IT auditor should reference for IAM include those found in the following list:

- **Control ID IAM-03—Identity Inventory**: Manage, store, and review information on system identities and level of access

- **Control ID IAM-05—Least Privilege**: Employ the least-privilege principle when implementing information system access

- **Control ID IAM-08—User Access Review**: Review and revalidate user access for least privilege and **separation of duties (SoD)** with a frequency that is commensurate with organizational risk tolerance

- **Control ID IAM-14—Strong Authentication**: Define, implement, and evaluate processes, procedures, and technical measures for authenticating access to systems, applications, and data assets, including MFA for at least privileged user and sensitive data access

- **Control ID IAM-15—Passwords Management**: Define, implement, and evaluate processes, procedures, and technical measures for the secure management of passwords

- **Control ID LOG-11—Transaction/Activity Logging**: Log and monitor key life-cycle management events to enable auditing and reporting on the usage of cryptographic keys

- **Control ID STA-07—Supply Chain Inventory**: Develop and maintain an inventory of all supply chain relationships

You can access more on the CCM matrix from CSA at `https://cloudsecurityalliance.org/artifacts/cloud-controls-matrix-v4/`. Please note that the matrix is periodically updated, so be sure you are accessing the latest version.

Now that we've taken a look at some example IT general controls from common frameworks that would apply to IaaS and PaaS enterprise cloud environments, let's take a look at some of the options where these controls may be configured or reviewed. In general, each of the cloud providers has a dedicated administrative area for configuring IAM controls. To understand more about where key configurable cloud IAM options exist, let's review some of the administration settings for each of the cloud providers in more detail.

Amazon AWS IAM

Within AWS, there are a few different options available for navigating to user authentication and authorization settings. Accessing those options will be dependent upon user permissions, as well as other options administrators may have previously configured. In many cases, an administrator may have used AWS Control Tower to configure a landing zone that aligns with the role- or job-based functions a user may need to access within a multi-account environment. Other options to navigate to organization-level authentication and authorization settings are in the dropdown for the login console, found in the top-right corner, as shown in *Figure 3.1*:

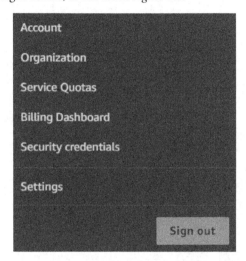

Figure 3.1 – Navigating to the Organization configuration settings

You may also use the left-side panel to navigate through the list of services and select the category of **Security, Identity, & Compliance** and the sub-level navigation option of **IAM**, as shown in *Figure 3.2*:

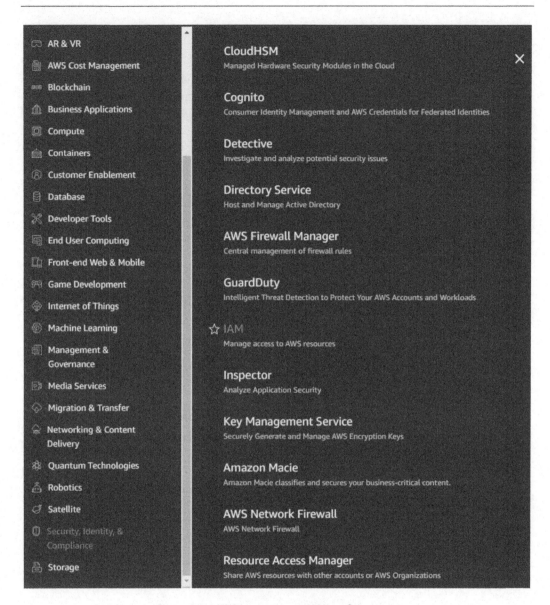

Figure 3.2 – AWS navigation to IAM configuration

Upon navigation to the AWS IAM console, you will find options for a dashboard as well as configuration options for areas such as **Users**, **User groups**, **Identity providers**, and password management settings, as seen in *Figure 3.3*. Direct navigation to the IAM console is also possible through https:// console.aws.amazon.com/iam/. Reviewing the configuration settings here will provide insight into any external **identity providers** in use, how accounts may or may not be synchronized with other systems, which password policies are in place, whether users may be restricted from managing their own credentials, and if MFA has been enabled. You should note that in AWS, MFA is enabled separately for root and IAM users. Enabling MFA for the root user does not impact the MFA settings for IAM users and vice versa, so special attention should be paid to this area:

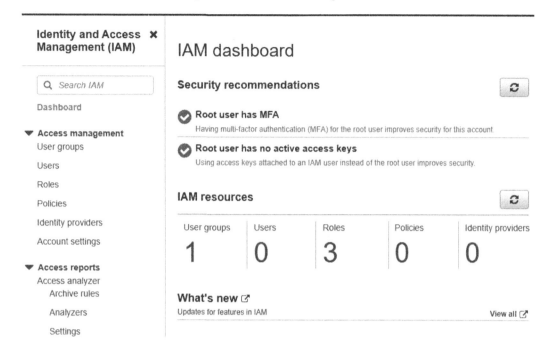

Figure 3.3 – AWS IAM configurations

In addition to navigating through the browser to the AWS console and IAM functions, you can also use a **command-line interface** (**CLI**). You can access more information on installing and using the AWS CLI at https://aws.amazon.com/cli, and you can find command references specific to IAM at https://docs.aws.amazon.com/cli/latest/reference/iam/index.html.

Now that we have reviewed navigating to IAM configurations in Amazon AWS IAM, let's now look at navigating to IAM configuration options within Microsoft Azure.

Microsoft Azure

As with AWS, you can use various options for navigating to user authentication and authorization settings in Microsoft Azure as well. One way to access identity settings within Microsoft Azure is to expand the left panel navigation for **All services** and select **Identity**, as seen in *Figure 3.4*. From there, you can navigate into **External Identities** to view information about federation and integration with identity provider services, to **Users** to view a full set of User Principal identities that exist within the tenant, or to Azure AD **Security** to view more on allowable authentication methods and MFA configuration:

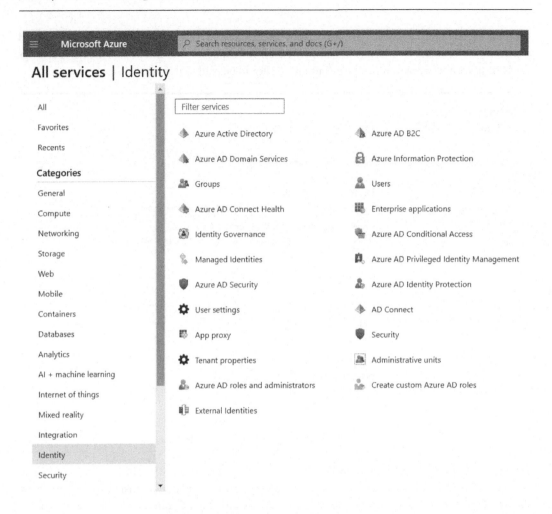

Figure 3.4 – Microsoft Azure IAM configurations

At the time of this writing, Microsoft has developed a new branded administrator experience for Azure Active Directory IAM functions that can be found at `https://entra.microsoft.com/` (*Figure 3.5*):

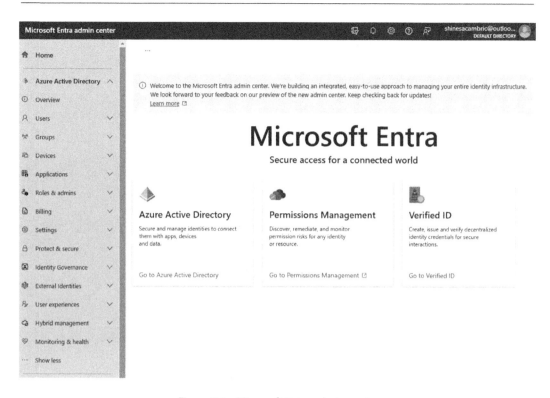

Figure 3.5 – Microsoft Entra admin center

This new branded experience aims to provide a simplified interface for configuration and administrative functions. Permission requirements for accessing and configuring these functions remain the same as accessing the administrative functions through `https://portal.azure.com`.

As with AWS, within Microsoft Azure, you can also use the CLI for navigation and accessing resources. Documentation and information on installing and using the Azure CLI, including tutorials, can be found at `https://learn.microsoft.com/en-us/cli/azure/`.

Now that we've identified one of the primary ways of accessing IAM configuration in Microsoft Azure, let's review where to find the configuration within GCP.

GCP

Similar to both AWS and Azure, GCP provides access to IAM functions through a few different navigation paths. GCP has a dedicated **IAM & Admin** product section, as seen in *Figure 3.6*; however, other relevant content exists within the **Security** product section as well, such as the management of service accounts and workload identities:

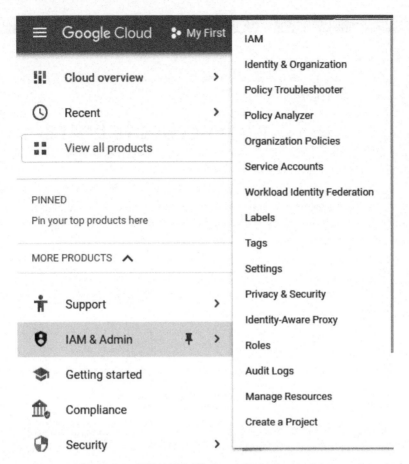

Figure 3.6 – GCP IAM & Admin configuration options

Also, similar to AWS, GCP uses the concept of establishing an organization (*Figure 3.7*) for use in structuring user accounts and managing access:

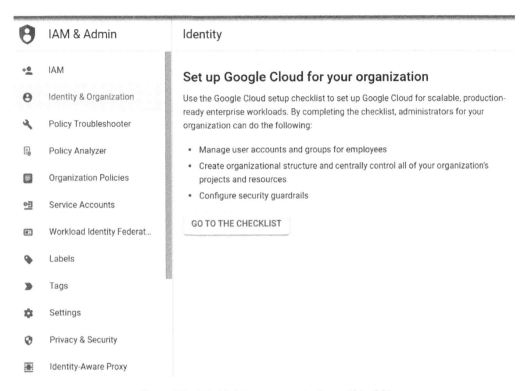

Figure 3.7 – Establishing an organization within GCP

Additionally, GCP has an "identity as a service" function known as **Cloud Identity** for providing a centrally managed user identity store.

Similar to AWS and Azure, we can also navigate within GCP using the CLI. More information about this can be found at `https://cloud.google.com/cli`.

As we've seen, there are a few differences but also many similarities in the way that IAM navigation is structured in AWS, Azure, and GCP. Now that we've looked at the key areas where configuration options for users and user authentication exist, let's look at concepts for defining and identifying permissions, roles, and groups.

Permissions, roles, and groups

Beyond establishing how identities are created and authenticated in a cloud environment, identities require some level of permissions to access resources within those cloud environments. In some cases, there may be a default level of access granted based on the type of account created (such as a default administrative user) or the assignment of users to a particular group that has been assigned an access policy (see *Figure 3.8* for an example of policies in AWS):

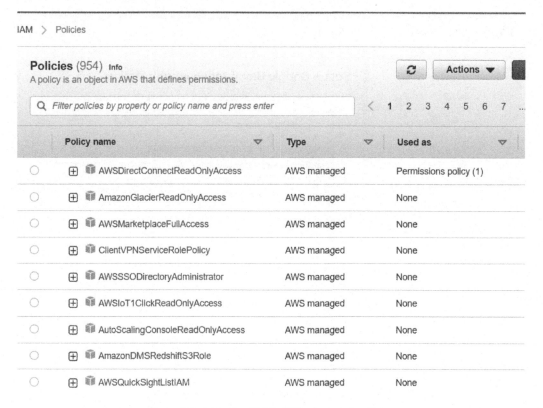

Figure 3.8 – List of available AWS managed policies

For some cloud components and services, the concept of inheritance also exists, as well as the ability to manage permissions through RBAC and ABAC. Administrators may manage users and their permissions within a portal **user interface** (**UI**); however, they may also do this through the CLI, **application programming interface** (**APIs**), the use of cloud provider SDKs, or through integrated user life-cycle and management applications.

When assessing a customer cloud environment, there are several things that an auditor should be familiar with in relation to access. The first is understanding the default high-privileged users and/or roles that exist within an environment and reviewing how that access is managed. Some cloud providers offer the ability for time-bound, temporary, logged access when elevated privileges are required. An example of time-bound access can be seen in *Figure 3.9*:

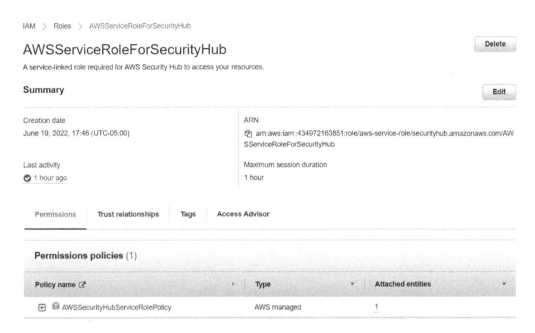

Figure 3.9 – AWS time-bound access

In the case of time-bound access, any configuration of time boundaries, workflows, or approval process for the temporary access should be reviewed. The auditor should note that using a workflow process may not be possible for all privileged role and user types and should determine through customer interviews whether there are alternative processes for controlling high-privileged access.

Another thing auditors should note is that for some cloud services, designating a user with a specific title within the cloud such as **Owner** or **Contributor** may effectively be the same as granting permissions or access rights. Additionally, such as in AWS, a user may be able to "assume" the permissions of another user or role, which could potentially elevate the permissions for the user, depending on the policy and existing permissions for that user. The concept of inheritance and delegation, such as in GCP, may also come into play. In *Figure 3.10*, you can see an example where policies have inheritance defined. Here, the user may not be granted access rights explicitly but due to inheritance may gain additional rights to a resource:

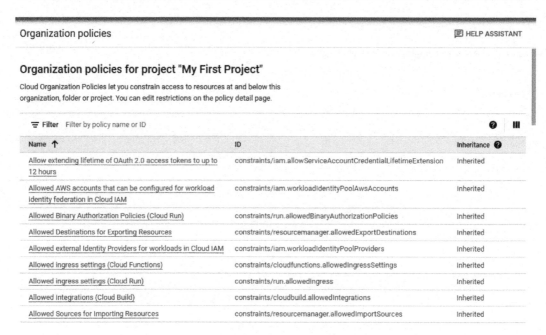

Figure 3.10 – Example GCP organization policies with inheritance

Other areas an auditor will want to review will include the use of individual user identities to run services and which permissions have been granted, the assignment of privileges to service and workload identities (and whether they may be over-privileged), and the use of custom roles or roles that have been cloned from the cloud provider's default roles. The definition of default (or built-in) roles can be found in cloud provider documentation. For custom or customer-defined roles, an auditor may need to request a more detailed listing of which permissions are included. As in *Figure 3.11*, a cloud provider will distinguish between which roles are provided as default roles. A cloud provider may offer hundreds or thousands of roles and permissions for use within the cloud customer environment. Here is a sample list of default privileged roles you should be aware of:

	Role		Description	Type	
☐	Application administrator		Can create and manage all aspects of app registrations and enterprise apps.	Built-in	···
☐	Application developer		Can create application registrations independent of the 'Users can register ...	Built-in	···
☐	Attack payload author		Can create attack payloads that an administrator can initiate later.	Built-in	···
☐	Attack simulation administrator		Can create and manage all aspects of attack simulation campaigns.	Built-in	···
☐	Attribute assignment administrator	🔖	Assign custom security attribute keys and values to supported Azure AD ob...	Built-in	···
☐	Attribute assignment reader	🔖	Read custom security attribute keys and values for supported Azure AD obj...	Built-in	···
☐	Attribute definition administrator	🔖	Define and manage the definition of custom security attributes.	Built-in	···
☐	Attribute definition reader	🔖	Read the definition of custom security attributes.	Built-in	···
☐	Authentication administrator		Has access to view, set, and reset authentication method information for an...	Built-in	···
☐	Authentication policy administrator		Can create and manage all aspects of authentication methods and passwor...	Built-in	···
☐	Azure AD joined device local administrator		Users assigned to this role are added to the local administrators group on ...	Built-in	···
☐	Azure Auditor		Azure Auditor	Custom	···

Figure 3.11 – Example Azure built-in and custom roles

Now that we've discussed attributes in defining access for users in cloud environments, let's take a deeper look at privileged permissions. As mentioned at the beginning of this chapter, it's important that auditors know and can identify highly privileged roles in cloud environments to properly assess governance and risk.

Key privileged access, roles, and policies

Although there may be thousands of roles, permissions, and policies, here are some examples of important ones to note. You may also find additional information on access permissions for each of the cloud providers at the noted URLs.

The following is a small sample of AWS ECS highly privileged roles, permissions, and policies that an auditor should be aware of. Learn more about specific access permissions and policies within AWS by going to https://docs.aws.amazon.com/IAM/latest/UserGuide/access.html:

- iam:CreateUser
- AmazonEC2ContainerRegistryFullAccess
- Billing
- AdministratorAccess
- AWSConfigUserAccess

In addition to the built-in available privileged access, as an auditor, you should also be aware of the following within AWS IAM:

- AWS IAM policy evaluation logic

- Identity versus resource-based policies

- The `AssumeRole` capability

You can find more in-depth information on these at `https://docs.aws.amazon.com/IAM/latest/UserGuide/id.html` and `https://docs.aws.amazon.com/IAM/latest/UserGuide/best-practices.html`.

A similar sample of Microsoft Azure highly privileged roles can be found in the following list, and you can get more details on roles and permissions at `https://docs.microsoft.com/en-us/azure/active-directory/roles/permissions-reference`:

- Global Admin

- Security Administrator

- Privileged role administrator

- Cloud device administrator

- Application administrator

Other things to note for Azure include the ability to create cybersecurity-risk policies that control enforcement of MFA and access to resources through Conditional Access and the ability for automated cybersecurity-risk-based reports and alerts based on **machine learning** (**ML**) detections for risk related to account compromise or fraud within the **Security** and **Identity Protection** blades. More information about these capabilities can be found at `https://learn.microsoft.com/en-us/azure/active-directory/identity-protection/`.

To complete our list of sample privileged access across the major cloud environments, the following is a sample list of privileged roles within Google Cloud. You can learn more about these, and other roles, at `https://cloud.google.com/iam/docs/understanding-roles`:

- Editor

- Security Admin

- Role Administrator

- Super Administrator

- Organization Administrator

Other things to note about GCP include IAM policy settings that can change whether or not inheritance is enforced. By default, policies are inherited and merged but be aware that a "deny" permission always takes precedence as part of any privilege or access assignment. You can learn more at https:// cloud.google.com/iam/docs/overview.

Now that we understand more about how permission can be managed for identities and identifying privileged levels of access (permissions, roles, and policies) within AWS, Azure, and GCP, let's look at the management of a specific type of identity—devices.

Device management

For a company, a necessary part of users connecting to resources is having devices that can successfully connect, and this holds true even for cloud environments. Although many companies have adopted **bring your own device** (**BYOD**) policies for accessing some or all company assets, in most cases, those devices require some form of device registration and security policy and posture management to prevent the risk of unauthorized or compromised devices from gaining access (*Figure 3.12*):

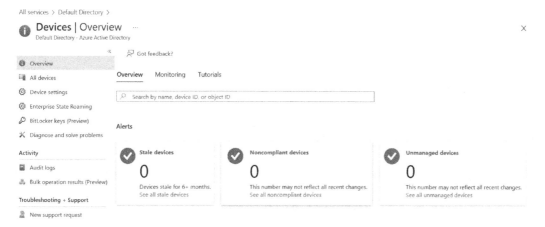

Figure 3.12 – Example Microsoft Azure device policy overview

There may be some default features within the portal environment for managing devices; however, in most instances, additional applications or specialized licensing for endpoint and **mobile device management** (**MDM**) is required to enforce and gain full visibility into device health and security compliance.

Important things to note for each cloud provider are assessing which administrators can modify device registration policies or register devices in the customer cloud and how these devices are validated. Another thing to consider is the impact and requirements of device policies for hybrid environments.

Now that we've reviewed important aspects of device administration in a portal environment, let's discuss ways to review activity logs related to IAM within a cloud environment.

Reviewing activity logs

As an auditor, one method that may be used to correlate processes and procedures that mitigate risk is to review activity logs. In cloud environments, these logs may be made up of separate sign-in and activity logs that are capturing activity for user accounts and service or workload identities. The activity may be occurring directly within the portal UI or through API calls by an identity. An important step in ensuring these various sign-ins and activities are being captured is to ensure that auditing has been enabled. This should not be assumed. There may be some auditing features enabled as default; however, this may not be a full set of what is required to satisfy a company's control process, and the company should not rely on the cloud provider for managing the capture of these logs (refer to shared responsibility, discussed in *Chapter 1, Cloud Architecture and Navigation*, and *Chapter 2, Effective Techniques for Preparing to Audit Cloud Environments*). In addition to the possibility that logs may not be enabled by default, the amount of logging details retained may be limited unless administrators are intentional about updating the retention period and storage of log information, and this retention may carry a cost or require additional applications or tools, such as exporting the logs to a **Security Information and Event Management** (**SIEM**) tool. A list of logs and identity auditing features that should be enabled or considered for auditing use is included next.

AWS

Within AWS, there are several logging and auditing features that are natively available that will facilitate control test evidence and monitoring for IAM controls. These include (but are not limited to):

- **Amazon CloudWatch**—Leverages AWS CloudTrail logs and provides the ability for alerts to be created for identity scenarios. An example use case is to trigger an alert if an IAM policy has been changed.

- **AWS CloudTrail**—Captures IAM user activities and provides a way to audit, either through CloudTrail directly or by sending this to other tools (such as CloudWatch). You should ensure this is enabled for all regions and for all billing accounts within scope.

- **Amazon GuardDuty**—Captures and alerts on cybersecurity-related identity risk based on information from AWS CloudTrail.

You can find more information about each of these features at `https://docs.aws.amazon.com/whitepapers/latest/introduction-aws-security/monitoring-and-logging.html`.

Azure

Similar to AWS, Microsoft Azure provides some native logging abilities that an auditor should review to confirm they are enabled, and also take advantage of as part of conducting the audit and collecting control evidence. In Azure, logging and monitoring areas for IAM include the following:

- **Audit, activity, and sign-in logs**—These are enabled by default; however, there should be awareness of the retention period and length of time for which the logs are available. This may be dependent upon your organization's licensing.

- **Azure Monitor and Log Analytics**—This requires enabling diagnostic settings and configuration within Microsoft Azure and provides a way to query various types of logs, as well as create "workbooks" for continued access to queries, and also offers alerting capabilities.

- **Azure Active Directory Identity Protection**—As mentioned in an earlier section, Azure offers a way to monitor and alert on cybersecurity-related identity risks. Certain features may be dependent upon the level of your organization's licensing.

To find out more information about these features, please visit `https://learn.microsoft.com/en-us/azure/active-directory/reports-monitoring/`.

GCP

As with AWS and Azure, GCP offers some native options for identity-related audit logging and monitoring. Many of the logging options for GCP (such as Admin Activity logs) are enabled by default and cannot be disabled; however, it's important to thoroughly review the logging settings across the entire GCP environment to ensure there is full coverage. You can learn more about GCP Cloud Logging at `https://cloud.google.com/logging/docs/audit/`.

Summary

In this chapter, we looked at where configuration options exist for IAM within the three major cloud providers. We covered where to find settings for authentication and authorization, permissions, and access management. We also reviewed concepts around device management, which is another type of identity, as well as the importance of understanding how logging may or may not be configured for a cloud environment.

In our next chapter, we'll look deeper into network, infrastructure, and security controls within cloud environments.

4

Network, Infrastructure, and Security Controls

In cloud networks, access is controlled primarily through virtual networks and their associated networking resources. Cloud systems use virtual networks to enable communication between components inside a cloud. A virtual network is a networking system that emulates a physical network by combining the hardware and software network resources into a single entity. A virtual network contains network resources and capabilities including firewalls, virtual routers, load balancers, and network management.

In the cloud, virtual networks are managed via **Software-Defined Networking** (**SDN**). SDN is a category of technologies designed to allow virtualized networking functions that can be managed through software. SDN enables the creation of virtual networks by emulating physical firewalls, routers, and other networking devices used in traditional networks.

Deploying virtual networks on the cloud is fairly simple. New infrastructure can be quickly provisioned with no direct involvement by the IT or security teams, unlike a traditional network. Without IT or security oversight, this increases the chance that new infrastructure isn't configured securely and thus is vulnerable to various attacks. In addition, cloud environments can be accessed directly from the public internet, which makes it easier for an attacker to gain unauthorized access to an organization's cloud-based resources.

In 2019, Capital One suffered a massive data breach where more than 100 million consumer records were accessed. The breach originated in part from a misconfigured **Web Application Firewall** (**WAF**) that Capital One was utilizing in **Amazon Web Services** (**AWS**).

To evaluate network security controls, the IT auditor must understand the shared responsibility model. The shared responsibility model describes what obligations the cloud customer is responsible for, and what the cloud service provider is responsible for. The shared responsibility model may vary, depending on the cloud service provider and the service models deployed. Generally, the cloud service provider is responsible for securing the physical data centers and physical infrastructure. The cloud customer is responsible for securing the virtual network resources they deploy within the cloud environment though this may vary.

Chapter 1, *Cloud Architecture and Navigation*, introduced us to the relationship between cloud shared responsibility and the three cloud service models: **Infrastructure as a Service (IaaS)**, **Platform as a Service (PaaS)**, and **Software as a Service (SaaS)**. In the IaaS model, the cloud customer manages the virtual network resources, while the cloud service provider is responsible for securing the underlying physical infrastructure.

In the PaaS model, the cloud service provider is generally responsible for securing both the physical and virtual infrastructure. Some PaaS implementations may support a limited set of built-in virtual networking features for the cloud customer's use.

In the SaaS model, the cloud service provider hosts and configures all the physical and virtual infrastructure, including virtual networking so that the cloud customer has no responsibility.

For illustration, if a cloud customer was to deploy an Amazon **Elastic Compute Cloud (EC2)** instance which is an IaaS, the cloud customer would have to configure the virtual network so that the EC2 instance cannot be accessed directly from the internet. Many of the IaaS virtual networks are exposed to the internet by default, which means anyone could theoretically access any data in the cloud customer instance if no virtual network configuration was done. In contrast, if a cloud customer were to deploy Salesforce, which is a SaaS, they would not have to worry about the physical or virtual network configurations as Microsoft would be responsible for that. SaaS applications are typically accessible from a web browser and do not need any additional configuration to the virtual infrastructure.

In addition, the IT auditor needs to review industry-standard security benchmarks such as CIS Amazon Web Services, CIS Microsoft Azure Benchmarks, and CIS Google Cloud Platform Benchmarks to understand their recommendations around the secure configuration of virtual networks.

In this chapter, we'll cover the following main topics:

- Security control centers
- Network controls
- Security policies
- Data security

By the end of this chapter, we will be able to identify the security control center within each cloud service provider portal and functionality and recognize features and policies for defining and controlling network access. In addition, we will also learn how to assess the implementation of features for protecting data, such as encryption and data loss prevention techniques.

Security control centers

Each of the three major cloud service providers offers functionality and configurable controls to support setting up virtual private networks for your cloud resources. The cloud service providers have designed their portals to make it intuitive for anyone to set up a virtual private network for cloud resources.

AWS refers to its virtual network as a **Virtual Private Cloud** (**VPC**), Azure refers to its virtual network as a **Virtual Network** (**VNet**), and GCP refers to its virtual network as a **Virtual Private Cloud**. A virtual network is divided into subnetworks, also known as subnets.

Amazon Virtual Private Cloud

Amazon's VPC is a core AWS service and allows you to create a virtual network for resources in an isolated section of the Amazon Web Services cloud. Within the VPC, a user can define network configurations such as IP address range as well as route tables and manage network gateways and subnets. Subnets are smaller separate parts of the overall network.

All VPCs are created and exist in one AWS Region. AWS Regions are separate geographic areas around the world that Amazon uses to house its cloud data centers and infrastructure. AWS Regions are distributed around the globe so that customers can choose a region closest to them to host their cloud infrastructure there. Because an AWS VPC is essentially moving network traffic into and around your AWS Regions, it's also your first line of defense. When configured correctly, a VPC acts as a secure, logically isolated non-public area inside your public cloud.

The most common way to create, access, and manage your VPCs is through the AWS Management Console. The AWS Management Console provides a web interface that you can use to access your VPCs. Let's look at how to create an AWS VPC:

1. Navigate to the AWS **Console home**, as shown in *Figure 4.1*:

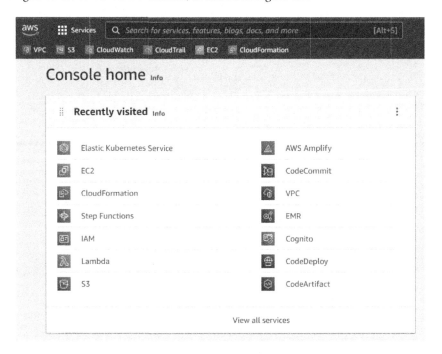

Figure 4.1 – AWS Console home

2. Next, navigate to the **Resources by Region** AWS interface, as shown in *Figure 4.2*:

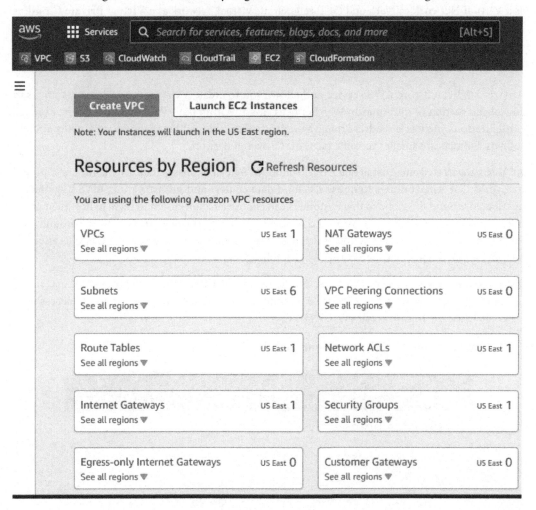

Figure 4.2 – AWS – Resources by Region

3. Finally, create the VPC with the settings shown in *Figure 4.3*:

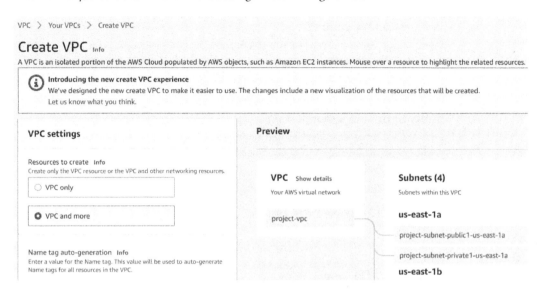

Figure 4.3 – AWS Create VPC configuration options

4. Specify IP address ranges, as shown in *Figure 4.4*:

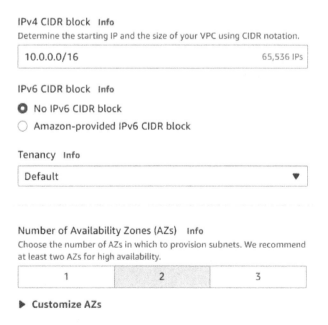

Figure 4.4 – AWS Create VPC – IP address options

5. Specify subnet information, as shown in *Figure 4.5*:

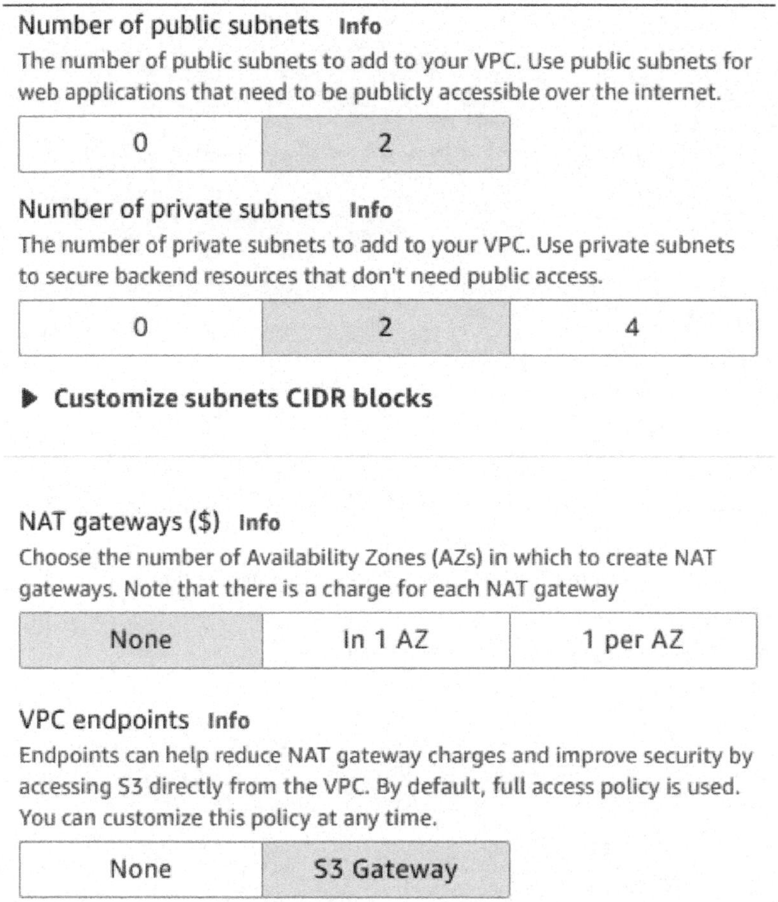

Number of public subnets   Info

The number of public subnets to add to your VPC. Use public subnets for web applications that need to be publicly accessible over the internet.

0	2

Number of private subnets   Info

The number of private subnets to add to your VPC. Use private subnets to secure backend resources that don't need public access.

0	2	4

▶ **Customize subnets CIDR blocks**

NAT gateways ($)   Info

Choose the number of Availability Zones (AZs) in which to create NAT gateways. Note that there is a charge for each NAT gateway

None	In 1 AZ	1 per AZ

VPC endpoints   Info

Endpoints can help reduce NAT gateway charges and improve security by accessing S3 directly from the VPC. By default, full access policy is used. You can customize this policy at any time.

None	S3 Gateway

Figure 4.5 – AWS Create VPC – subnet options

6.   Specify NAT gateway options, VPC endpoints, and DNS options, as shown in *Figure 4.6*:

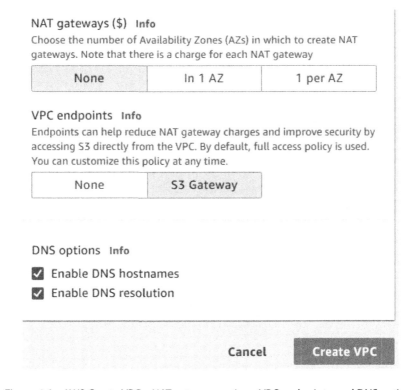

Figure 4.6 – AWS Create VPC – NAT gateway options, VPC endpoints, and DNS options

7.   Finally, create the VPC, as shown in *Figure 4.7*:

Figure 4.7 – AWS – Creating VPC Resources

Deploy the AWS VPC, as shown in *Figure 4.8*:

Figure 4.8 – AWS VPC deployed

Now that we've looked at how to create and configure an AWS VPC, let's look at how to build an Azure VNet.

Azure Virtual Network

An Azure VNet is an isolated network within the Microsoft Azure cloud. A VNet in Azure provides a range of networking functions similar to the AWS or GCP VPC. These functions include connectivity between **virtual machines** (**VMs**), routing, and **virtual private networks** (**VPNs**). A VNet can be broken down into single or multiple subnets. The scope of a virtual network is a single region.

You can create a VNet by performing the following steps:

1. Navigate to the Microsoft Azure portal and search for `virtual networks`, as shown in *Figure 4.9*:

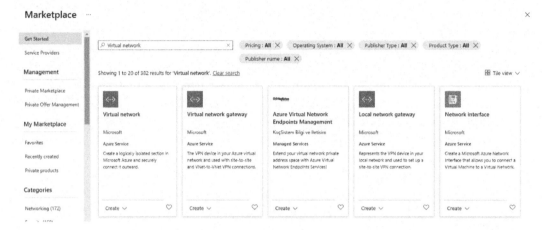

Figure 4.9 – Azure portal

2. Next, create the virtual network with the various VNet settings, as shown in *Figure 4.10*:

Figure 4.10 – Creating an Azure VNet

3. Specify the IP addresses, as shown in *Figure 4.11*:

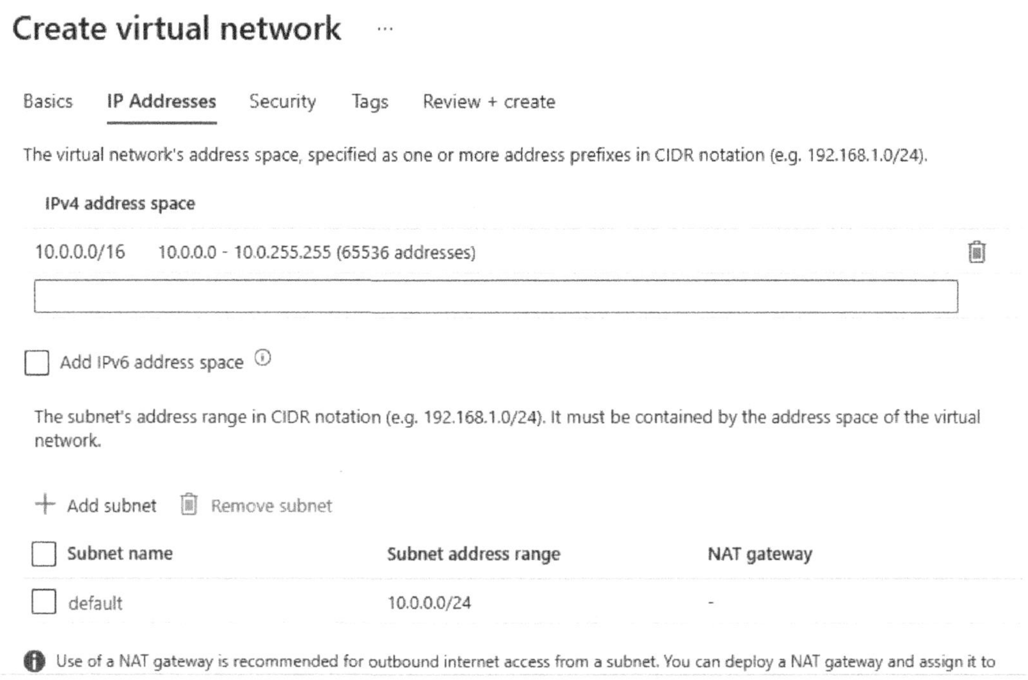

Create virtual network   ⋯

Basics   **IP Addresses**   Security   Tags   Review + create

The virtual network's address space, specified as one or more address prefixes in CIDR notation (e.g. 192.168.1.0/24).

IPv4 address space

10.0.0.0/16 10.0.0.0 - 10.0.255.255 (65536 addresses)	🗑

☐ Add IPv6 address space ⓘ

The subnet's address range in CIDR notation (e.g. 192.168.1.0/24). It must be contained by the address space of the virtual network.

+ Add subnet   🗑 Remove subnet

☐ Subnet name	Subnet address range	NAT gateway
☐ default	10.0.0.0/24	-

ⓘ Use of a NAT gateway is recommended for outbound internet access from a subnet. You can deploy a NAT gateway and assign it to

Figure 4.11 – Azure VNet IP address configuration options

4. Specify security settings such as **DDoS Protection Standard** and **Firewall**, as shown in *Figure 4.12*:

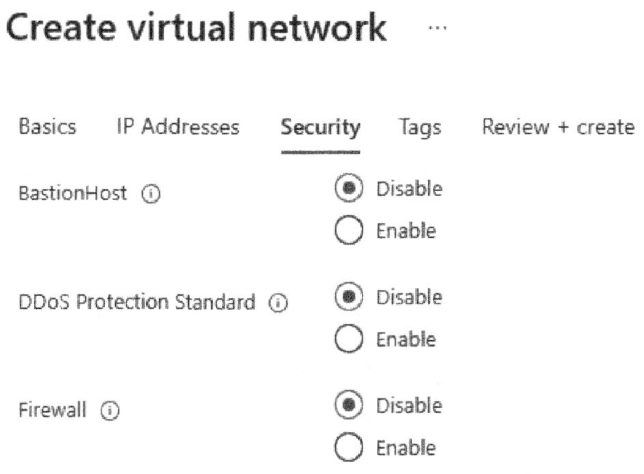

Create virtual network   ⋯

Basics   IP Addresses   **Security**   Tags   Review + create

BastionHost ⓘ
  ⦿ Disable
  ○ Enable

DDoS Protection Standard ⓘ
  ⦿ Disable
  ○ Enable

Firewall ⓘ
  ⦿ Disable
  ○ Enable

Figure 4.12 – Azure VNet security configuration options

5.   Lastly, review the configuration and create a virtual network, as shown in *Figure 4.13*:

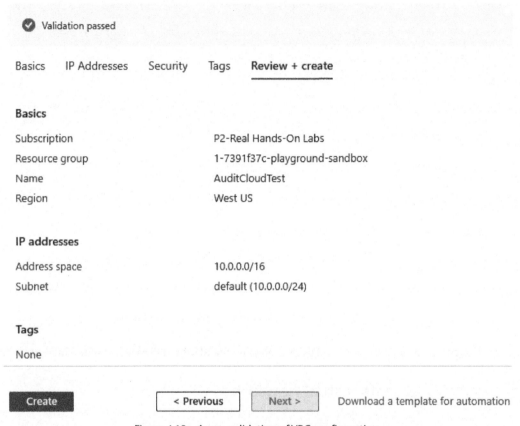

Figure 4.13 – Azure validation of VPC configuration

6. With that, virtual network deployment is complete, as shown in *Figure 4.14*:

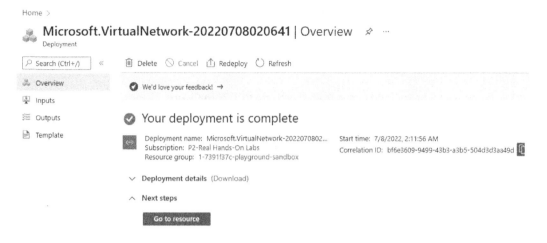

Figure 4.14 – Azure VNet deployed

So far, we've reviewed how to build an Azure VNet. We will now look at how to create and configure a GCP VPC.

Google Cloud Platform Virtual Private Cloud

A GCP VPC provides virtual networks very similar to physical networks, except that it is virtualized within the GCP. GCP VPC differs from AWS VPC and Azure VNet as it is not scoped to an individual region. Both AWS VPC and Azure VNet are scoped to an individual region. To create a GCP VPC, perform the following steps:

1. Go to the Google Cloud Console and navigate to **VPC network**, as shown in *Figure 4.15*:

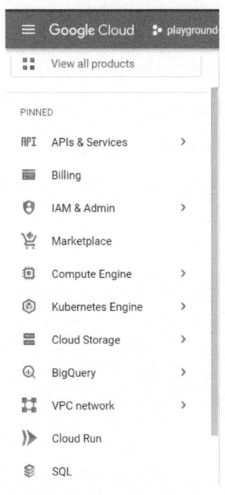

Figure 4.15 – Google Cloud Console

Review the existing VPCs. Note the existence of several default VPC networks. The IT auditor should take keen note of this as default VPC networks on GCP are inherently insecure. This is shown in *Figure 4.16*:

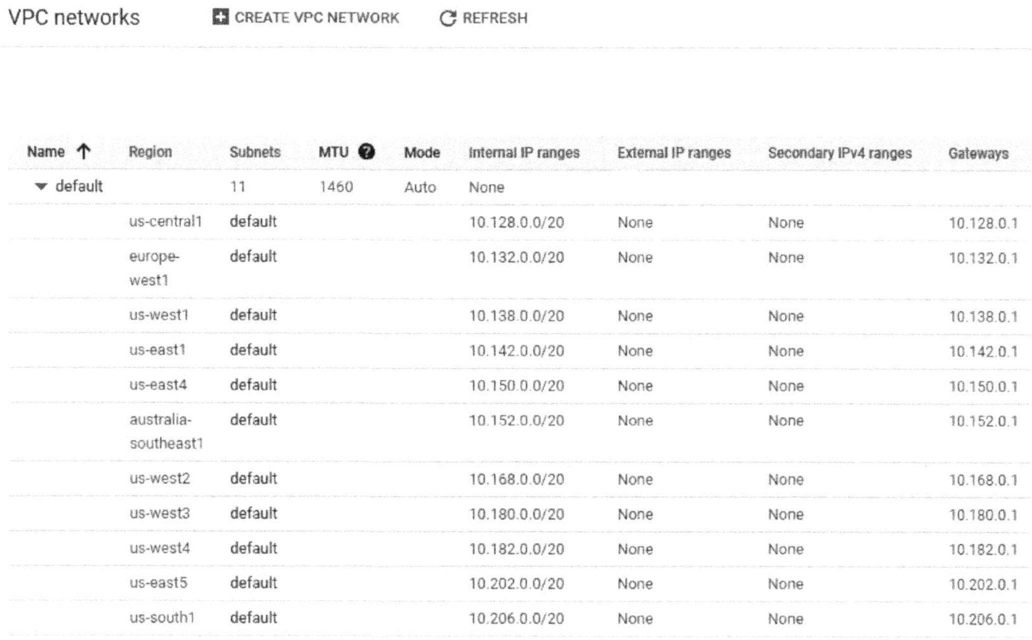

VPC networks   ➕ CREATE VPC NETWORK   ⟳ REFRESH

Name ↑	Region	Subnets	MTU ❔	Mode	Internal IP ranges	External IP ranges	Secondary IPv4 ranges	Gateways
▼ default		11	1460	Auto	None			
	us-central1	default			10.128.0.0/20	None	None	10.128.0.1
	europe-west1	default			10.132.0.0/20	None	None	10.132.0.1
	us-west1	default			10.138.0.0/20	None	None	10.138.0.1
	us-east1	default			10.142.0.0/20	None	None	10.142.0.1
	us-east4	default			10.150.0.0/20	None	None	10.150.0.1
	australia-southeast1	default			10.152.0.0/20	None	None	10.152.0.1
	us-west2	default			10.168.0.0/20	None	None	10.168.0.1
	us-west3	default			10.180.0.0/20	None	None	10.180.0.1
	us-west4	default			10.182.0.0/20	None	None	10.182.0.1
	us-east5	default			10.202.0.0/20	None	None	10.202.0.1
	us-south1	default			10.206.0.0/20	None	None	10.206.0.1

Figure 4.16 – GCP VPC networks

2.   Next, create a GCP VPC, as shown in *Figure 4.17*:

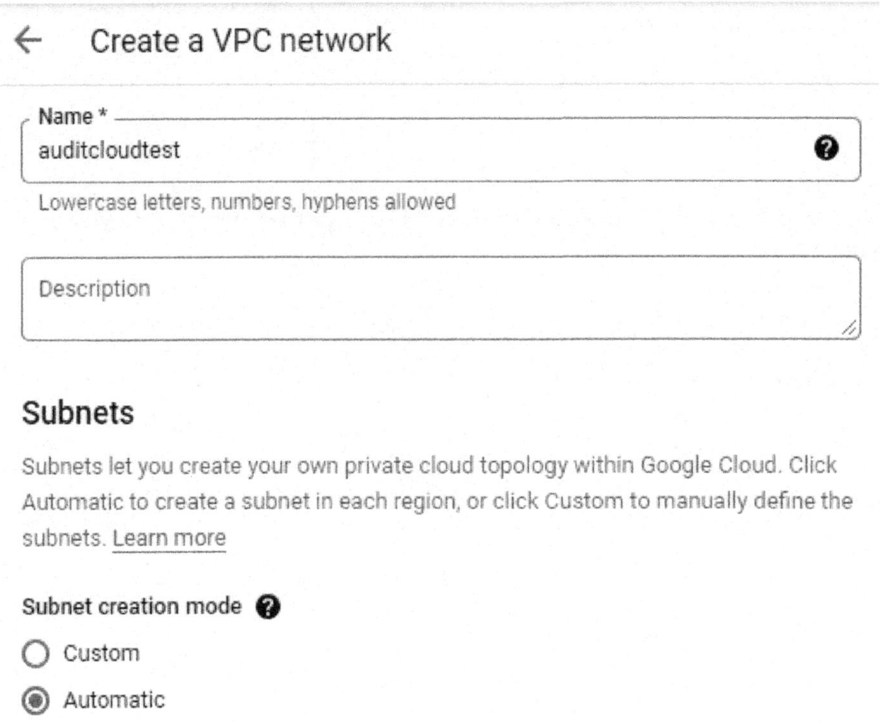

←   Create a VPC network

Name *

auditcloudtest   ❓

Lowercase letters, numbers, hyphens allowed

Description

Subnets

Subnets let you create your own private cloud topology within Google Cloud. Click Automatic to create a subnet in each region, or click Custom to manually define the subnets. Learn more

Subnet creation mode ❓

○ Custom

◉ Automatic

Figure 4.17 – GCP – Create a VPC network

3. Specify inbound and outbound firewall rules, as shown in *Figure 4.18*:

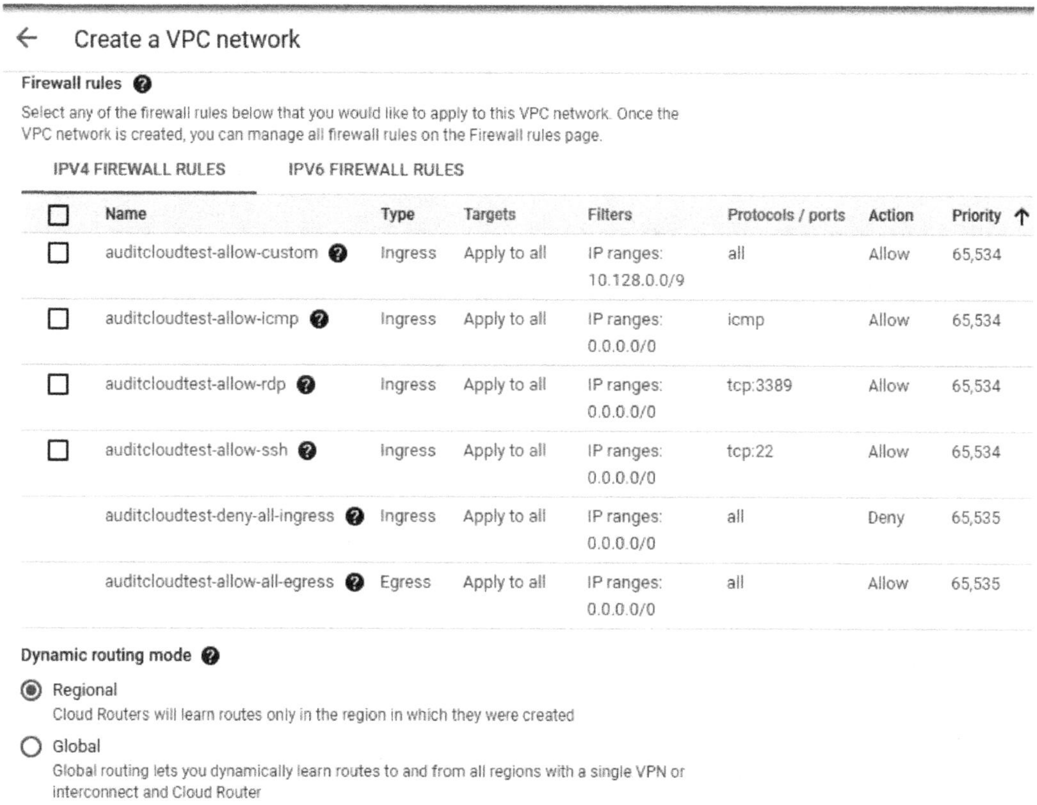

← Create a VPC network

Firewall rules ❓

Select any of the firewall rules below that you would like to apply to this VPC network. Once the VPC network is created, you can manage all firewall rules on the Firewall rules page.

IPV4 FIREWALL RULES   IPV6 FIREWALL RULES

	Name	Type	Targets	Filters	Protocols / ports	Action	Priority ↑
☐	auditcloudtest-allow-custom ❓	Ingress	Apply to all	IP ranges: 10.128.0.0/9	all	Allow	65,534
☐	auditcloudtest-allow-icmp ❓	Ingress	Apply to all	IP ranges: 0.0.0.0/0	icmp	Allow	65,534
☐	auditcloudtest-allow-rdp ❓	Ingress	Apply to all	IP ranges: 0.0.0.0/0	tcp:3389	Allow	65,534
☐	auditcloudtest-allow-ssh ❓	Ingress	Apply to all	IP ranges: 0.0.0.0/0	tcp:22	Allow	65,534
	auditcloudtest-deny-all-ingress ❓	Ingress	Apply to all	IP ranges: 0.0.0.0/0	all	Deny	65,535
	auditcloudtest-allow-all-egress ❓	Egress	Apply to all	IP ranges: 0.0.0.0/0	all	Allow	65,535

Dynamic routing mode ❓

◉ Regional
   Cloud Routers will learn routes only in the region in which they were created

◯ Global
   Global routing lets you dynamically learn routes to and from all regions with a single VPN or interconnect and Cloud Router

Figure 4.18 – GCP – Firewall rules configuration options

4. Next, create the GCP VPC, as shown in *Figure 4.19*:

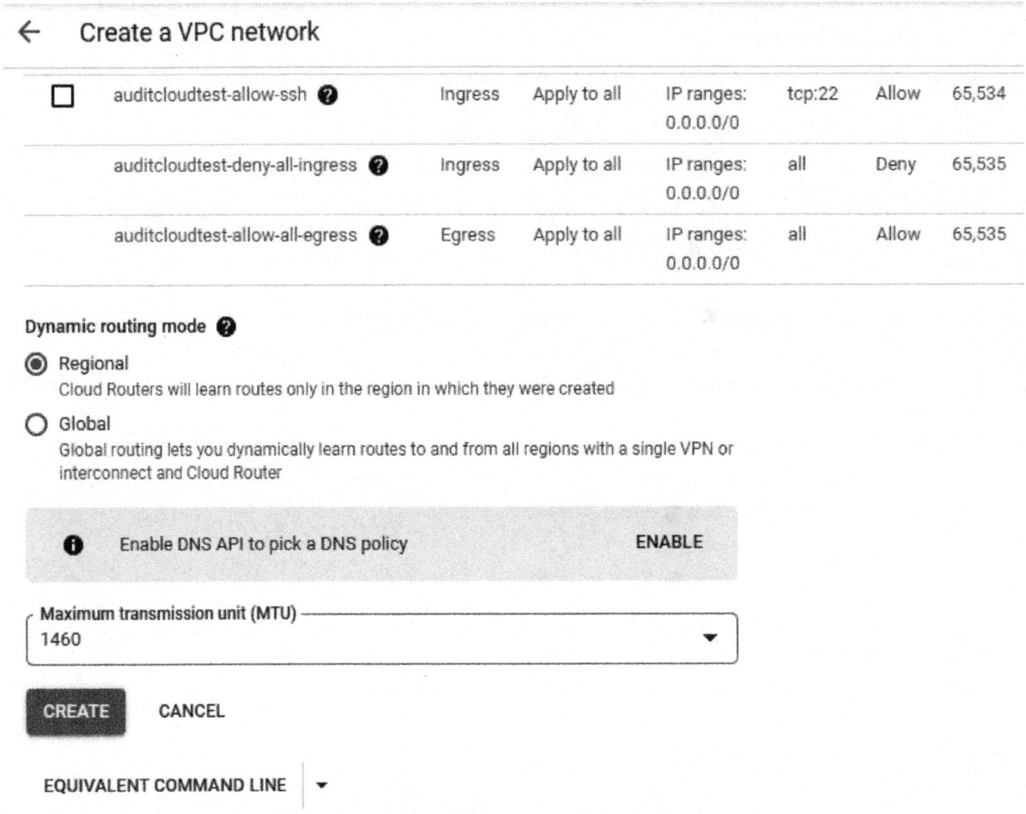

←   **Create a VPC network**

☐ auditcloudtest-allow-ssh ❓	Ingress	Apply to all	IP ranges: 0.0.0.0/0	tcp:22	Allow	65,534
auditcloudtest-deny-all-ingress ❓	Ingress	Apply to all	IP ranges: 0.0.0.0/0	all	Deny	65,535
auditcloudtest-allow-all-egress ❓	Egress	Apply to all	IP ranges: 0.0.0.0/0	all	Allow	65,535

Dynamic routing mode ❓

◉ Regional
Cloud Routers will learn routes only in the region in which they were created

◯ Global
Global routing lets you dynamically learn routes to and from all regions with a single VPN or interconnect and Cloud Router

> ℹ   Enable DNS API to pick a DNS policy   **ENABLE**

┌ Maximum transmission unit (MTU) ─────────────────
│ 1460   ▼

CREATE   CANCEL

EQUIVALENT COMMAND LINE │ ▼

Figure 4.19 – GCP – creating VPC resources

With that, the GCP VPC network has been created, as shown in *Figure 4.20*:

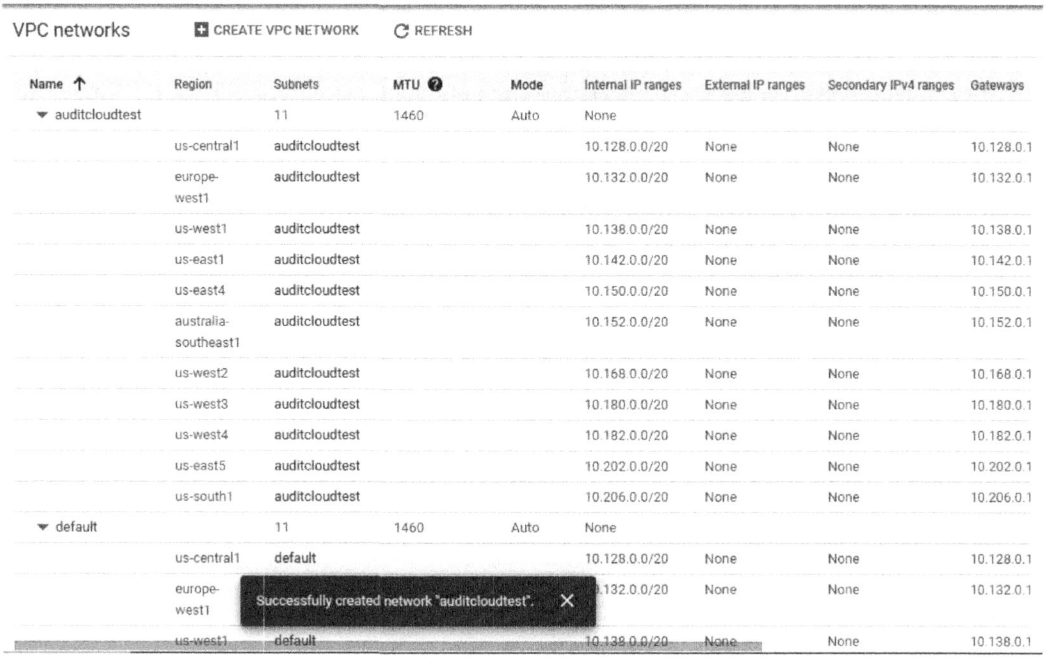

Name ↑	Region	Subnets	MTU ❓	Mode	Internal IP ranges	External IP ranges	Secondary IPv4 ranges	Gateways
▼ auditcloudtest		11	1460	Auto	None			
	us-central1	auditcloudtest			10.128.0.0/20	None	None	10.128.0.1
	europe-west1	auditcloudtest			10.132.0.0/20	None	None	10.132.0.1
	us-west1	auditcloudtest			10.138.0.0/20	None	None	10.138.0.1
	us-east1	auditcloudtest			10.142.0.0/20	None	None	10.142.0.1
	us-east4	auditcloudtest			10.150.0.0/20	None	None	10.150.0.1
	australia-southeast1	auditcloudtest			10.152.0.0/20	None	None	10.152.0.1
	us-west2	auditcloudtest			10.168.0.0/20	None	None	10.168.0.1
	us-west3	auditcloudtest			10.180.0.0/20	None	None	10.180.0.1
	us-west4	auditcloudtest			10.182.0.0/20	None	None	10.182.0.1
	us-east5	auditcloudtest			10.202.0.0/20	None	None	10.202.0.1
	us-south1	auditcloudtest			10.206.0.0/20	None	None	10.206.0.1
▼ default		11	1460	Auto	None			
	us-central1	default			10.128.0.0/20	None	None	10.128.0.1
	europe-west1	default			10.132.0.0/20	None	None	10.132.0.1
	us-west1	default			10.138.0.0/20	None	None	10.138.0.1

Successfully created network "auditcloudtest".   ✕

Figure 4.20 – GCP VPC deployed

In this section, we reviewed how to create and configure virtual networks in AWS, Azure, and GCP. Next, we will look at how to securely configure network controls to protect these networks.

Network controls

Virtual networks in the cloud are exposed to the internet by default. As a result, they can be susceptible to attacks such as denial-of-service attacks or data exfiltration among others. It is critical to ensure network controls have been configured securely to protect cloud resources from unauthorized access or attack.

The basic network control in the cloud is the security group, which represents a virtual firewall for your instance/server/virtual machine. You can use a security group to manage inbound and outbound network traffic to your instance/server/virtual machine.

In traditional networks, network traffic is protected via a dedicated network firewall. A network firewall is essentially the barrier that sits between a private internal network and the public internet. The network firewall's main purpose is to allow traffic in from authorized sources and to keep malicious traffic out. In contrast, in the cloud, instead of having a dedicated network firewall, each instance/server/virtual machine is associated with a security group.

Cloud misconfiguration is one of the top security risks in the cloud. Cloud misconfiguration refers to any errors or gaps sustained while constructing a cloud environment that could pose a security risk. One of the most common misconfigurations relating to networks is a security groups rule allowing for unrestricted **Secure Shell** (**SSH**) access (for example, 0.0.0.0/0 on port 22). This simple configuration error allows an attacker to attempt remote server access from anywhere with internet access.

To mitigate bad actors from accessing an organization's data, the cloud customer should configure their ports and protocols so that they're only accessible by trusted IP addresses and networks. For example, remote administration ports such as 22 (SSH) and 3389 (RDP) should only allow access from your private network and not the entire internet (which is specified in security groups as 0.0.0.0/0).

While the cloud service providers have embedded some network security controls into their virtual network resources, it is not enough to rely on the cloud service provider configurations. Many of the cloud service provider network implementations come with default settings that are not inherently secure. These default settings have to be scrutinized closely to ensure they are secure for the cloud customer. Generally, the best way to mitigate attacks is to create secure VPCs, virtual networks, subnetworks, and their associated security groups.

As IT auditors, we have to assess if controls for managing network access have been implemented securely. We will highlight the core network controls we need to examine for each cloud service provider

Amazon Virtual Private Cloud

Several levels of controls can be leveraged to secure Amazon VPCs. We will highlight two main network controls: **network access control lists** (**ACLs**) and **security groups**.

Cloud customers can restrict both inbound and outbound network traffic using network ACLs and/ or security groups. Restricting inbound and outbound network traffic protects the cloud customers' network against unauthorized access to its resources. An IT auditor needs to ensure network ACLs, security groups, and firewalls have been configured securely.

Network ACLs

Network ACLs manage network traffic at the subnetwork level. Network ACLs keep unwanted network traffic out of the subnets. Subnets or subnetworks are smaller separate parts of the overall VPC. Network ACLs allow or disallow network traffic based on the configured policy. NACLs are stateless, so they must be configured inbound or outbound. NACLs rules are processed in order, so order matters.

Network ACLs control network traffic to or from a subnet according to a set of inbound and outbound rules. This means they represent network-level security. For example, an inbound rule might deny incoming network traffic from a range of IP addresses originating from a hostile country, while an outbound rule might allow all network traffic to leave the subnet.

All AWS accounts come with a default VPC. A default VPC comes with a public subnet. As an IT auditor, it is important to ensure no sensitive company data is placed in a public subnet. In addition, the default VPC has a network ACL, which allows all inbound and outbound network traffic. The IT auditor needs to review the rules in the default VPC network ACL to ensure inbound and outbound network traffic is authorized by the organization. In particular, pay close attention to the source, destination, protocol, and port ranges for both inbound and outbound rules. In addition, AWS rules are evaluated in numerical order, starting with the lowest-numbered rule getting processed first. Therefore, it is important to examine if the rules have been placed in the proper order.

To review network ACLs in AWS, click on **Network ACLs** under the **Resources by Region** AWS interface, as shown in *Figure 4.21*:

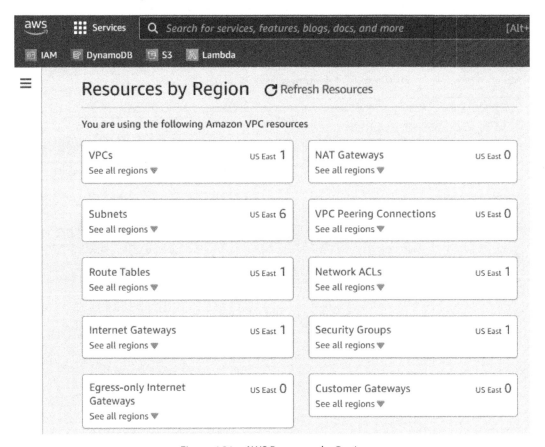

Figure 4.21 – AWS Resources by Region

A list of network ACLs will be displayed, as shown in *Figure 4.22*:

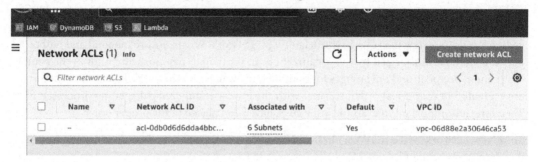

Figure 4.22 – AWS – Network ACLs

Review **Inbound rules**, as shown in *Figure 4.23*:

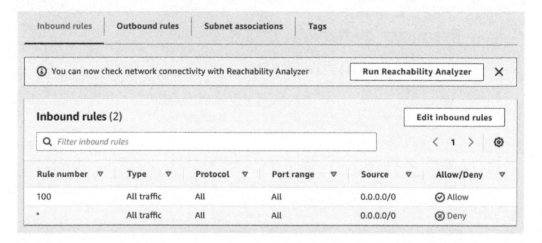

Figure 4.23 – AWS Inbound rules

Review **Outbound rules**, as shown in *Figure 4.24*:

| Inbound rules | Outbound rules | Subnet associations | Tags |

ⓘ You can now check network connectivity with Reachability Analyzer   [Run Reachability Analyzer]   ✕

Outbound rules (2)   [Edit outbound rules]

🔍 *Filter outbound rules*   ⟨ 1 ⟩   ⚙

Rule number ▽	Type ▽	Protocol ▽	Port range ▽	Destination ▽	Allow/Deny ▽
100	All traffic	All	All	0.0.0.0/0	⊘ Allow
*	All traffic	All	All	0.0.0.0/0	⊗ Deny

Figure 4.24 – AWS Outbound rules

In the example shown in *Figure 4.23*, rule 100 for inbound rules with source 0.0.0.0/0 means the VPC allows inbound access from all IP addresses for all port ranges and protocols. In the example in *Figure 4.24*, rule 100 for outbound rules with destination 0.0.0.0/0 means the VPC allows outbound access from all IP addresses for all port ranges and protocols. In this scenario, the IT auditor should question the organization as to the business case of maintaining a VPC with insecure rules.

Security groups are another network control for managing network traffic. We'll look at them next.

Security groups

Security groups control network traffic to or from an AWS EC2 instance according to a set of inbound and outbound rules. Security groups evaluate all the rules in them before allowing network traffic. Security groups, by default, do not allow any inbound network traffic but allow all outbound network traffic. When you create a VPC, AWS automatically creates a default security group for it. Similar to network ACLs, the IT auditor needs to review the rules in the security group to ensure inbound and outbound network traffic is authorized by the organization. In particular, pay close attention to the source, destination, protocol, and port ranges for both inbound and outbound rules.

While you could implement security groups independent of network ACLs, it is recommended to implement both as security groups and network ACLs are two layers that complement each other as part of defense in depth. Network ACLs are the first line of defense, whereas security groups are the second line of defense for inbound network traffic. For outbound network traffic, security groups are the first line of defense, while network ACLs are the second layer of defense.

To review security groups in AWS, click on **Security Groups** under the **Resources by Region** AWS interface, as shown in *Figure 4.25*:

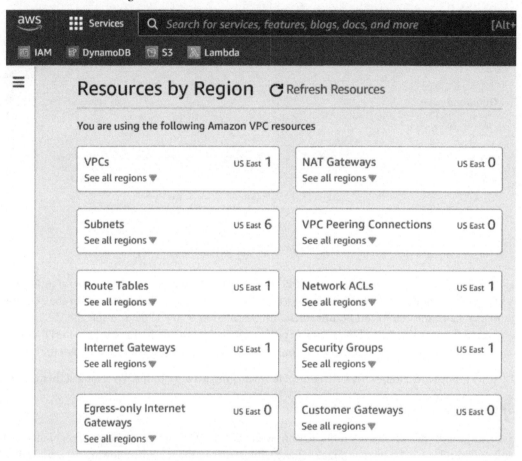

Figure 4.25 – AWS Resources by Region

A list of security groups will be displayed, as shown in *Figure 4.26*:

Figure 4.26 – AWS – Security Groups

Details of the Security Group are shown in *Figure 4.27*:

Figure 4.27 – AWS Security Group details

Review **Inbound rules**, as shown in *Figure 4.28*:

Figure 4.28 – AWS Inbound rules

Review **Outbound rules**, as shown in *Figure 4.29*:

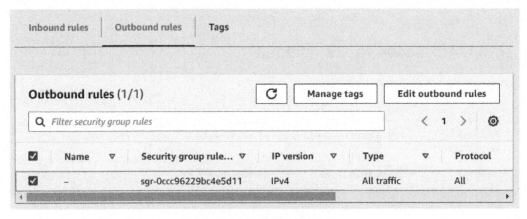

Figure 4.29 – AWS Outbound rules

Now that we've looked at how to secure network controls for an AWS VPC, let's look at how to implement network security controls in an Azure VNet.

Azure Virtual Network

Azure VNet manages network traffic via network security groups. A network security group contains security rules that manage inbound and outbound security rules that enable you to filter network traffic. For each rule, you can specify the source and destination, port, and protocol. With a network security group, you can allow or deny network traffic to and from a single IP address, to and from multiple IP addresses, or to and from entire subnets.

To review network security groups in Azure, go to the portal and type `security group` in the search bar, as shown in *Figure 4.30*:

Figure 4.30 – Azure security group search

Review **Inbound port rules**, as shown in *Figure 4.31*:

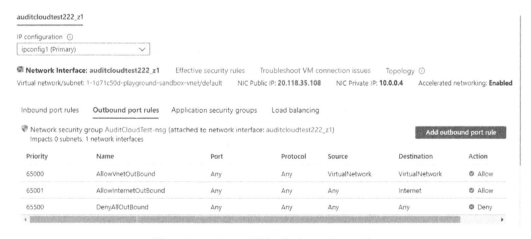

Figure 4.31 – Azure NSG – Inbound port rules

In this example, we get a warning on rule **300**. SSH, which runs on port 22, is a powerful network protocol that gives users, particularly system administrators, a secure way to access a computer over an unsecured network. In this scenario, SSH is directly exposed to the internet. As an IT auditor, we would flag this and recommend the organization use a VPN or a private connection if there was a business need for SSH.

In addition, review the **Outbound port rules** section to ensure secure configuration, as shown in *Figure 4.32*:

auditcloudtest222_z1

IP configuration ⓘ

ipconfig1 (Primary)   ⌄

🖥 **Network Interface: auditcloudtest222_z1**   Effective security rules   Troubleshoot VM connection issues   Topology ⓘ
Virtual network/subnet: 1-1d71c50d-playground-sandbox-vnet/default   NIC Public IP: **20.118.35.108**   NIC Private IP: **10.0.0.4**   Accelerated networking: **Enabled**

Inbound port rules   **Outbound port rules**   Application security groups   Load balancing

🔰 Network security group AuditCloudTest-nsg (attached to network interface: auditcloudtest222_z1)   **Add outbound port rule**
    Impacts 0 subnets, 1 network interfaces

Priority	Name	Port	Protocol	Source	Destination	Action
65000	AllowVnetOutBound	Any	Any	VirtualNetwork	VirtualNetwork	✓ Allow
65001	AllowInternetOutBound	Any	Any	Any	Internet	✓ Allow
65500	DenyAllOutBound	Any	Any	Any	Any	⊗ Deny

Figure 4.32 – Azure NSG – Outbound port rules

Now that we've looked at how to secure network controls for Azure VNet, let's look at how to implement network security controls in a GCP VPC.

Google Cloud Platform Virtual Private Cloud

Network traffic in GCP is managed by VPC firewall rules and network firewall policies. The firewall contains rules that are scoped to a single VPC. Network traffic is evaluated against each rule in priority order until there is a matching rule to make the final determinations.

Every GCP project comes with a default VPC and this default VPC is pre-populated with firewall rules that allow incoming connections to all instances. The default VPC has over-permissive, insecure firewall rules, so the IT auditor needs to examine these default rules closely to ensure they match the organization's risk posture.

Organizations are strongly recommended to create custom VPC networks and avoid using GCP default VPCs. GCP firewall rules are defined at the VPC network level and are specific to the network in which they are defined. GCP firewall rules are specific to a VPC network. Each rule either allows or denies traffic when its conditions are met. The IT auditor should review ports, protocols, and the source or destination of the network traffic.

To review the VPC firewall, follow these steps:

1. Go to the Google Cloud Console and navigate to **VPC network**. Then, click on **Firewall**, as shown in *Figure 4.33*:

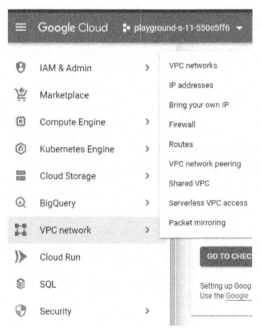

Figure 4.33 – Google Cloud Console

2. Next, navigate to **Firewall resources**, as shown in *Figure 4.34*:

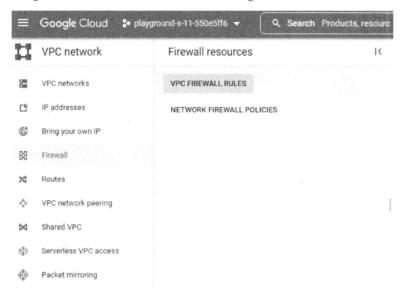

Figure 4.34 – GCP VPC – Firewall resources

3. Navigate to **VPC firewall rules** to review the current rules, as shown in *Figure 4.35*:

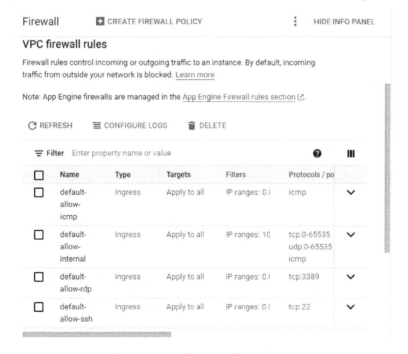

Figure 4.35 – GCP – VPC firewall rules

4.   Navigate to **Network firewall policies** to review the current policies, as shown in *Figure 4.36*:

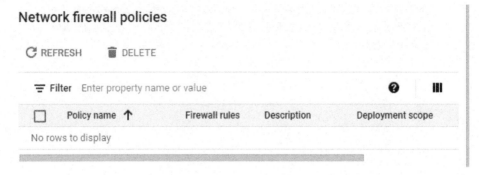

Figure 4.36 – GCP VPC – Network firewall policies

In this section, we reviewed how to securely configure core network controls in AWS, Azure, and GCP. Next, we will look at how to implement industry-standard security benchmarks within security policies in AWS, Azure, and GCP.

Security policies

As we said earlier in this chapter, it is important to review industry-standard security benchmarks such as CIS Amazon Web Services, CIS Microsoft Azure Benchmarks, and CIS Google Cloud Platform Benchmarks to understand best practices around security policies when configuring virtual networks. At the time of writing, the benchmarks from the Center for Internet Security can be found at https://www.cisecurity.org/cis-benchmarks.

For each benchmark, we will look at the recommendations around the networking policies.

Amazon Virtual Private Cloud

The following security policies related to networking in the CIS Amazon Web Services are recommended:

- 5.1 Ensure no network ACLs allow ingress from 0.0.0.0/0 to remote server administration ports

- 5.2 Ensure no security groups allow ingress from 0.0.0.0/0 to remote server administration ports

- 5.3 Ensure the default security group of every VPC restricts all traffic

- 5.4 Ensure routing tables for VPC peering are "least access"

For each control, the CIS benchmarks provide detailed instructions on why the policy is recommended, as well as the rationale. For example, for **5.1 Ensure no network ACLs allow ingress from 0.0.0.0/0 to remote server administration ports**, it is recommended that "no NACL allows unrestricted ingress access to remote server administration ports, such as SSH to port 22 and RDP to port 3389." The rationale given is "public access to remote server administration ports, such as 22 and 3389, increases the resource attack surface and unnecessarily raises the risk of resource compromise."

Azure Virtual Network

Similarly, in Azure, the following security policies related to networking in the CIS Microsoft Azure Benchmarks are recommended:

- 6.1 Ensure that RDP access is restricted from the internet
- 6.2 Ensure that SSH access is restricted from the internet
- 6.3 Ensure no SQL databases allow ingress 0.0.0.0/0 (ANY IP)
- 6.4 Ensure that the Network Security Group Flow Log retention period is "greater than 90 days"
- 6.5 Ensure that Network Watcher is "Enabled" (manual)
- 6.6 Ensure that UDP services are restricted from the internet

For each control, the CIS benchmarks provide detailed instructions on why the policy is recommended, as well as the rationale. For example, for **6.2 Ensure that SSH access is restricted from the internet**, it is recommended that you "Disable SSH access on network security groups from the internet." The rationale given is "attackers can use various brute-force techniques to gain access to Azure Virtual Machines. Once the attackers gain access, they can use a virtual machine as a launch point for compromising other machines on the Azure Virtual Network or even attack networked devices outside of Azure."

Google Cloud Platform Virtual Private Cloud

Similarly, for GCP, the following security policies related to networking in the CIS Google Cloud Platform are recommended:

- 3.1 Ensure that the Default Network Does Not Exist in a Project
- 3.2 Ensure Legacy Networks Do Not Exist for Older Projects
- 3.3 Ensure that DNSSEC is Enabled for Cloud DNS
- 3.4 Ensure that RSASHA1 is Not Used for the Key-Signing Key in Cloud DNS DNSSEC
- 3.5 Ensure that RSASHA1 is Not Used for the Zone-Signing Key in Cloud DNS DNSSEC
- 3.6 Ensure that SSH Access is Restricted From the Internet
- 3.7 Ensure that RDP Access Is Restricted From the Internet
- 3.8 Ensure that VPC Flow Logs are Enabled for Every Subnet in a VPC Network
- 3.9 Ensure No HTTPS or SSL Proxy Load Balancers Permit SSL Policies With Weak Cipher Suites
- 3.10 Use **Identity Aware Proxy** (**IAP**) to Ensure Only Traffic From Google IP Addresses are "Allowed"

For each control, the CIS benchmarks provide detailed instructions on why the policy is recommended, as well as the rationale. For example, for **3.1 Ensure that the Default Network Does Not Exist in a Project**, it is recommended that "To prevent the use of default network, a project should not have a default network." The rationale given is that "The default network has a preconfigured network configuration and automatically insecure firewall rules."

With that, we've looked at how to implement industry-standard security benchmarks within security policies for each of the three cloud providers. Next, let's look at security attributes we can apply to protect data within virtual networks in the cloud.

Data security

Cloud networks have public frontends and the ability to communicate with the broader internet. As we said earlier in this chapter, cloud infrastructure is exposed to the internet. As a result, it can be susceptible to attacks such as denial-of-service attacks, data exfiltration, and so on.

A denial-of-service attack is the act of flooding your network with tons of illegitimate network traffic to overload your network and prevent you from fulfilling the real requests. Data exfiltration is a type of security breach that leads to the unauthorized transfer of data. There are many attack paths an adversary can take once they have obtained some sort of access to a cloud network.

Securing networks running in the cloud is essential to providing data security. The following security controls can mitigate the risks presented by the cloud:

- **Encryption**: To protect data in transit, network traffic should be encrypted, regardless of whether the traffic goes over public networks or within a secure private network. Encryption should be implemented to avoid **man-in-the-middle (MiTM)** attacks. Network traffic should be encrypted using a secure protocol such as **Transport Layer Security (TLS)**. The IT auditor should check that deprecated ciphers are not being used, such as TLS 1.0 or TLS 1.1. TLS 1.2 or above is encouraged. Another option is to encrypt data in cloud storage before it is transmitted so that it is secure as it travels from point A to B. For instance, you could enable **Server Message Block (SMB)** encryption for Azure VMs. SMB encryption provides end-to-end encryption of data. This would ensure the data is encrypted in transit as it travels over Azure VNets. In addition, the IT auditor should be cognizant of any organization using unsecure protocols such as Telnet or FTP.

- **Firewalls**: Firewalls separate trusted network traffic from untrusted. Use additional security solutions such as firewalls and WAFs to actively detect and block malicious traffic. A firewall should be placed at the edge of the network. WAFs will block connections at edge locations long before they can get onto your network. For example, in Azure VNets, you can enable a firewall. Navigate to **Virtual network | Capabilities**, as shown in *Figure 4.37*:

AuditCloudTest
Virtual network
Search (Ctrl+/)
Overview
Activity log
Access control (IAM)
Tags
Diagnose and solve problems
Settings
Address space
Connected devices
Subnets
Bastion
DDoS protection
Firewall
Microsoft Defender for Cloud
Network manager
DNS servers
Resource group (move) : 1-7391f37c-playground-sandbox
Location (move) : West US
Subscription (move) : P2-Real Hands-On Labs
Subscription ID : 964df7ca-3ba4-48b6-a695-1ed9db5723f8
Address space : 10.0.0.0/16
DNS servers : Azure provided DNS service
Flow timeout : Configure
BGP community string : Configure
Virtual network ID : bef7ea00-1f23-406b-b9a0-659883f397e1
Tags (edit) : Click here to add tags
Topology
Capabilities (5)
Recommendations
Tutorials
DDoS protection
Configure additional protection from distributed denial of service
Not configured
Azure Firewall
Protect your network with a stateful L3-L7 firewall.
Not configured
Peerings
Seamlessly connect two or more virtual networks.
Not configured
Security
Filter network traffic to and from Azure resources.
Private endpoints
Privately access Azure services without sending traffic across
Not configured

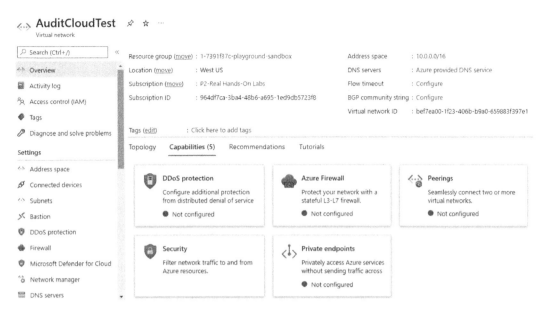

Figure 4.37 – Azure VNet – Capabilities

Navigate to **Azure Firewall** to either enable Azure Firewall or create a new firewall, as shown in *Figure 4.38*:

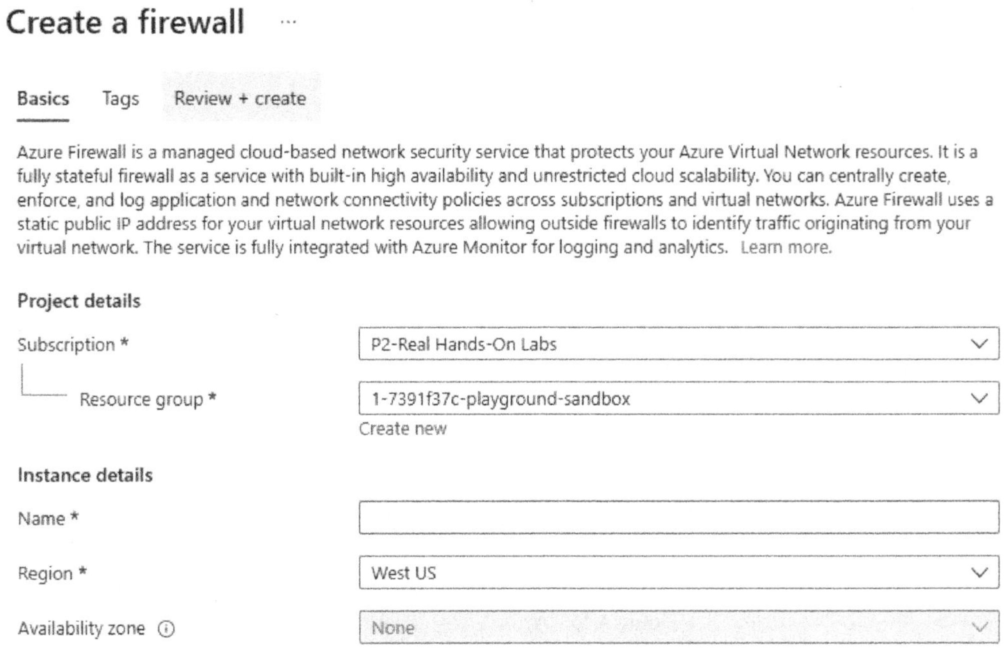

Create a firewall
Basics
Tags
Review + create
Azure Firewall is a managed cloud-based network security service that protects your Azure Virtual Network resources. It is a fully stateful firewall as a service with built-in high availability and unrestricted cloud scalability. You can centrally create, enforce, and log application and network connectivity policies across subscriptions and virtual networks. Azure Firewall uses a static public IP address for your virtual network resources allowing outside firewalls to identify traffic originating from your virtual network. The service is fully integrated with Azure Monitor for logging and analytics. Learn more.
Project details
Subscription *
P2-Real Hands-On Labs
Resource group *
1-7391f37c-playground-sandbox
Create new
Instance details
Name *
Region *
West US
Availability zone
None

Figure 4.38 – Azure VNet – Create a firewall

In addition, you can navigate to **DDos protection** and enable the capability to mitigate denial-of-service attacks, as shown in *Figure 4.39*:

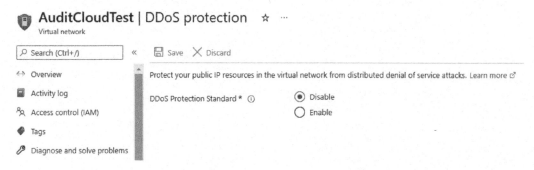

Figure 4.39 – Azure VNet – DDos protection

- **Peering**: Peering is a technique for securely connecting two or more virtual private clouds, or virtual networks. When peering is implemented, resources running in separate clouds can communicate with each other as if they were running on the same private network. Without peering, resources running in distinct clouds would have to communicate over the public internet, which would significantly increase their exposure to potential attack or abuse. Peering can help mitigate further risks of exploitation when data is transferred outside of the spaces you control, which is the internet. For example, in Azure, you can enable **Peerings**. Navigate to **Virtual network | Capabilities**, as shown in *Figure 4.40*:

Figure 4.40 – Azure VNet – Peerings

Next, **Add peering**, as shown in *Figure 4.41*:

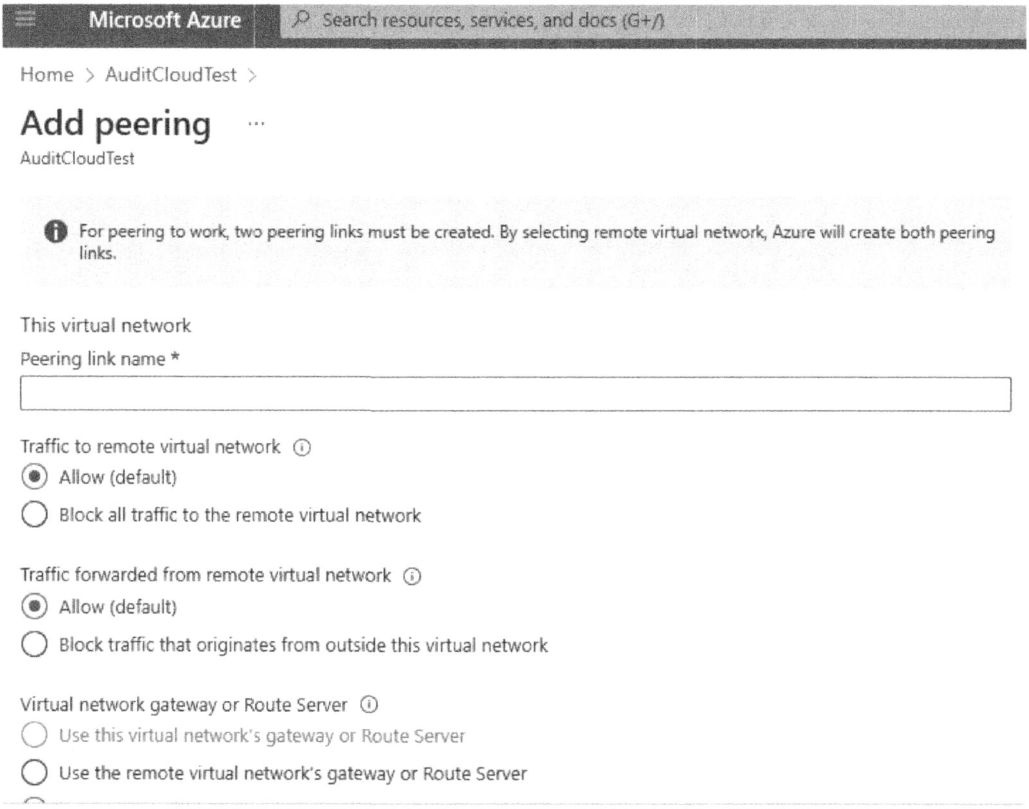

Figure 4.41 – Azure VNet – Add peering

- **Network Address Translation Gateway**: Also known as a **NAT gateway**, this is used to enable instances present in a private subnet to access the internet. In addition to this, the NAT gateway makes sure that the internet doesn't initiate a connection with the instances. To prevent unwanted traffic from entering a VPC, you can create a NAT gateway that enables instances in a private subnet to initiate outbound traffic but prevents receipt of inbound traffic from the internet.

- **Logging via Network Flow Logs**: Network Flow Logs is a feature that captures information about the network traffic going to and from network interfaces in a VPC. Flow logs can be used to help monitor the traffic that is going across the network. All three main cloud service providers have Network Flow Logs capabilities. For illustration purposes, in AWS, navigate to **VPCs**, select your VPC, and click on the **Flow logs** tab, as seen in *Figure 4.42*. Alternatively, you can view the logs in Amazon CloudWatch Logs:

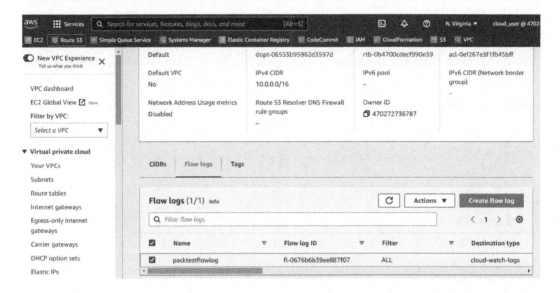

Figure 4.42 – AWS VPC – Flow logs

In this section, we reviewed some techniques to secure data in the cloud. This includes implementing core security controls to mitigate the risks presented by the cloud.

Summary

In this chapter, we looked at network security controls for the three major cloud providers: AWS, Azure, and GCP. We covered how to identify the security control center within each cloud service provider portal and functionality, as well as how to implement industry-standard security benchmarks within security policies. In addition, we also learned how to examine data security controls.

In the next chapter, we'll review financial resources and change management.

5
Financial Resource and Change Management Controls

Due to the dynamic and automated capabilities that enable the quick procurement, deployment, and modification of cloud services, understanding how to review and assess the configuration of financial and change management controls in cloud systems is an essential skill for auditing these environments.

In this chapter, we'll cover the following main topics:

- Policies for resource management
- Policies for change management
- Change management integration and workflows
- Reviewing change history
- Financial billing and cost controls
- Financial resource ownership

By the end of this chapter, we will be able to identify policies and tags and know some options for configuring or applying these across the three cloud providers. We'll also gain insight into how tags impact resource management and learn why tags might be used. We'll learn how native DevSecOps tools may be integrated for change management within the cloud providers, and finally, we'll build knowledge of where options exist for billing and cost controls and the impact financial management has on resource allocation.

Example resource management controls

As mentioned in *Chapter 2, Effective Techniques for Preparing to Audit Cloud Environments,* several frameworks can be used as guidelines for a list of applicable controls and test procedures when defining the scope of your audit. As a reference for this chapter, we'll highlight a few example controls from the **Center for Internet Security** (**CIS**) and **Cloud Security Alliance** (**CSA**) that are relevant to resource management, tagging, change management, change history, and financial features within an enterprise cloud environment.

Center for Internet Security (CIS) benchmark controls

As a reminder, determining all applicable controls will need to be based on system architecture and integration, business risk management goals, and enterprise operational procedures:

- CIS Control 3 Sub-Control 3.7 – Establish and Maintain a Data Classification Scheme: Establish and maintain an overall data classification scheme for the enterprise.

- CIS Control 3 Sub-Control 3.12 – Segment Data Processing and Storage Based on Sensitivity: Segment data processing and storage based on the sensitivity of the data. Do not process sensitive data on enterprise assets intended for lower sensitivity.

- CIS Control 8 Sub-Control 8.5 – Collect Detailed Audit Logs: Configure detailed audit logging for enterprise assets containing sensitive data.

- CIS Control 12 Sub-Control 12.2 – Establish and Maintain a Secure Network Architecture: Establish and maintain a secure network architecture. A secure network architecture must address segmentation, least privilege, and availability, at a minimum.

To find a comprehensive list of CIS benchmark controls, go to `https://www.cisecurity.org/benchmark`.

Now that we've taken a look at some example controls from CIS, let's take a look at controls from the CSA **Cloud Controls Matrix** (**CCM**).

CSA Cloud Controls Matrix

Within the CSA CCM v4.0 framework, controls that would be relevant to the technical assessment of functions in this chapter would fall under several domains, including Change Control and Configuration Management, Data Security and Privacy Life Cycle Management, and Infrastructure and Virtualization Security. Examples of CCM controls an IT auditor should reference for this chapter are as follows:

- Control ID CCC-04 – Unauthorized Change Protection: Restrict the unauthorized addition, removal, update, and management of organization assets

- Control ID CCC-07 – Detection of Baseline Deviation: Implement detection measures with proactive notification in case of changes deviating from the established baseline

- Control ID DSP-03 – Data Inventory: Create and maintain a data inventory, at least for any sensitive data and personal data

- Control ID IVS-08 – Network Architecture Documentation: Identify and document high-risk environments

You can find out more about the CCM matrix from CSA at `https://cloudsecurityalliance.org/artifacts/cloud-controls-matrix-v4/`. Please note that the matrix is periodically updated, so be sure you are accessing the latest version.

Policies for resource management

To ensure that cloud resources (particularly when using IaaS and PaaS services) align with operational and security policies, it's often necessary to leverage technical policies to enforce these within a cloud environment. These technical policies allow organizations to configure a technical template of standards that the cloud resources are either configured to adhere to at the time of setup, reconfigured to adhere to as changes are made, or potentially create alerts for an administrator when the resource is no longer in compliance. In many cases, different policies might be assigned to different resources based on the intent and use of the resource. For example, there may be a need to apply more restrictive policies to a resource that is in a production environment versus a sandbox environment, or those resources that are accessible to external users versus those that are only accessible to users within a corporate directory. The determination of *what* policies an organization applies should be based on the system architecture and integration of the environment. Developing an effective method to control *how*, *where*, and *when* different policies are applied can be done using tagging. In addition to tags supporting the application of policies, another use case for tags in some cloud environments, such as AWS, is to enable **Attribute-Based Access Controls** (**ABACs**). These tags can be used to control who and what can access a particular resource and what actions they can take. Other use cases for tagging are to ensure resources are mapped correctly to architecture and technical requirements for segmentation, quota allocation, business continuity, and disaster recovery. In short, tagging is a way of associating metadata with resources using key-value pairing, and provides a method for grouping resources, controlling access to those resources, and understanding the expectations of what type of security controls the resource should be in adherence to. Although, in some cases, tags may systematically control who has access, this may not always be the case and should be verified. Some tags may be used to provide identifiers for architecture (production and non-production), sensitive data or data classification (**Personally Identifiable Information** (**PII**)), ownership (IT team versus a business team), or applicable compliance and regulatory controls (Sox, PCI and GDPR).

When using policies and tags, organizations must leverage automation where possible to ensure the application of policies and tags is consistently enforced. There should also be a documented policy for the use of policies and tagging that outlines when and how these attributes are applied and the roles and responsibilities related to and impacted by different tags. This policy should also support a documented and agreed-upon naming convention for the tagging key-value pairs, as well as outline ownership for ensuring consistency of what these pairs mean. This should be done for all cloud environments the organization is operating in and the use of tagging and definitions for the key-value pairs should be captured, along with the asset inventory to be provided at the start of an audit. In assessing the application of policies and tags, important areas to identify are where policy and tags have **not** been applied, where there are policy exemptions, and the process for periodic review of any automated applications of policies and tagging. Keep in mind that there may be some areas where default tagging capabilities have been enabled by the cloud provider. You should also assess whether there is any default-enabled policy configuration for the cloud environment and review any policies that may have been disabled.

Each of the cloud providers enables multiple paths to access tagging and policy information. They also each have a concept of Blueprints or Landing Zones, which enable preconfigured environments that can be automatically provisioned through code (**Infrastructure as Code (IaC)** and Policy as Code) and include default compliance policies (often including tagging) and enabled security services and best practices. These options generally intend to apply security and governance policies at scale for multi-account organizations and should greatly minimize potential misconfigurations or misapplication of policies and tags. To learn more about the Blueprint or Landing Zone features of the three major cloud providers, visit the following links:

- AWS: `https://docs.aws.amazon.com/controltower/latest/userguide/what-is-control-tower.html`

- Azure: `https://learn.microsoft.com/en-us/azure/cloud-adoption-framework/ready/landing-zone/`

- Google Cloud Platform (GCP): `https://cloud.google.com/anthos-config-management/docs/concepts/blueprints`

As an IT auditor, you should be aware of where options that directly modify and review policy and tagging settings exist. These features may be spread out between identity or security features or have a dedicated feature area, and this will vary by cloud provider.

In the Microsoft Azure portal, one way to see and edit tags (depending on access permissions) is by accessing an individual resource and selecting **Tags** from either the **Overview** area or directly selecting **Tags** from the left navigation panel, as shown in *Figure 5.1*:

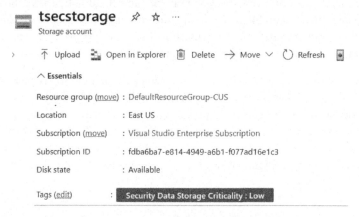

Figure 5.1 – Example Microsoft Azure resource tagging

Another way to find features related to **Policy** and **Tags** in Microsoft Azure is by using the search bar and searching for resources. By performing a search in the Azure portal and navigating to **Tags**, as in *Figure 5.2*, we have the option to look at existing key-value tag pairs and get more insight into how tags can be defined and used within Microsoft Azure:

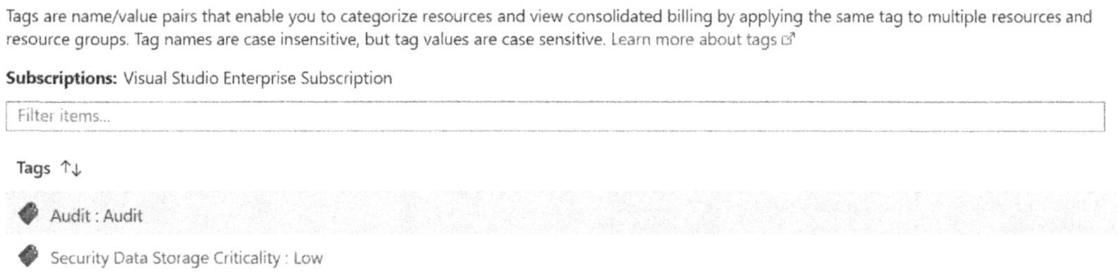

Tags are name/value pairs that enable you to categorize resources and view consolidated billing by applying the same tag to multiple resources and resource groups. Tag names are case insensitive, but tag values are case sensitive. Learn more about tags ☐

Subscriptions: Visual Studio Enterprise Subscription

Filter items...

Tags ↑↓

◆ Audit : Audit

◆ Security Data Storage Criticality : Low

Figure 5.2 – Microsoft Azure key-value tag pairing

In *Figure 5.3*, a search on **Policy** allowed us to navigate directly to the **Policy** blade, where we can see there is a resource that appears to be non-compliant with a default policy:

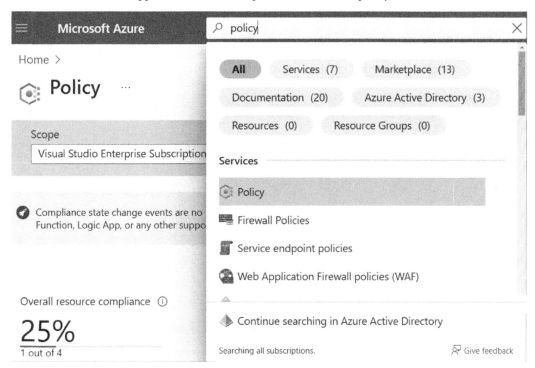

Figure 5.3 – Microsoft Azure Policy blade

Selecting the policy that appears as non-compliant provides additional details on the policy and why the resource has been flagged as non-compliant, as shown in *Figure 5.4*. This would be a great option for an IT auditor as they can have this report extracted and compared against the organization's IT controls:

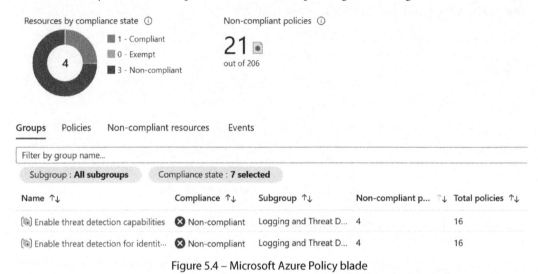

Figure 5.4 – Microsoft Azure Policy blade

Additional details about the use of tags and policies within Microsoft Azure can be found at `https://docs.microsoft.com/en-us/azure/azure-resource-manager/management/tag-policies`.

In AWS, one location where you can find configuration for tags is under **AWS Resource Groups**, as shown in *Figure 5.5*:

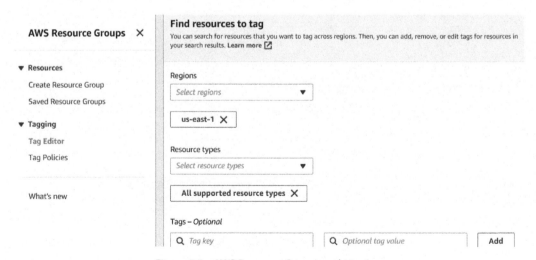

Figure 5.5 – AWS Resource Groups and tagging

As the name suggests, you can group resources, as well as apply tagging to individual resources and edit tag policies. As mentioned earlier, AWS allows ABAC via the use of tags, so it's important to understand the taxonomy and tagging design an organization is using since it may influence access controls. To learn more about this, you can check out `https://docs.aws.amazon.com/ IAM/latest/UserGuide/tutorial_attribute-based-access-control.html`.

Within **Google Cloud**, much of the policy, tagging, and resource management abilities exist within the **IAM & Admin** product, as shown in *Figure 5.6*. Here, you can easily identify a list of built-in inherited policies that have been applied. The option for **Tags** is visible in the left-hand side navigation:

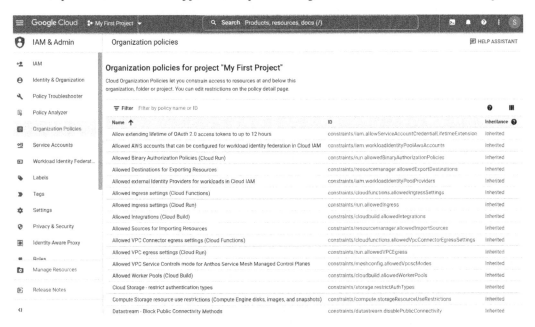

Figure 5.6 – Google Cloud Platform organizational-level policies

Now that we've reviewed how policies and tags may be used to impact compliance, let's review other options for controlling changes to resources.

Performing changes

Beyond using policies and tags to control compliant management of resources, these same features, along with others, may be used to restrict changes. Each of the cloud providers offers a way of grouping resources together for ease of classification. Both at a group and individual level, settings can be applied to lock the resource against changes or to restrict the level of changes that can be made (as shown in *Figure 5.7*), in addition to role assignments and access policies, as covered in *Chapter 3*, *Identity and Access Management Controls*:

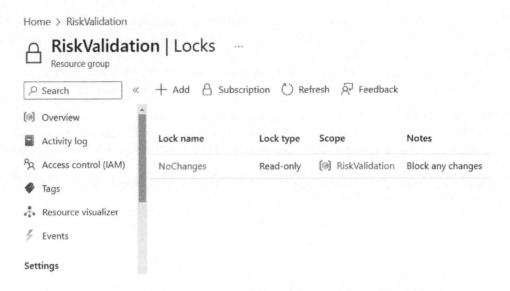

Figure 5.7 – Example Microsoft Azure read-only lock applied

This level of restriction may not be readily apparent when discussing access controls, which is why organizations must document their system architecture. As auditors, we must understand that cloud providers offer a complex mix of controls that can be applied.

Now that we have looked at additional options for controlling changes, let's gain insight into what cloud provider tools are available for managing changes.

Change management integration and workflows

When adopting IaaS or PaaS cloud services, many companies also choose to adopt change management processes that support **continuous integration/continuous deployment (CI/CD)**. By necessity, this means there should be automated processes embedded into their change management procedures. From an auditing standpoint, this becomes important for a few different reasons. Removing manual processes also reduces the opportunity for manual IT control failures, but organizations now need to ensure that there are safeguards within the automated process that enforce separation of duties, automated policy applications, effective testing and approval gates, and rollback procedures. Automation workflows themselves will need to be regularly reviewed to ensure they adhere to change controls requirements, are not allowing compliance checks to be bypassed, and there is clear visibility and approval for those individuals with access to change the automation workflows or perform approvals as part of the workflows. Both the code and the automated workflows themselves should now be in scope for periodic review. Automation templates and workflows will need to be assessed for security-related controls such as the following:

- Are the latest security patches being applied through IaC templates?

- Who has access to maintain templates? Are changes to templates visible in logging?

- What is the mechanism that is enforcing all changes to go through the CI/CD pipeline? Are there any exceptions to this process?

- Who has access to login or account details for any workload identities or automation accounts being used to manage change integrations and deployments?

- Is there automated alerting to detect non-compliant changes? Who receives this alerting?

Each of the cloud providers has a set of capabilities that can be used to automate the deployment of resources, whether that is **virtual machines** (**VMs**), code, or even security and configuration policies. As shown in *Figure 5.8*, for AWS, some of these capabilities, such as **CodeCommit**, **CodeDeploy**, and **CodePipeline**, can be found under **Developer Tools**:

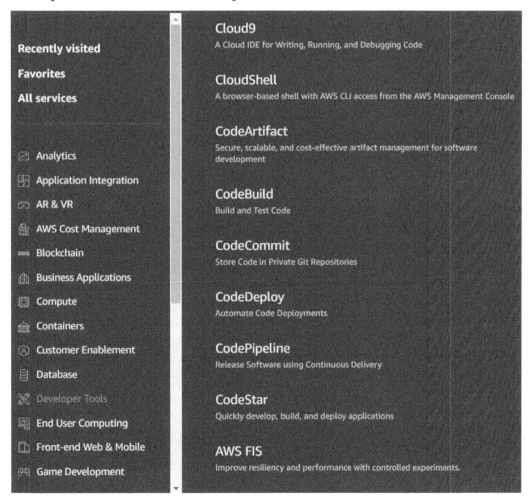

Figure 5.8 – AWS Developer Tools

These tools may be integrated with other third-party change management and CI/CD tools, or third-party tools may be used in place of these. As discussed in *Chapter 1, Cloud Architecture and Navigation,* organizations must provide a sound architectural diagram that outlines these types of integrations.

Like AWS, Microsoft Azure offers a set of tools for managing changes under the **DevOps** feature. As shown in *Figure 5.9,* in addition to deployment pipelines and change repositories, there is an option to view and track artifacts and test plans:

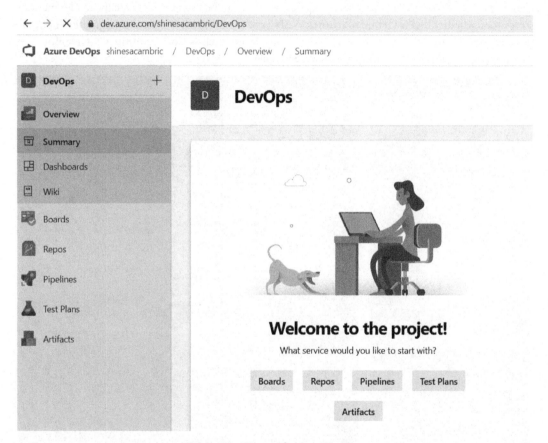

Figure 5.9 – Microsoft Azure DevOps

And in Google Cloud, you can find a set of available native CI/CD options, as shown in *Figure 5.10*:

CI/CD		Name	Description		
Integrate and deliver continuously	🪛	Cloud Build	Continuous integration delivery platform	🗐	⌄
	🪛	Container Registry	Private container registry storage	🗐	⌄
	🪛	Source Repositories	Hosted private git repos	🗐	⌄
	🪛	Artifact Registry	Universal build artifact management	🗐	⌄
	🪛	Cloud Deploy	Managed continuous delivery to GKE	🗐	⌄

Figure 5.10 – Google Cloud Platform CI/CD features

Keep in mind that these are only some of the built-in or native options available with each of the cloud providers. Other resources, such as AWS Config (`https://aws.amazon.com/config/features/`) and Google Anthos Config Management (`https://cloud.google.com/anthos/config-management`), can be used for auditing and deploying automating compliance deviation and Policy as Code configurations. Several popular open source options exist as well for managing policy and code automation. These include the following:

- Cloud Custodian, which is focused on AWS compliance and Policy as Code. More information can be found at `https://aws.amazon.com/blogs/opensource/compliance-as-code-and-auto-remediation-with-cloud-custodian/`.

- Gatekeeper is a general Compliance-as-Code tool that allows administrators to identify and reject any policy violations and also perform audits to see what existing resources may be violating policy. More information can be found at `https://github.com/open-policy-agent/gatekeeper`.

- Terraform by HashiCorp offers a general IaC tool with the ability to define policies and an ancillary tool, Terraform Compliance, that tests for policy compliance. Additional information can be found at `https://developer.hashicorp.com/terraform/intro` and `https://terraform-compliance.com/`.

In the interview and discovery phases of your audit, you may identify that different tools are used in different scenarios, along with integration to third-party products, which will need to be assessed.

Now that we have covered some of the available ways for managing and performing changes in cloud environments, let's investigate some ways that we can see the history of changes that have been made.

Change history

As an auditor, one method that may be used to correlate processes and procedures that mitigate risk is to review activity logs. In cloud environments, these logs may be made up of separate sign-in and event logs that are capturing change history and actions performed by user accounts, service accounts, or workload identities.

In each of the cloud environments, you will find multiple options for tracking the activity that's occurred. The amount of this activity that is tracked, where it is tracked, and for how long this information is made directly available will change based on licensing, cloud system configuration, and cloud provider. In some cases, supplementary data storage tools or platforms may need to be used to ensure longer retention that meets compliance requirements. As an IT auditor, you should also note that not all items are logged by default. In some cases, an organization may need to manually enable logging or the settings to log certain activities, and there may be a cost for doing so. An organization may have the assumption that the cloud provider has the default responsibility of logging activity and making logs available, but an organization should refer to the Shared Responsibility Model referenced in *Chapter 1, Cloud Architecture and Navigation*, as well as periodically review logging settings within their environments.

Change history is typically found in audit logs. Depending on the cloud provider and the event, the navigation to these logs could be dispersed throughout the environment. In Microsoft Azure, for example, you may need to search through audit logs, sign-in logs, log analytics, and provisioning logs, as well as enable diagnostics settings to use workbooks to further query log information. The ability to read these audit logs is tied to specific permissions, as shown in *Figure 5.11*:

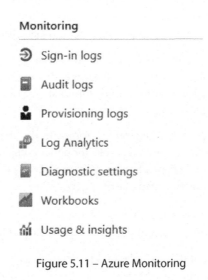

Figure 5.11 – Azure Monitoring

As part of assessing changes to a particular resource or object in a cloud environment, in some cases, it is possible to get the activity by selecting it and identifying its **Activity log**, as shown in *Figure 5.12*:

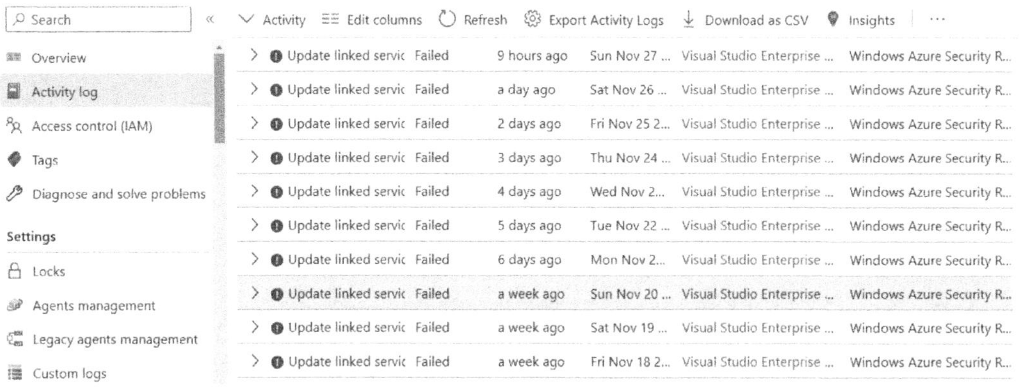

Figure 5.12 – Microsoft Azure Activity log for a resource

In AWS, an organization might use CloudTrail (as shown in *Figure 5.13*) to view event history, or they may be routing to an S3 bucket for storage or out to a third-party SIEM tool. And depending on the environment and control being tested, you may also need to ensure that Amazon network logs, known as VPC Flow Logs, are enabled and available. To find out more about VPC Flow Logs, go to https://docs.aws.amazon.com/vpc/latest/userguide/flow-logs.html.

As an IT auditor, it will be important to ask and understand all logging for all event types. Also, be aware that there may be significant cost implications to logging data and the methods used to retain those logs. This cost may impact the organization's architecture and operational choices, also leading to new or additional risks being identified or controls being adopted. Leveraging cost monitoring and alerting, which will be covered later in this chapter, may be of increased importance in scenarios that require a high degree of logging:

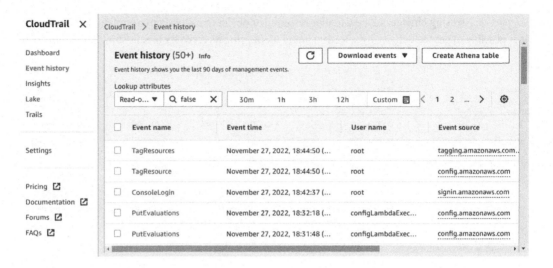

Figure 5.13 – AWS CloudTrail

In many GCP scenarios, logs are enabled by default, but that is not the case for every type of log. In *Figure 5.14*, we can see that for this Google Cloud environment, the log types for Data Access audit logs need to be explicitly selected:

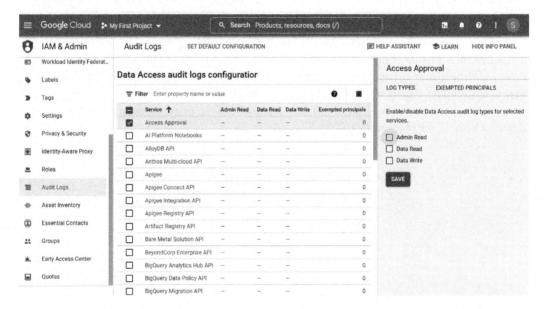

Figure 5.14 – Google Cloud audit log configuration

As an IT auditor, understanding that this is configurable and reviewing who has the access to modify this configuration (and when this configuration is changed, where is it logged) should be an essential part of your audit program.

In *Figure 5.15*, we can see that the retention period for **Log buckets** varies by the log type and whether it is a default log versus what is determined as a required audit log:

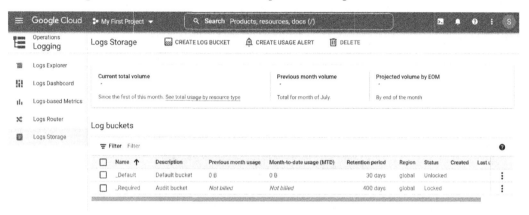

Figure 5.15 – Google Cloud audit log storage configuration

As we wrap up this section, the importance of making sure all pertinent logging is enabled and capturing all in-scope activities for the period required cannot be understated. More information on audit log options for each of the three providers can be found at the following links:

- AWS: https://docs.aws.amazon.com/whitepapers/latest/introduction-aws-security/monitoring-and-logging.html

- Microsoft Azure: https://learn.microsoft.com/en-us/azure/active-directory/reports-monitoring/

- GCP: https://cloud.google.com/logging/docs/audit/

Now that we've covered some important aspects of both managing change and reviewing change history, let's look at billing and cost controls.

Financial billing and cost controls

In a cloud environment, setting up services can be as easy as providing a credit card number. Although this provides the benefit of making cloud services easy to enable and consume, this also adds risk in terms of business continuity (what if the credit card holder leaves the company?), as well as a company being financially liable for overages or the misuse of services (someone stands up a rogue server for crypto mining). Like controls in legacy environments that may check who is authorized to approve purchases at a given amount, this should be assessed within the cloud environment as well. Additionally, the IT auditor should ensure there are controls in place that allow an organization to limit potential cost overages and that proper alerting and notification are in place to monitor billing and cost status.

Depending on how the environment has been configured, some access controls may be defined around who can access billing and cost information. In some cases, an individual may be named as an account owner and retain access to billing and cost details based on that status. In AWS, you may see information about billing in the top-right navigation area, as shown in *Figure 5.16*:

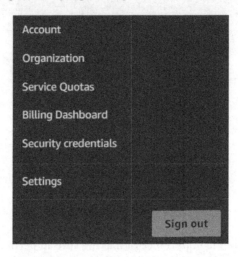

Figure 5.16 – AWS navigation to Service Quotas and Billing Dashboard

Here, you can see there are navigation links to both **Service Quotas** and **Billing Dashboard**. Quotas are an important component of capacity and thus cost.

When accessing the **Billing Dashboard** area in AWS, as shown in *Figure 5.17*, information regarding usage reports, cost categories, and allocation tags is also available:

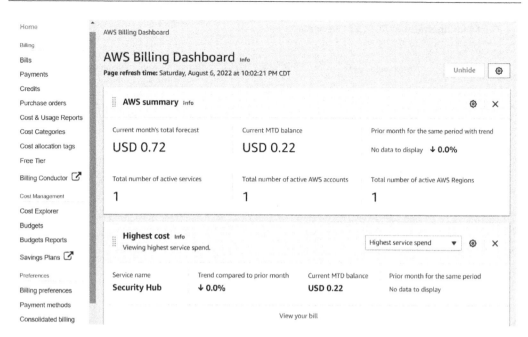

Figure 5.17 – AWS Billing Dashboard

Earlier in this chapter, we reviewed the use and importance of tagging from a change management perspective. Now, we can see that they are also relevant for financial change management.

Within the Microsoft Azure portal, there are a few different places where you can review cost management options. One way to navigate is by searching for billing and then going to the **Cost Management + Billing** blade (as shown in *Figure 5.18*). From here, you can select the option for **Billing scopes**, as shown in the left-hand side navigation menu:

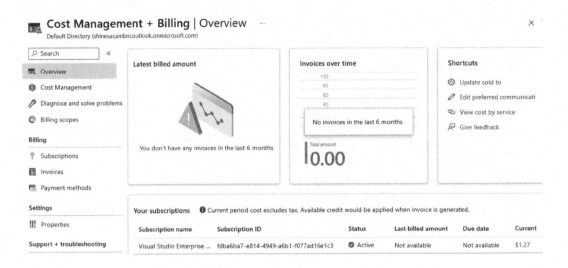

Figure 5.18 – Azure navigation to Cost Management + Billing

After you've selected a billing scope, as shown in *Figure 5.19*, you can view more information regarding the configuration and setup of cost alerts and analysis:

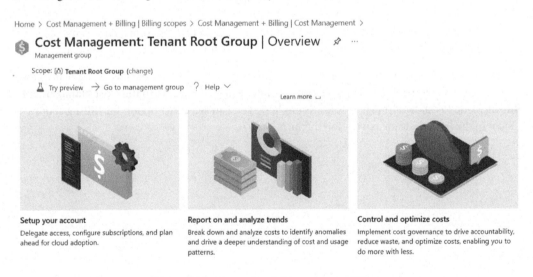

Figure 5.19 – Azure Cost Management + Billing

After selecting a scope, you can also see or create budget alerts (as shown in *Figure 5.20*):

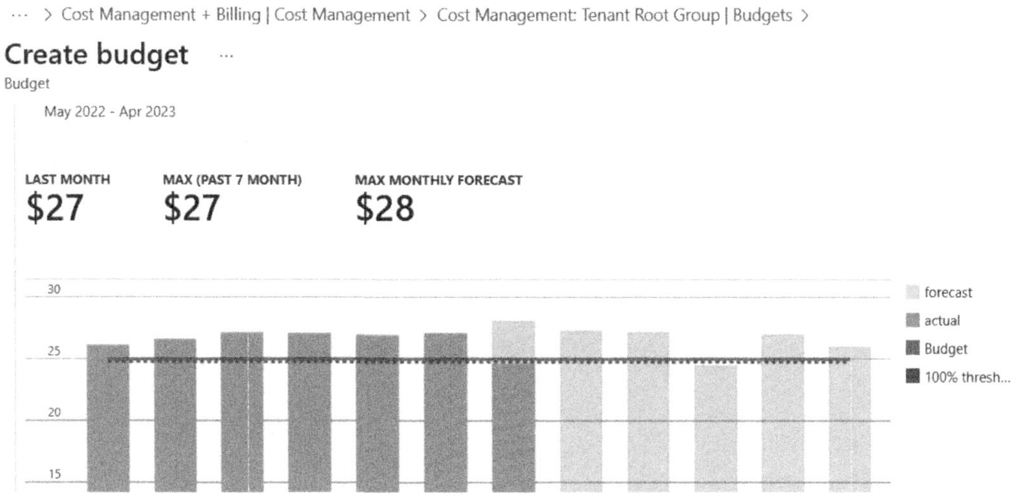

Figure 5.20 – Azure – Create budget

Like AWS and Microsoft Azure, **GCP** offers options to view and control billing. You can see this information by selecting the **Billing** product in the left navigation panel, as shown in *Figure 5.21*:

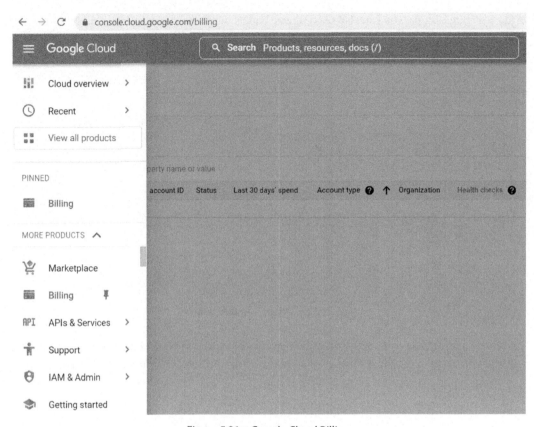

Figure 5.21 – Google Cloud Billing

In GCP, you can also see details regarding quota limits, quota usage, and requests for increases (as shown in *Figure 5.22*):

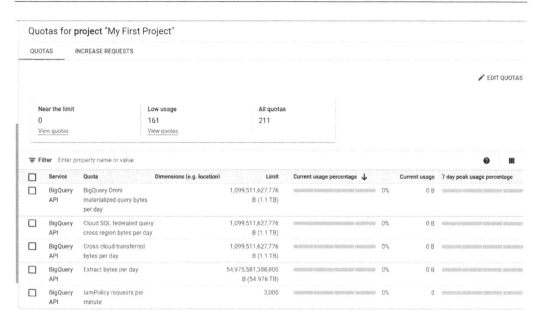

Figure 5.22 – Google Cloud quota increase

Now that we've reviewed how to view billing and cost controls, let's discuss financial resource ownership in cloud environments.

Financial resource ownership

As we reviewed in *Chapter 1, Cloud Architecture and Navigation*, cloud services operate on the Shared Responsibility Model. Understanding this becomes increasingly important as you begin to assess change management controls, which is the ability to log and view changes in a cloud environment and protect against unexpected costs. In most scenarios, it is not the responsibility of the cloud provider to prevent an organization from occurring overages because they have consumed more resources than planned or because there is a lack of controls around who can request increased quota and services. An organization must be vigilant in establishing and communicating a financial ownership and responsibility structure, with both process and technical controls that enforce that structure.

Summary

In this chapter, we looked at some essential areas for IT controls, change management, and financial resource management, where configuration options exist for identity and access management within the three major cloud providers. We covered where policy and tagging configuration can be found and how this information may be automated and influence access.

We also reviewed tools available for change management controls in a CI/CD cloud environment, as well as how to view change history. We finished this chapter by reviewing some features available for billing and cost controls and the importance of determining financial resource ownership.

In the next chapter, we'll look at executing an effective cloud portal audit plan and some tips and techniques that will support that.

Part 3:
Executing an Effective
Enterprise Cloud Audit Plan

On completing this section, the reader will bring together the knowledge gained in previous chapters to effectively assess their cloud environments for risk, compliance, and adherence to IT general computing controls and standard compliance frameworks. This section provides an opportunity to practice performing some basic audit test steps, and allows the reader to get foundational hands-on experience to prepare for more complex auditing.

This part comprises the following chapters:

- *Chapter 6, Tips and Techniques for Advanced Auditing*
- *Chapter 7, Tools for Monitoring and Assessing*
- *Chapter 8, Walk-Through – Assessing IAM Controls*
- *Chapter 9, Walk-Through – Assessing Policy Settings and Resource Controls*
- *Chapter 10, Walk-Through – Assessing Change Management, Logging, and Monitoring Policies*

6

Tips and Techniques for Advanced Auditing

The cloud provides organizations with flexibility, scalability, increased collaboration, and speed. However, IT auditors need to be aware of the potential pitfalls that can increase the security risk for organizations. In this chapter, we want to equip IT auditors with a few tips and techniques they can leverage to make audits in the cloud more efficient. In addition, we will build awareness of considerations IT auditors need to know as they prepare for more advanced auditing requirements.

In this chapter, we'll cover the following main topics:

- Common pitfalls
- Tips, tricks, and techniques
- Preparing for more advanced auditing
- Other clouds – IBM, Oracle, Alibaba

By the end of this chapter, we will be able to identify the common pitfalls IT auditors need to be cognizant of as they approach their audits. We will also have knowledge of some tips and techniques that can be utilized for more effective audits and the considerations for more advanced audits, including other cloud environments.

Common pitfalls

With the scale, speed, and flexibility of the cloud comes complexity. This complexity leads to inherent pitfalls. We will review two broad areas that are common pitfalls for organizations that the IT auditor should be aware of. The first area involves administrative pitfalls that include not managing resource usage, an inability to control shadow IT, and a lack of automation. The second area concerns technical pitfalls that include misconfiguration, providing overly permissive access to users, and the inadvertent exposure of data, such as credentials.

Let's look at the most common pitfalls IT auditors should focus on during an audit, and recommendations they may consider providing to a cloud customer.

Inability to forecast resource usage and costs

Cloud service providers such as **Amazon Web Services** (**AWS**), Azure, and GCP have hundreds of services to choose from. Many cloud customers usually choose services not suited to their business needs due to poor planning including not understanding the requirements of the business.

Cloud service providers have complex pricing models with rates that change according to service, region, and many other parameters. If an organization doesn't fully understand a cloud service provider's pricing model, or how it will progress with the cloud customer usage of service, the organization may incur unexpected costs.

Unused resources left running can easily cause cloud costs to spiral out of control. Organizations need to know the type of resources their applications consume, their quantity, and their corresponding price dimension. In addition, organizations should automate resource provisioning with the various cloud-respective auto-scaling features.

An IT auditor should look to examine if the organization is utilizing tools for tracking and licensing their cost. Such tools include third-party tools, such as **CloudCheckr** and **CloudHealth**.

In addition, an IT auditor should evaluate if the organization is leveraging tags as a means of identification for forecasting. Tags can be defined as applying metadata to help describe and identify the resources running across an organization's cloud environments. Therefore, utilizing tags is an essential tool for gaining visibility into an organization's cloud consumption and expenditure.

The impact of shadow IT

Cloud computing has made it easier for users to bypass organizational procurement processes in order to access the cloud solutions they want. For instance, it's very easy to spin up accounts in AWS, Azure, or GCP without the knowledge of the organization. This is also referred to as shadow IT.

Shadow IT is the practice of bypassing organizational processes and installing IT solutions without the knowledge or approval of the organization. The risk with shadow IT is that it creates a situation in which corporate data is placed outside of the protection provided by the organization's security controls. As a result, shadow IT increases the risk of a data breach.

An IT auditor should evaluate whether an organization leverages tools to track which cloud services are being accessed, to ensure there are no cloud services being used that aren't authorized or supported.

Avoiding automation

Many organizations execute processes in the cloud manually, including installation processes, configuring virtual servers, setting up a network, storage volumes, or other cloud resources. Manual processes are time-consuming, error-prone, and hard to scale.

Automation encompasses solutions and tools that help eliminate repetitive aspects managed by one or more manual processes in the cloud. Cloud automation can increase security and the efficiency of workflows and tasks in the cloud. Automating routine security tasks will mitigate the majority of the manual risks presented by human error.

An IT auditor should examine if the organization utilizes automation within its cloud environments. One popular way to implement cloud automation is by using **infrastructure as code (IaC)**. IaC is a process of creating cloud infrastructure through templates defined by code. Once developed, IaC becomes the building blocks for creating compute, storage, networking, and security policy in a cloud environment.

Misconfiguration

The cloud is still a novel concept and many organizations are unfamiliar with securing cloud infrastructure. As a result, it is easy for a security oversight to leave an organization's cloud-based resources exposed to attackers. An example of a misconfiguration is mistakenly making a cloud-based repository public when you meant to make it private. This makes the repository accessible to anyone on the internet. Tools exist specifically for searching the internet for these unsecured cloud deployments.

To address cloud misconfiguration, the IT auditor should evaluate if the organization scans and reviews its cloud workloads for common vulnerabilities, such as exposed access points, resources labeled as public, and so on. This can be done by using cloud security posture management tools. Cloud security posture management tools are automated solutions that identify misconfiguration issues and compliance risks in cloud environments.

The inadvertent exposure of credentials

Credentials are the keys used to access cloud services. Credentials include user credentials, passwords, access keys, encryption, and decryption keys among others.

Software developers with poor security practices often embed credentials into their code to save time during the code development process. The code containing the credentials may then be uploaded into a public repository service. This can be considered the same as closing the entrance door of a house and forgetting the key in the lock: this is the most straightforward and obvious way to cause a data breach. Tools exist that enable adversaries to find credentials in public cloud accounts.

The IT auditor should examine whether the organization has enforced secure coding standards, along with a secrets management strategy. This is to ensure that software developers code their applications securely, minimizing any vulnerabilities that may be exploited.

Overly permissive access

Cloud environments usually include both human and non-human identities. Cloud environments are often created with overly broad permissions that allow unregulated access to cloud resources. Threat actors who have managed to get initial entry into a cloud environment might be able to leverage these broad permissions to escalate access and move laterally inside the cloud infrastructure.

Identity access management (**IAM**) is a framework of policies, processes, and technologies that enable organizations to manage digital identities and control user access to an organization's data.

Some practices an IT auditor should look out for ways to minimize access risks are as follows:

- Implementing IAM wherever feasible
- Utilizing role-based access control and the least privilege principle
- Enabling multi-factor authentication
- Performing regular reviews of all identity roles and policies

Now that we've looked at the common pitfalls organization face in cloud adoption, let's look at tips and tricks to perform an effective audit.

Tips, tricks, and techniques

Cloud environments are complex and have low visibility. In a traditional data center, there was a finite number of assets that IT auditors could examine and report on. However, in a cloud environment, there can be exponential growth in the number of assets, which may include **virtual machines** (**VMs**), virtual networks, containers, serverless functions, and so on. It can be very challenging to inventory what is running in an organization's cloud.

Asset inventory plays such a foundational role in a cyber security program, that CIS Critical Security Controls and the NIST Cybersecurity Framework list the need to inventory and control infrastructure assets as their first security controls.

The first thing the IT auditor needs to do is to understand the cloud asset inventory to be able to perform an effective audit. The IT auditor needs to understand what applications are running within the cloud and whether they are approved by the organization, or if they represent shadow IT. In this section, we will demonstrate how to leverage native tools from each cloud service provider to get inventory and a quick snapshot security posture of the cloud environment.

It is important to note that the tips and tricks provided in this chapter should be incorporated and aligned based on the cloud customer's cloud security policies, standards, and procedures.

AWS

In AWS, you can use the AWS Tag Manager to inventory cloud resources. AWS allows you to assign metadata to a cloud customer's AWS resources using tags. All tags serve as simple labels that consist of a user-defined key and an optional value. The Tag Editor can be found under **AWS Resource Groups**. To list all resources using the Tag Editor, you can either manually select specific regions, or all of the regions listed under **Region** by selecting **All supported resource types**, and not specifying a tag. Then, click **Find resources** and this will show all resources that were created, as shown in *Figure 6.1*:

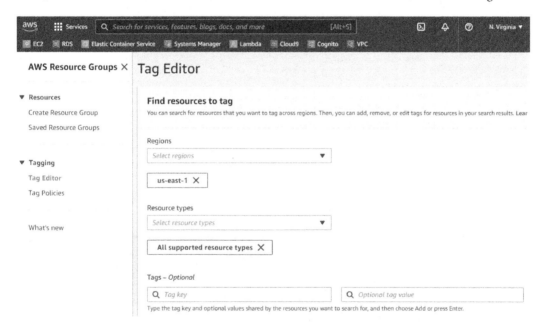

Figure 6.1 – Finding resources to tag

All the resources are identified, as shown in *Figure 6.2*:

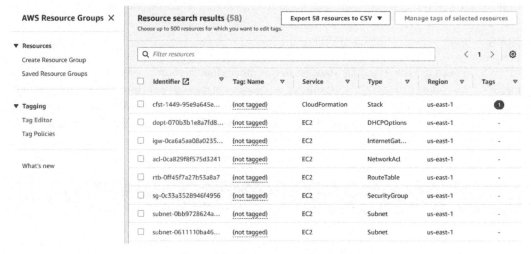

Figure 6.2 – Resource search results

To get a snapshot of the AWS security posture, we can use AWS Security Hub. According to the AWS documentation, "*AWS Security Hub is a cloud security posture management service that performs security best practice checks, aggregates alerts, and enables automated remediation.*"

To use AWS Security Hub, we first have to enable the service. We can simply search for the service using the AWS search function, as seen in *Figure 6.3*:

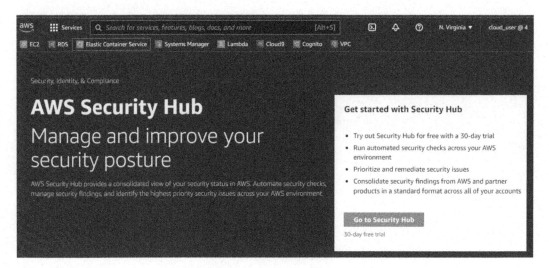

Figure 6.3 – AWS Security Hub

Before you can enable Security Hub standards and controls, you must first enable AWS Config, as seen in *Figure 6.4*:

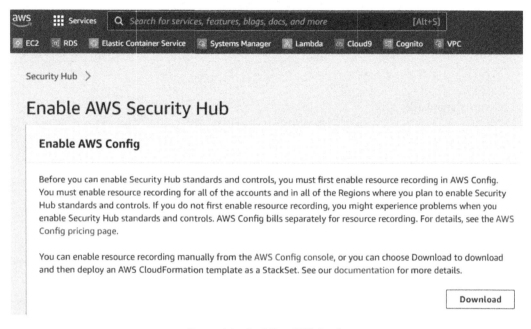

Figure 6.4 – Enabling AWS Config

To enable AWS Security Hub, select the security standards you would like it to perform security checks against as seen in *Figure 6.5*. AWS Security Hub security checks are currently mapped to AWS Foundational Security Best Practices, the CIS AWS Foundation Benchmark, and **Payment Card Industry Data Security Standard** (**PCI DSS**).

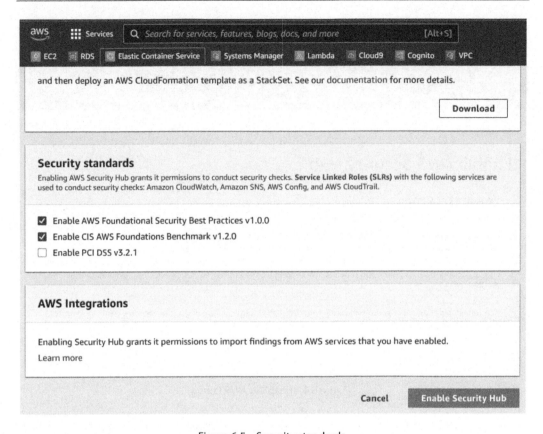

Figure 6.5 – Security standards

Once you have enabled Security Hub, you may have to wait up to two hours for it to populate. There are three important tabs for the IT auditor to review:

- **Summary**
- **Findings**
- **Insights**

Let's start by reviewing the **Summary** tab. It has different information such as security standards passed and failed, **Resources with the most failed security checks**, findings by region, and so on:

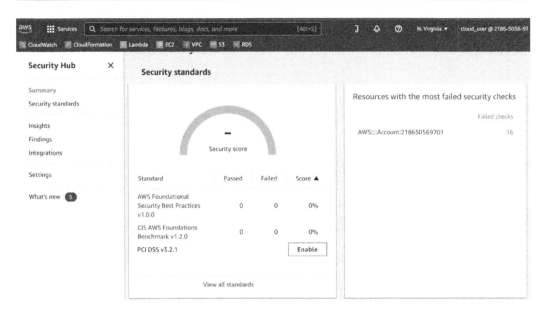

Figure 6.6 – The Summary tab

You can view findings across multiple regions, as seen in *Figure 6.7*. As you can see, we have 1 moderate finding and 15 low findings:

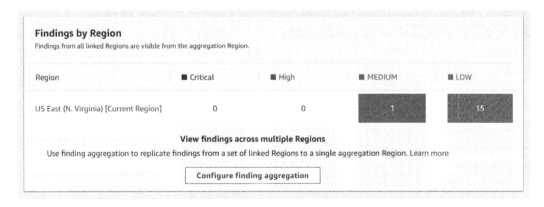

Figure 6.7 – Findings by region

Another tab the IT auditor should review in AWS Security Hub is the **Findings** tab. Here, you can get the details of a finding and what security checks it failed, as seen in *Figure 6.8*:

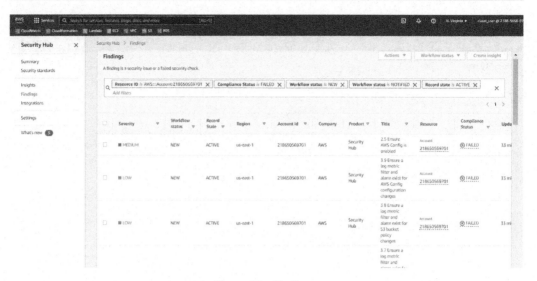

Figure 6.8 – Findings

Another useful tab the IT auditor should review in AWS Security Hub is the **Insights** tab. Here, you can get insight into the type of finding. The information presented on this tab include: **AWS resources with the most findings, S3 buckets with public write or read permissions, AMIs that are generating the most findings**, and so on, as seen in *Figure 6.9*:

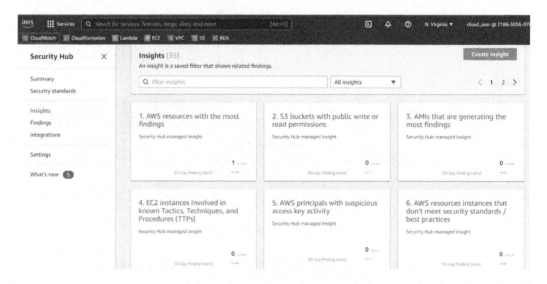

Figure 6.9 – The Insights tab

The second tool an IT auditor should leverage is AWS Config. As per the AWS documentation, *"AWS Config is a service that enables you to assess, audit, and evaluate the configurations of your AWS resource."* AWS Config provides AWS-managed rules, which are predefined, customizable rules that AWS Config uses to evaluate whether your AWS resources align with prescribed best practices. AWS Config can be quite valuable to an IT auditor as the service lets you define your own rules. To get to AWS Config, search for it on the AWS console, as seen in *Figure 6.10*:

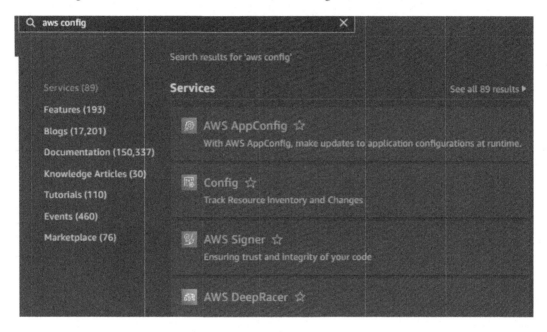

Figure 6.10 – AWS Config search

You can enable AWS Config with 1-click setup, as shown in *Figure 6.11*:

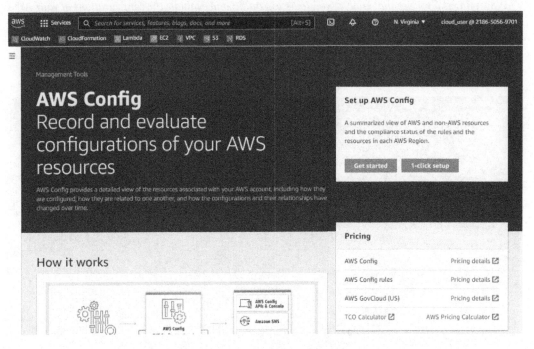

Figure 6.11 - Enabling AWS Config

Select **General settings | Rules**, then click **Confirm**, as seen in *Figure 6.12*:

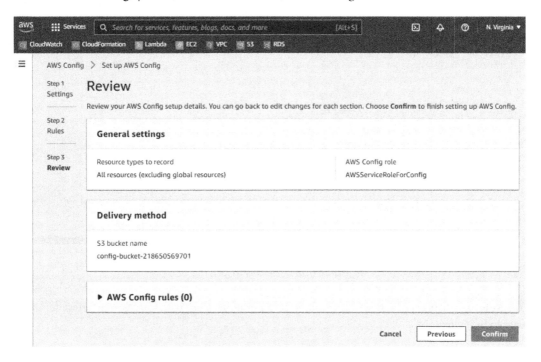

Figure 6.12 – Setting up AWS Config

Once AWS Config has launched, the three most valuable tabs for an IT auditor are the **Dashboard**, **Rules**, and **Resources** tabs. In the **Dashboard** tab, you can find information such as **Configuration Items**, **Compliance status**, and **AWS Config success metrics**, as seen in *Figure 6.13*:

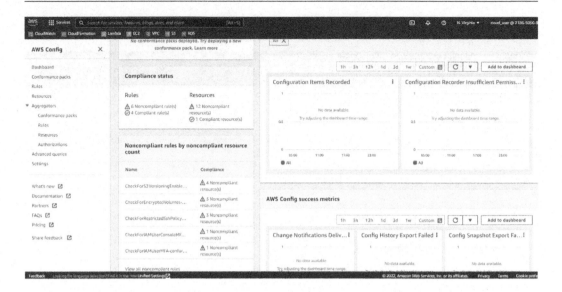

Figure 6.13 – The Dashboard tab

The **Rules** tab displays whether your resource configurations align with the relevant rules identified, as seen in *Figure 6.14*:

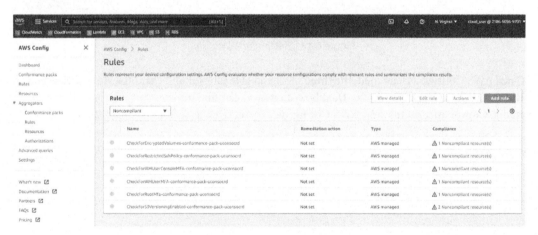

Figure 6.14 – The Rules tab

The **Resources** tab displays an inventory of supported resources and their compliance status, as shown in *Figure 6.15*:

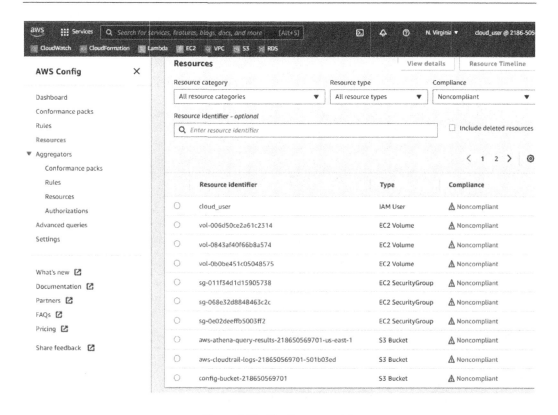

Figure 6.15 – The Resources tab

In our example, you can see we have the **IAM User**, **EC2 Volume,** and **S3 Bucket** types that are **Noncompliant**. You can click on each resource identifier for more information. The IT auditor would have to investigate relevant findings and collaborate with the cloud customer to come up with appropriate remediation.

A third useful tool for an IT auditor is **AWS Trusted Advisor**.

AWS Trusted Advisor

AWS Trusted Advisor provides real-time best practice guidance to help provision, monitor, and maintain AWS resources. You can then follow AWS Trusted Advisor recommendations to optimize your services and resources. These best practice recommendations span five categories:

- Cost optimization
- Performance
- Security

- Fault tolerance
- Service limits

To launch AWS Trusted Advisor, search for the service in the AWS console, as seen in *Figure 6.16:*

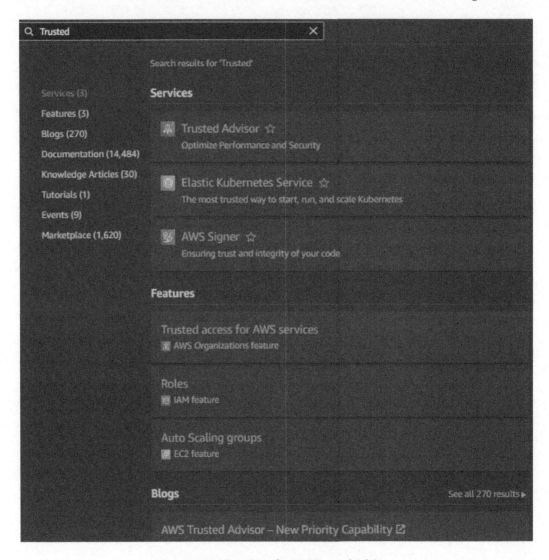

Figure 6.16 – Searching for AWS Trusted Advisor

The following screenshot is from AWS documentation and shows an example of the AWS Trusted Advisor interface, as seen in *Figure 6.17*:

Figure 6.17 – The AWS Trusted Advisor interface

Azure

A core tool an IT auditor should leverage in the Azure environment is Microsoft Defender for Cloud.

Microsoft Defender for Cloud

Microsoft Defender for Cloud (formerly known as **Azure Security Center**) is Azure's native solution. The service helps measure, maintain, and improve the level of security by continuously assessing resources and providing recommendations. You can use Microsoft Defender to determine the population of cloud resources. To launch Microsoft Defender, search for it in the search bar. The **Overview** tab has information such as **Security posture**, **Azure Subscriptions**, and **Active Recommendations**, as seen in *Figure 6.18*:

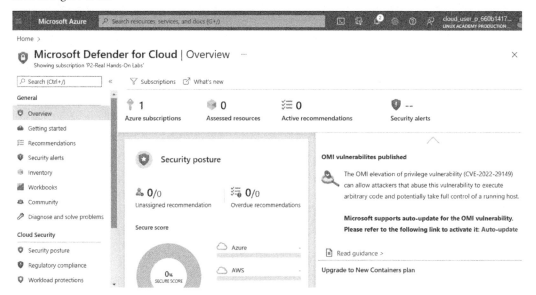

Figure 6.18 – The Overview tab

The **Inventory** tab displays the total resources running in Azure. It gives information such as resource type and health status, as seen in *Figure 6.19*:

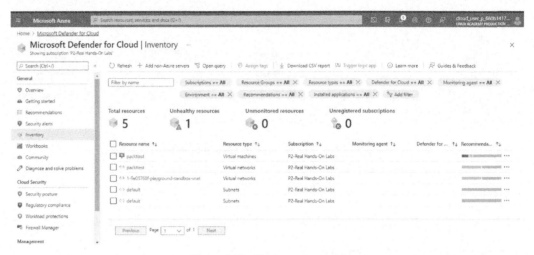

Figure 6.19 – The Inventory tab

In our example, we have **1** unhealthy resource. The auditor would need to investigate this resource further.

The **Recommendations** tab provides Azure recommendations with related severity of issues. As you can see in our example, we have wide open network ports and Microsoft Defender recommends we should restrict them:

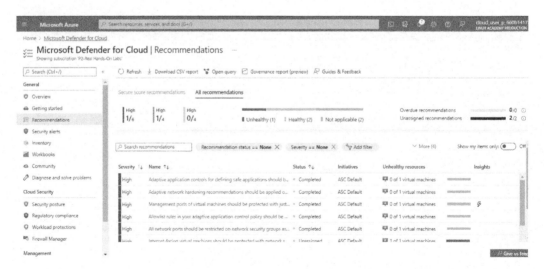

Figure 6.20 – The Recommendations tab

Under the **Cloud Security** section is **Security posture**, which provides a holistic view and a secure score as seen in *Figure 6.21*:

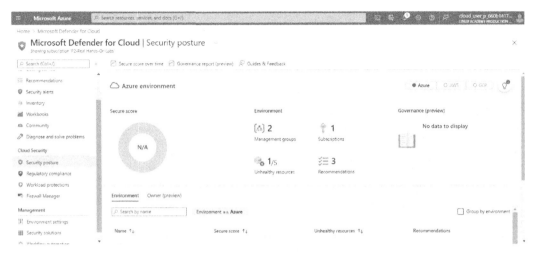

Figure 6.21 – The Security posture tab

Another item under the **Cloud Security** section is **Regulatory compliance**. In this section, you can add and track customized regulations that you want your organizations to align with, as seen in *Figure 6.22*:

Figure 6.22 – Regulatory compliance

Another tool an IT auditor can leverage is Microsoft Purview.

Microsoft Purview

Microsoft Purview (formerly **Azure Purview**) is a centralized data governance and risk management service that helps manage data. To set up Microsoft Purview, you can search for it on any browser, or go to `https://azure.microsoft.com/en-us/products/purview/#overview`, as seen in *Figure 6.23*:

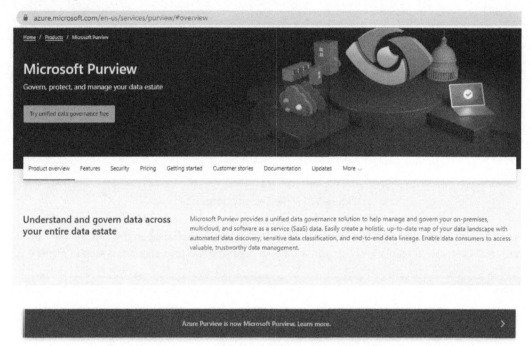

Figure 6.23 – Azure Purview

You will need to set up a Microsoft Purview account, as shown in *Figure 6.24*:

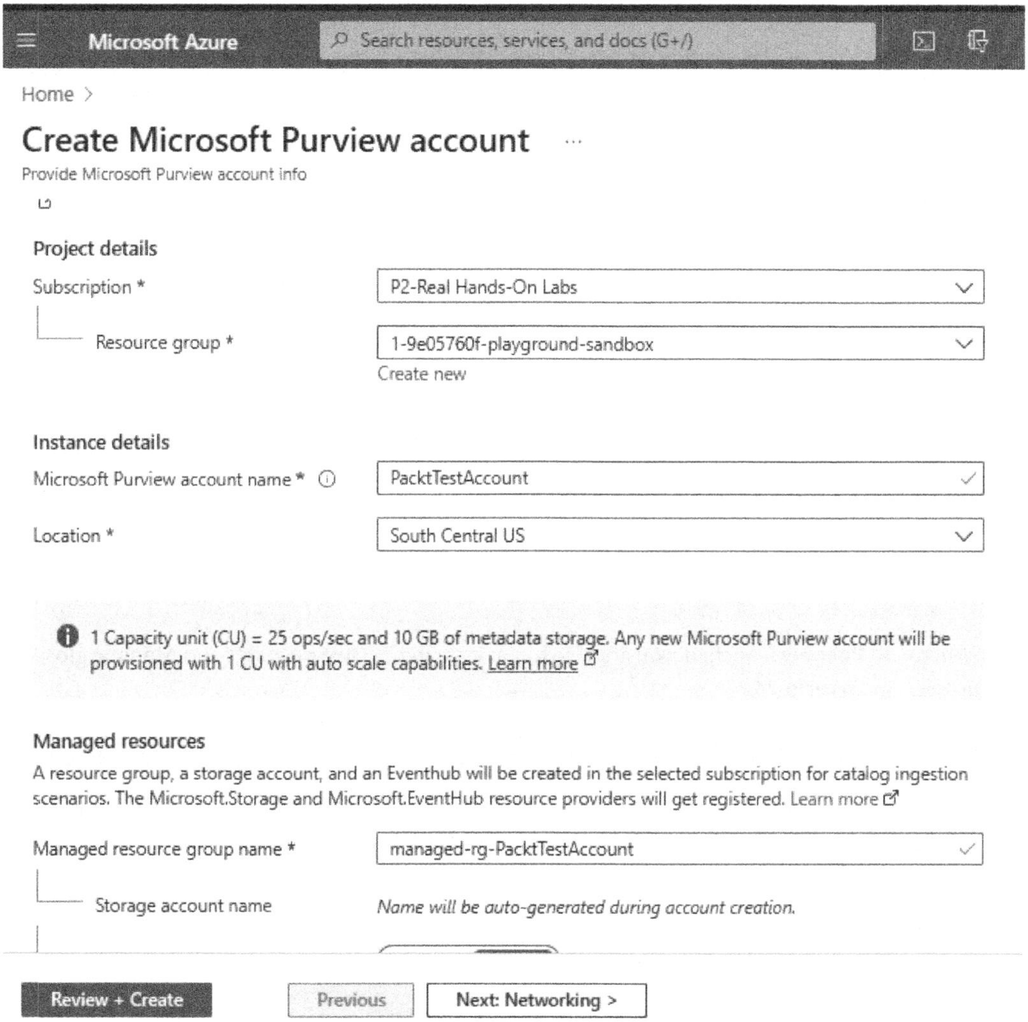

Figure 6.24 – Creating the Microsoft Purview account

With the account created, launch the Microsoft Purview workspace from the Azure portal, as shown in *Figure 6.25*.

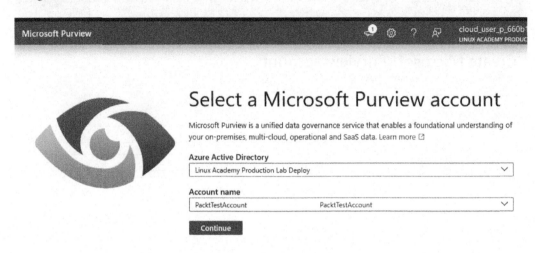

Figure 6.25 – Selecting an account

With Microsoft Purview launched, you are able to navigate to the **Browse assets** and **Manage glossary** tabs, as seen in *Figure 6.26*:

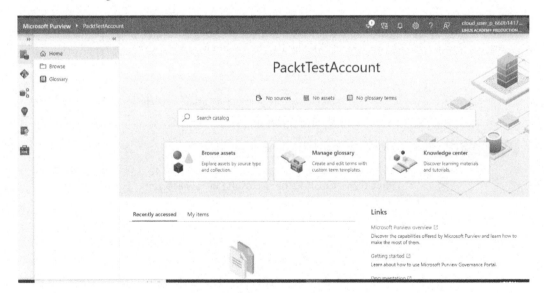

Figure 6.26 – Microsoft Purview Home page

If you click on **Browse assets**, it displays the population discovered, as seen in *Figure 6.27*.

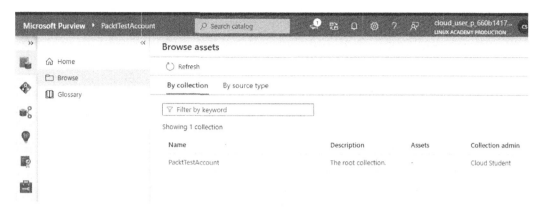

Figure 6.27 – Browse assets

Before Microsoft Purview scans your data, Microsoft Purview will need to be given access to data sources. You can do this by assigning Microsoft Purview managed identity access rights.

Once configured, Purview can create a holistic, up-to-date map of your data landscape with automated data discovery, sensitive data classification, and many other data insights, as shown in *Figure 6.28*:

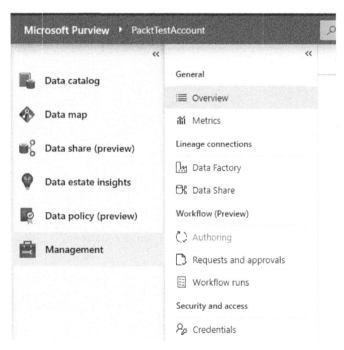

Figure 6.28 – Management | Overview

GCP

IT auditors can leverage a tool called Security Command Center for GCP.

Security Command Center

Security Command Center provides centralized visibility into the security posture and status of the GCP environment. According to GCP's documentation, "*Security Command Center ingests data about new, modified, and deleted assets from Cloud Asset Inventory, which continuously monitors assets in your cloud environment. Security Command Center supports a large subset of Google Cloud assets. For most assets, configuration changes, including IAM and organization policies, are detected in near-real time.*" You can get to Security Command Center from the Google Cloud Console, as shown in *Figure 6.29*:

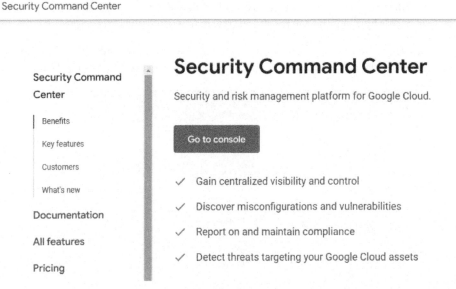

Figure 6.29 – Security Command Center

Security Command Center requires an organization resource that is associated with a domain. As a result, you will need to create an organization, as shown in *Figure 6.30*.

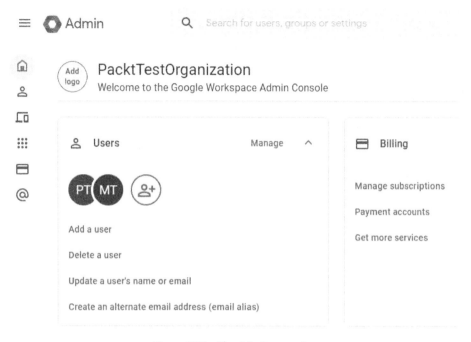

Figure 6.30 – The Admin console

Note

For detailed information on setting up Security Command Center, please view the Google Cloud Documentation at `https://cloud.google.com/security-command-center/docs/set-up`.

Once the organization is set up, you need to enable the Security Command Center dashboard, as shown in *Figure 6.31*:

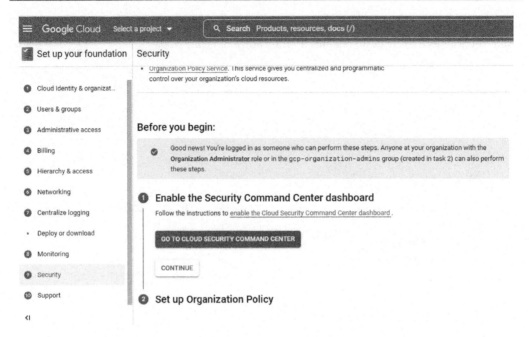

Figure 6.31 – The Security tab

Next, select the services you would like to set up, as shown in *Figure 6.32*:

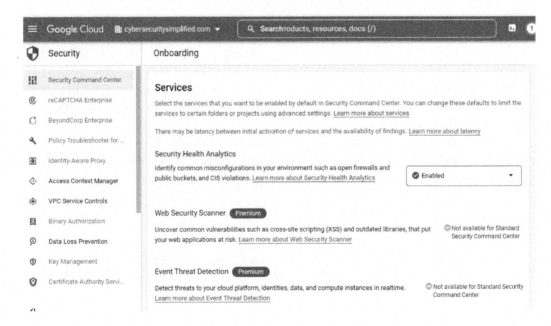

Figure 6.32 – Services setup

Once Security Command Center is fully configured, we can go and review the security posture of the GCP environment. There are five important tabs to review; they include **OVERVIEW**, **VULNERABILITIES**, **ASSETS**, **FINDINGS**, and **SOURCES**:

- **OVERVIEW**: Provides a snapshot of the security state, as seen in *Figure 6.33*:

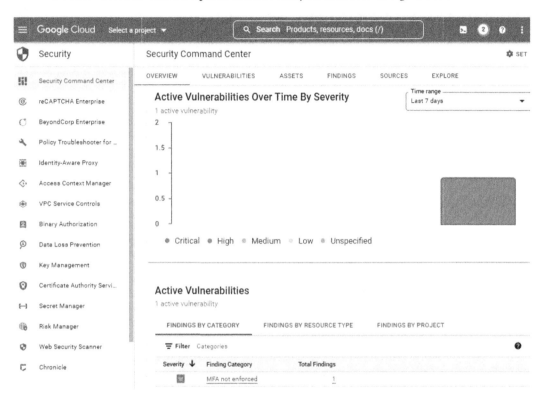

Figure 6.33 – Security Command Center | OVERVIEW

- **VULNERABILITIES**: Provides a list of the vulnerabilities found when last scanned. In our example, we have an **MFA not enforced** vulnerability with a **High** severity, as seen in *Figure 6.34*:

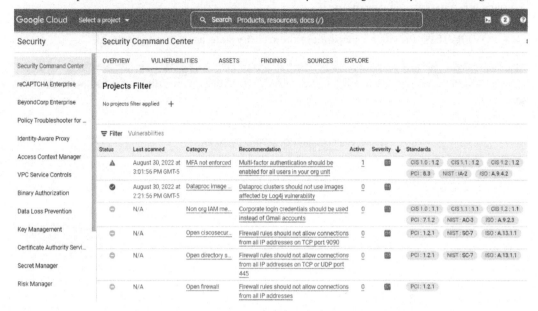

Figure 6.34 – Security Command Center | VULNERABILITIES

- **ASSETS**: Displays the Google Cloud resources, as shown in *Figure 6.35*:

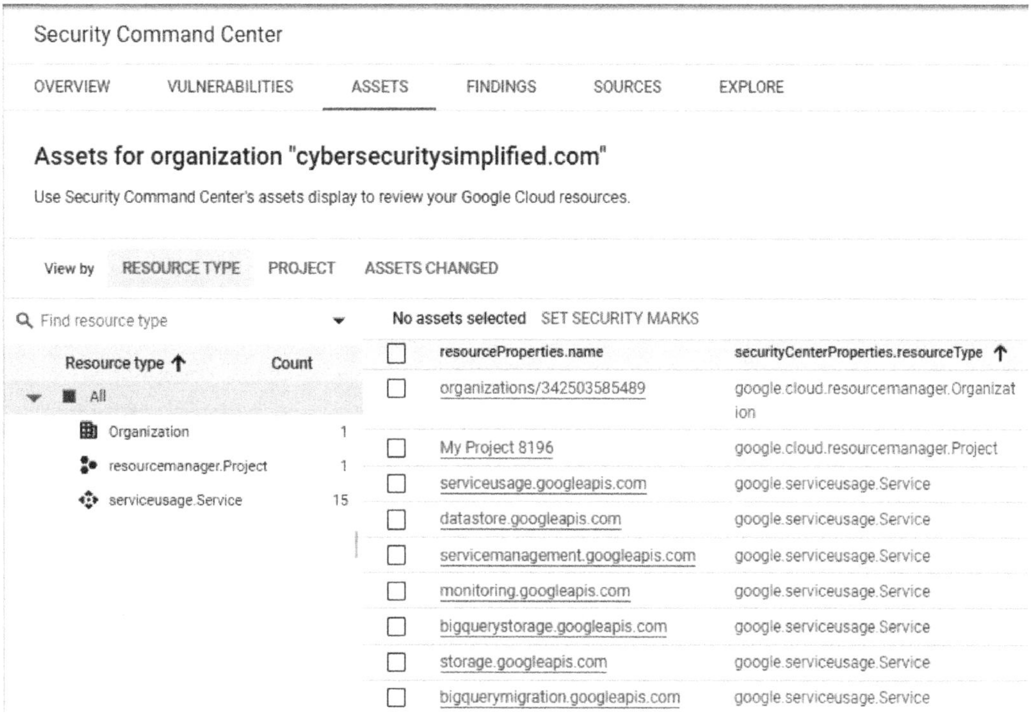

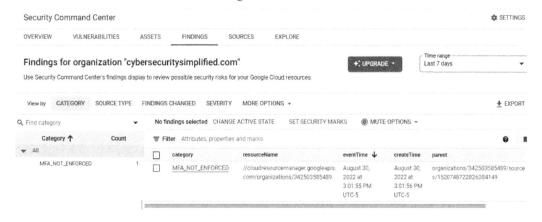

Figure 6.35 – Security Command Center | ASSETS

- **FINDINGS**: Provides detail around the security risks identified and what organizations they have been found under, as seen in *Figure 6.36*:

Figure 6.36 - Security Command Center | FINDINGS

- **SOURCES**: Displays a summary of assets and findings from the relevant security sources that are enabled, as seen in *Figure 6.37*:

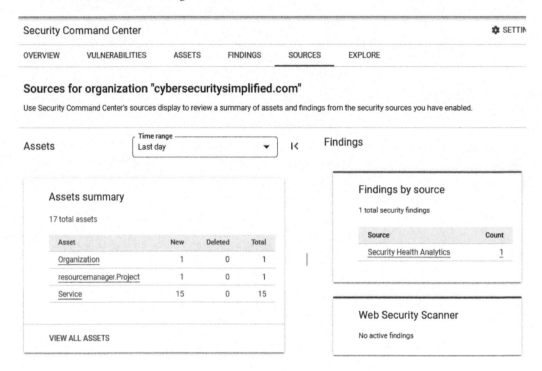

Figure 6.37 – Security Command Center | SOURCES

A second tool an IT auditor can leverage in GCP is Cloud Asset Inventory.

Cloud Asset Inventory

Cloud Asset Inventory is a service that allows one to view, monitor, and analyze GCP assets. To access Cloud Asset Inventory, you can either go to the Google Console under **IAM & Admin** or go through a browser, as shown in *Figure 6.38*:

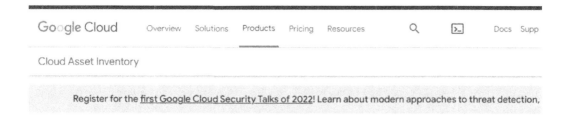

Figure 6.38 – Cloud Asset Inventory

Three tabs are important for the IT auditor to review; **OVERVIEW**, **RESOURCE**, and **IAM POLICY**. The **OVERVIEW** tab provides a snapshot of resources in use, as shown in *Figure 6.39*:

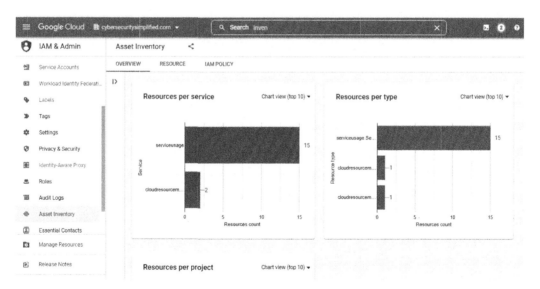

Figure 6.39 – The Asset Inventory OVERVIEW tab

The **RESOURCES** tab displays the resource name, type, and location, as shown in *Figure 6.40*:

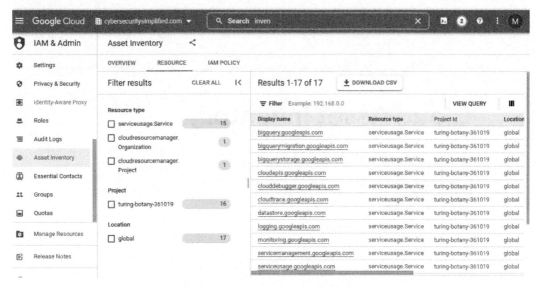

Figure 6.40 – The Asset Inventory RESOURCES tab

IAM policies display all the IAM policies across services, and resource types with information such as roles, permissions, and so on:

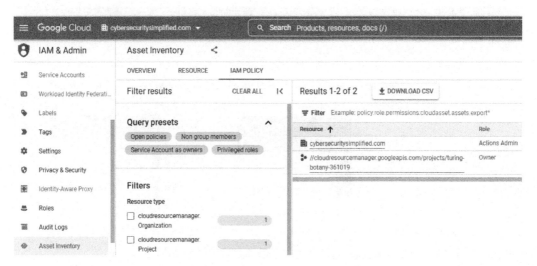

Figure 6.41 – The Asset Inventory IAM policy

A third tool an IT auditor can leverage to assess GCP is Cloud Overview.

Cloud Overview

Cloud Overview has three tabs; **DASHBOARD**, **ACTIVITY**, and **RECOMMENDATION**. The **DASHBOARD** tab has a summary of **Resources**, CPU usage, **APIs**, **Billing**, and **Monitoring**, as seen in *Figure 6.42*:

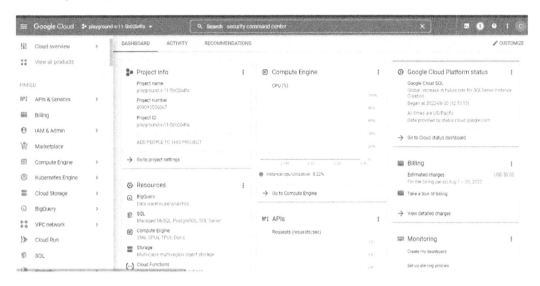

Figure 6.42 – The Cloud Overview DASHBOARD

The **ACTIVITY** tab provides a log of recent activities. In our example, we can see a VM and a network were deployed recently, as seen in *Figure 6.43*:

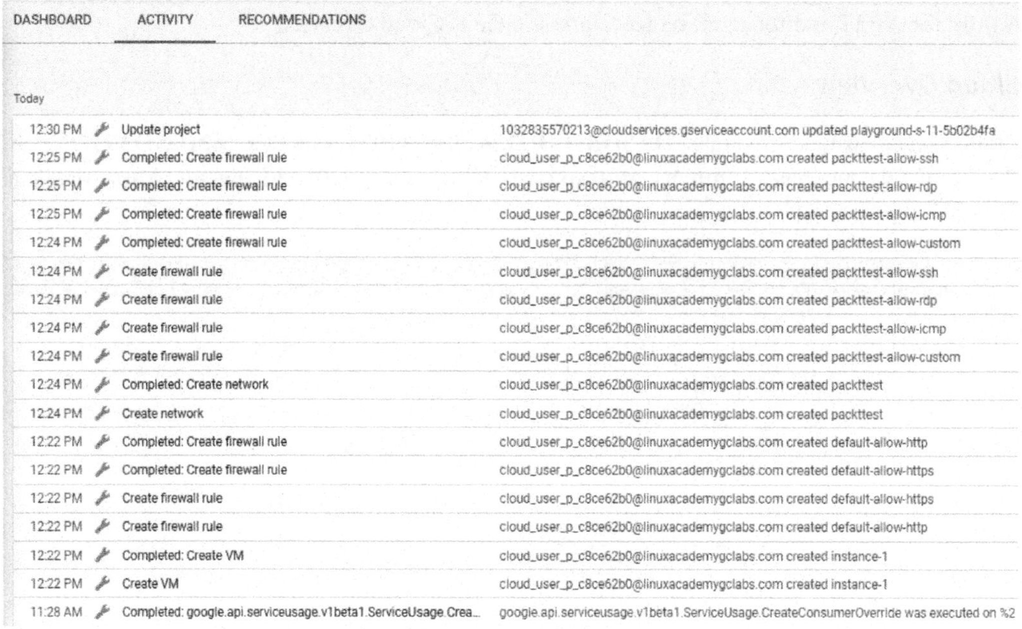

| DASHBOARD | ACTIVITY | RECOMMENDATIONS |

Today

12:30 PM	🔧 Update project	1032835570213@cloudservices.gserviceaccount.com updated playground-s-11-5b02b4fa
12:25 PM	🔧 Completed: Create firewall rule	cloud_user_p_c8ce62b0@linuxacademygclabs.com created packttest-allow-ssh
12:25 PM	🔧 Completed: Create firewall rule	cloud_user_p_c8ce62b0@linuxacademygclabs.com created packttest-allow-rdp
12:25 PM	🔧 Completed: Create firewall rule	cloud_user_p_c8ce62b0@linuxacademygclabs.com created packttest-allow-icmp
12:24 PM	🔧 Completed: Create firewall rule	cloud_user_p_c8ce62b0@linuxacademygclabs.com created packttest-allow-custom
12:24 PM	🔧 Create firewall rule	cloud_user_p_c8ce62b0@linuxacademygclabs.com created packttest-allow-ssh
12:24 PM	🔧 Create firewall rule	cloud_user_p_c8ce62b0@linuxacademygclabs.com created packttest-allow-rdp
12:24 PM	🔧 Create firewall rule	cloud_user_p_c8ce62b0@linuxacademygclabs.com created packttest-allow-icmp
12:24 PM	🔧 Create firewall rule	cloud_user_p_c8ce62b0@linuxacademygclabs.com created packttest-allow-custom
12:24 PM	🔧 Completed: Create network	cloud_user_p_c8ce62b0@linuxacademygclabs.com created packttest
12:24 PM	🔧 Create network	cloud_user_p_c8ce62b0@linuxacademygclabs.com created packttest
12:22 PM	🔧 Completed: Create firewall rule	cloud_user_p_c8ce62b0@linuxacademygclabs.com created default-allow-http
12:22 PM	🔧 Completed: Create firewall rule	cloud_user_p_c8ce62b0@linuxacademygclabs.com created default-allow-https
12:22 PM	🔧 Create firewall rule	cloud_user_p_c8ce62b0@linuxacademygclabs.com created default-allow-https
12:22 PM	🔧 Create firewall rule	cloud_user_p_c8ce62b0@linuxacademygclabs.com created default-allow-http
12:22 PM	🔧 Completed: Create VM	cloud_user_p_c8ce62b0@linuxacademygclabs.com created instance-1
12:22 PM	🔧 Create VM	cloud_user_p_c8ce62b0@linuxacademygclabs.com created instance-1
11:28 AM	🔧 Completed: google.api.serviceusage.v1beta1.ServiceUsage.Crea...	google.api.serviceusage.v1beta1.ServiceUsage.CreateConsumerOverride was executed on %2

Figure 6.43 – The Cloud Overview ACTIVITY tab

The **RECOMMENDATIONS** tab provides GCP recommendations for the project. Currently, we either have no recommendations or the tab hasn't populated, as seen in *Figure 6.44*:

DASHBOARD   ACTIVITY   RECOMMENDATIONS   ⬆ EXPORT   🕐 HISTORY

ⓘ   If you don't have the relevant IAM permissions, you may not see all of the Recommendations available for this project. Please select a Recommendation type from this pag
required permissions.

DISMISS

Check back for recommendations

When more data is available for this project,
recommendations to optimize your cloud's
security, performance, and cost will appear here.
Learn more

Figure 6.44 – The Cloud Overview RECOMMENDATIONS tab

In this section, we've reviewed some tips and techniques to utilize for a more effective audit. This included leveraging cloud-native solutions in AWS, Azure, and GCP to review the security posture of an organization. Next, we will talk about how IT auditors can become prepared for more advanced auditing.

Preparing for more advanced auditing

So far we have been leveraging native **graphical user interface (GUI)** tools to perform audits. To prepare for more advanced auditing, the IT auditor should familiarize themselves with the **command-line interface (CLI)**. A GUI permits users to interact with the cloud platform using graphical features such as icons, windows, and menus. In contrast, a CLI allows users to interact with the system via commands. A CLI gives the IT auditor more autonomy to write custom scripts that could be used to automate processes.

Let's start by looking at the **AWS CLI**.

> **Note**
>
> Instructions on getting started and installing the AWS CLI can be found at `https://docs.aws.amazon.com/cli/latest/userguide/cli-chap-getting-started.html`.

Once you have the AWS CLI installed, you will need to configure the basic settings that the AWS CLI uses to interact with AWS. These include security credentials, `Default region name`, and `Default output format`, as shown in *Figure 6.45*:

```
Command Prompt - aws configure

C:\Users\antagonist>aws configure
AWS Access Key ID [None]: AKIA6GPHQ7SD2ZQY2G63
AWS Secret Access Key [None]: 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
Default region name [None]: us-east-1
Default output format [None]: json
```

Figure 6.45 – The AWS CLI configuration settings to interact with AWS

Now that we have the AWS CLI configured, we can run simple commands to perform audit actions. I will demonstrate two commands that an IT auditor can leverage. To list the number of users within AWS, we type in the following command:

```
aws iam-list users
```

Note that `UserId`, `CreateDate`, and `PasswordLastUsed` are displayed, as shown in *Figure 6.46*:

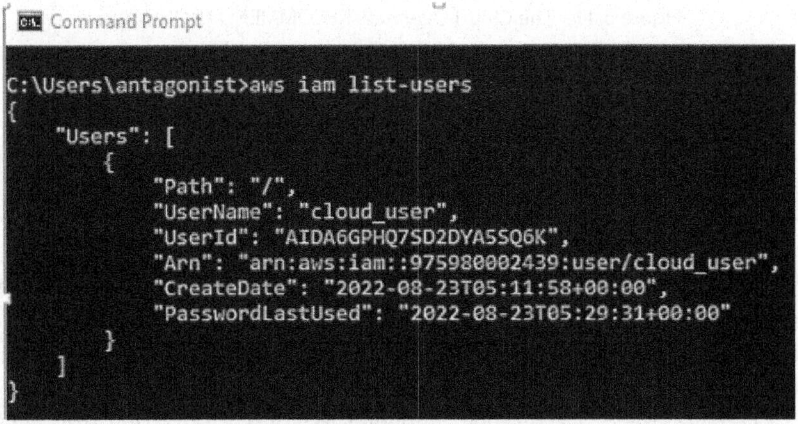

```
Command Prompt

C:\Users\antagonist>aws iam list-users
{
    "Users": [
        {
            "Path": "/",
            "UserName": "cloud_user",
            "UserId": "AIDA6GPHQ7SD2DYA5SQ6K",
            "Arn": "arn:aws:iam::975980002439:user/cloud_user",
            "CreateDate": "2022-08-23T05:11:58+00:00",
            "PasswordLastUsed": "2022-08-23T05:29:31+00:00"
        }
    ]
}
```

Figure 6.46 – AWS list users in IAM

As another example, if you need to know which groups are connected to AWS VPCs, you can type the following command:

```
aws ec2 describe-security-groups
```

This is shown in *Figure 6.47*:

Command Prompt - aws ec2 describe-security-groups

C:\Users\antagonist>aws ec2 describe-security-groups

Figure 6.47 – AWS describe-security-groups

VPC security groups and their respective attributes are shown in *Figure 6.48*:

Command Prompt - aws ec2 describe-security-groups

    "SecurityGroups": [
        {
            "Description": "default VPC security group",
            "GroupName": "default",
            "IpPermissions": [
                {
                    "IpProtocol": "-1",
                    "IpRanges": [],
                    "Ipv6Ranges": [],
                    "PrefixListIds": [],
                    "UserIdGroupPairs": [
                        {
                            "GroupId": "sg-0b7a1022de50fd306",
                            "UserId": "975980002439"
                        }
                    ]
                }
            ],
            "OwnerId": "975980002439",
            "GroupId": "sg-0b7a1022de50fd306",
            "IpPermissionsEgress": [
                {
                    "IpProtocol": "-1",
                    "IpRanges": [
                        {
                            "CidrIp": "0.0.0.0/0"
                        }
                    ],
-- More --

Figure 6.48 – AWS security groups and their attributes

In *Chapter 4*, *Network, Infrastructure, and Security Controls*, we stated that all AWS accounts come with a default VPC. A default VPC comes with a public subnet. As an IT auditor, it is important to ensure that sensitive company data is not placed in a public subnet.

AWS has a command library that can be found at `https://awscli.amazonaws.com/v2/documentation/api/latest/index.html`. In addition, you can type in `aws help` on the AWS CLI for information about a specific command.

Next, we will look at the **Azure CLI**.

> **Note**
> Instructions on getting started and installing the Azure CLI can be found at `https://docs.microsoft.com/en-us/cli/azure/get-started-with-azure-cli`.

Once you have the Azure CLI set up, you need to log in to Azure:

```
C:\Users\antagonist>az login
A web browser has been opened at https://login.microsoftonline.com/organizations/oauth2/v2.0/authorize. Please continue
the login in the web browser. If no web browser is available or if the web browser fails to open, use device code flow
ith `az login --use-device-code`.
[
  {
    "cloudName": "AzureCloud",
    "homeTenantId": "3617ef9b-98b4-40d9-ba43-e1ed6709cf0d",
    "id": "0f39574d-d756-48cf-b622-0e27a6943bd2",
    "isDefault": true,
    "managedByTenants": [],
    "name": "P3-Real Hands-On Labs",
    "state": "Enabled",
    "tenantId": "3617ef9b-98b4-40d9-ba43-e1ed6709cf0d",
    "user": {
      "name": "cloud_user_p_52b4d0dd@azurelabs.linuxacademy.com",
      "type": "user"
    }
  }
]
C:\Users\antagonist>
```

Figure 6.49 – Logging in to Azure

I will demonstrate two commands an IT auditor can leverage to perform an audit. To list all the resource groups we have, use the following command:

```
az resource list
```

```
C:\WINDOWS\system32\cmd.exe                                              —    □    ×

C:\Users\antagonist>az resource list
[
  {
    "changedTime": "2022-09-02T05:29:32.856764+00:00",
    "createdTime": "2022-09-02T05:19:12.202035+00:00",
    "extendedLocation": null,
    "id": "/subscriptions/0f39574d-d756-48cf-b622-0e27a6943bd2/resourceGroups/1-f151d2ee-playground-sandbox/providers/Mi
crosoft.Storage/storageAccounts/packtestaccount",
    "identity": null,
    "kind": "StorageV2",
    "location": "eastus",
    "managedBy": null,
    "name": "packtestaccount",
    "plan": null,
    "properties": null,
    "provisioningState": "Succeeded",
    "resourceGroup": "1-f151d2ee-playground-sandbox",
    "sku": {
      "capacity": null,
      "family": null,
      "model": null,
      "name": "Standard_RAGRS",
      "size": null,
      "tier": "Standard"
    },
    "tags": {},
    "type": "Microsoft.Storage/storageAccounts"
  },
```

Figure 6.50 – The resource list

To get a list of IP addresses associated with a VM, we can use the following command:

```
az vm list-ip-addresses
```

```
C:\WINDOWS\system32\cmd.exe                                             —    □    >

C:\Users\antagonist>az vm list-ip-addresses
[
  {
    "virtualMachine": {
      "name": "PacktTest",
      "network": {
        "privateIpAddresses": [
          "10.0.0.4"
        ],
        "publicIpAddresses": [
          {
            "id": "/subscriptions/0f39574d-d756-48cf-b622-0e27a6943bd2/resourceGroups/1-f151d2ee-playground-sandbox/pro
iders/Microsoft.Network/publicIPAddresses/PacktTest-ip",
            "ipAddress": "20.102.115.122",
            "ipAllocationMethod": "Static",
            "name": "PacktTest-ip",
            "resourceGroup": "1-f151d2ee-playground-sandbox",
            "zone": "1"
          }
        ]
      },
      "resourceGroup": "1-f151d2ee-playground-sandbox"
    }
  }
]
C:\Users\antagonist>
```

Figure 6.51 – Listing IP addresses associated with a VM

The full Azure CLI command reference can be found at `https://docs.microsoft.com/en-us/cli/azure/reference-index?view=azure-cli-latest`. In addition, you can type in `az help` on the Azure CLI for information on a specific command.

Next, we will look at the **Google Cloud CLI**.

> **Note**
>
> Instructions on getting started and installing the Google Cloud CLI can be found at `https://cloud.google.com/sdk/docs/install`.

Once you have installed the CLI, you need to authenticate using Google credentials:

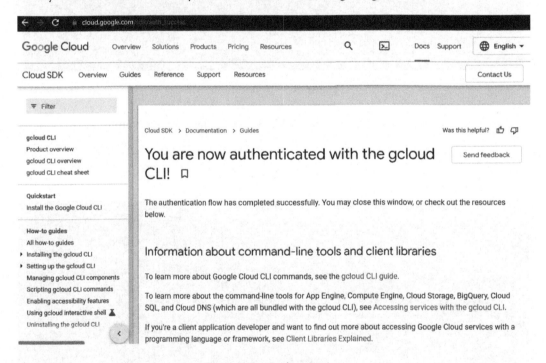

Figure 6.52 – Authentication

I will demonstrate two commands an IT auditor can leverage to perform an audit. To list all credential accounts, type the following command:

```
gcloud auth list
```

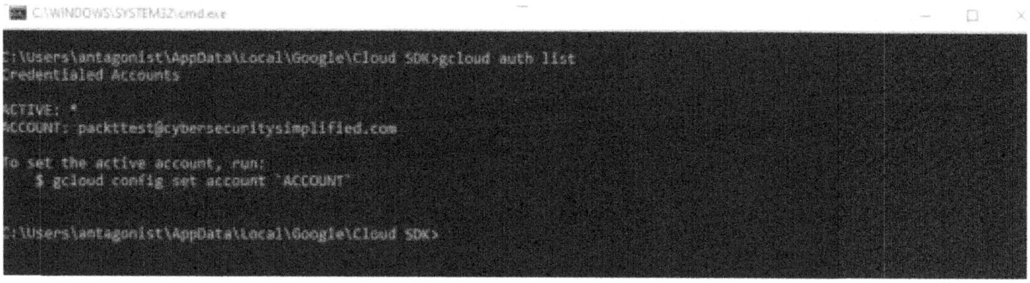

Figure 6.53 – Listing credential accounts

To list your project's logs, type the following command:

```
gcloud logging logs list
```

Figure 6.54 – Listing logs

The Google Cloud CLI cheat sheet can be found at `https://cloud.google.com/sdk/docs/cheatsheet`. In addition, you can type in the following command on the Google Cloud CLI for information on a specific command:

```
gcloud help
```

In this section, we've reviewed how to leverage CLI for more advanced auditing. All the tools we have talked about in this chapter are native cloud tools.

It is important to acknowledge there are open source tools that can assist IT auditors in advanced auditing. One such tool is Cloud Custodian. Cloud Custodian is an open source tool developed by Capital One for implementing automated security, compliance, and governance. IT auditors can use Cloud Custodian to monitor cloud environments as it generates a set of outputs for any given security policies. In the next section, we will briefly touch on other cloud platforms on the market.

Other clouds

Although the book focuses on the "big three" cloud providers, we recognize that there are other cloud infrastructure solutions and want to briefly highlight these and options for learning more outside of this book.

Oracle Cloud Infrastructure

Oracle Cloud Infrastructure or **(OCI)** has a unique attribute in the concept of compartments, which are used to segment and manage access as well as develop logical groupings of resources. OCI also offers features such as Security Zones, which are compartments where security can't be disabled. Similar to other clouds, OCI has available features for finance and change management, tagging of resources for management, as well as options for logging and notification of log events through a feature known as Service Connector Hub.

Learn more at `https://education.oracle.com/`.

IBM Cloud

One of the more unique things about IBM Cloud is the amount of open source technology that is used throughout the platform, and the availability of product solutions known as Cloud Paks, which range from security and compliance tooling to AI and chatbot. Like other cloud environments, IBM Cloud offers an interface for viewing security and compliance-related information. However, the creation and configuration of a "collector" may be required in order for the IBM Cloud Security and Compliance center to display this information. As part of the discovery and assessment for audit, this should be reviewed.

Learn more at `https://www.ibm.com/training/cloud`.

Alibaba Cloud

Alibaba Cloud is another global cloud option and has a strong presence primarily in Asia. Alibaba Cloud is also known as **Aliyun**. In terms of structure, Alibaba Cloud is comparable in many ways to AWS. Some of the more interesting and unique features include the ability to configure both user and role-based SSO and the availability of a service known as Cloud Config, which tracks and records configuration changes. Similar to other cloud providers, logging is available (through a feature known as ActionTrail). However, it will need to be assessed to ensure it's been activated and is logging all in-scope components.

Learn more at `https://edu.alibabacloud.com/`.

For other cloud providers, it is critical to understand if there are any sub-service organization dependencies that need to be taken into consideration. A sub-service organization is a supporting vendor that is engaged by the cloud service provider to perform some services for the cloud service provider. For example, a cloud service provider may utilize a sub-service organization for infrastructure hosting. In these instances, the IT auditor will also have to evaluate controls at the sub-service organization. The IT auditor will also want to verify that the scope of any assessments performed on the sub-service organization is sufficient for the services used by the cloud customer.

In this section, we've reviewed the options for other clouds outside the "big three" cloud service providers (AWS, Azure, and GCP).

Summary

In this chapter, we looked at tips, tricks, and techniques that you can utilize for the three major cloud providers AWS, Azure, and GCP. We covered how to identify the common pitfalls IT auditors need to be cognizant of as they approach their audits; tips and techniques to utilize for more effective audits, and considerations for more advanced audits, including other cloud environments.

In our next chapter, we'll review tools for monitoring and assessing the cloud.

7

Tools for Monitoring and Assessing

Cloud monitoring is one of the keys to ensuring that cloud services and resources remain secure and cost-effective. AWS, Azure, and **Google Cloud Platform** (**GCP**) offer native solutions that an IT auditor can leverage to monitor and assess cloud environments. Cloud monitoring is a method of reviewing, observing, and managing the health and security of a cloud. Cloud monitoring is performed with the aim of detecting cyber threats, data breaches, and anomalous behavior. Using monitoring tools, organizations can proactively monitor their cloud environments to identify security events before they become security incidents.

We will cover the following topics in this chapter:

- Basic cloud auditing tools within AWS

- Basic cloud auditing tools within Azure

- Basic cloud auditing tools within GCP

In *Chapter 6, Tips and Techniques for Advanced Auditing*, we went over tools that an IT auditor can leverage to perform monitoring specifically for resources. This includes **AWS Config** for AWS, **Microsoft Defender Cloud** for Azure, and **Google Cloud Asset Inventory** for GCP. In this chapter, we'll cover the standard tools for holistic monitoring of the performance, availability, and security of infrastructure and applications for AWS, Azure, and GCP environments. We will start by looking at the tools offered by AWS.

Basic cloud auditing tools within AWS

In the sections that follow, as a prerequisite, you may require a minimum level of view or read access to obtain the test evidence independently. Depending upon your specific organization's configuration and any additional customizations, you may require additional access rights or group memberships to directly access specific content, or you may be required to work with an administrative point of contact for your organization as you observe them pulling control evidence. For reference, any screenshots in the following sections are based on a user with administrative privileges to the cloud environment. In addition, some of the tools may need to be enabled by the cloud customer, if they have not yet been.

We will begin with the basic cloud auditing tools within the AWS platform.

Amazon CloudWatch

The first tool an IT auditor can leverage in AWS is Amazon CloudWatch. Amazon CloudWatch is an AWS native monitoring and management service, which is designed for the purpose of maintaining the services and resources that are used. Amazon CloudWatch can be used to collect and track metrics, monitor log files, and set alarms, among many other functions. To navigate to Amazon Cloudwatch, you can simply search for it on the AWS console, as seen in *Figure 7.1*:

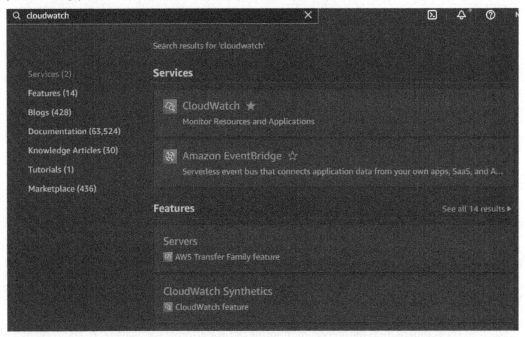

Figure 7.1 – Searching for Amazon CloudWatch

Once you launch Amazon CloudWatch, you have several options you can configure. These vary from creating alarms to custom dashboards, monitoring logs and creating events, and so on, as seen in *Figure 7.2*:

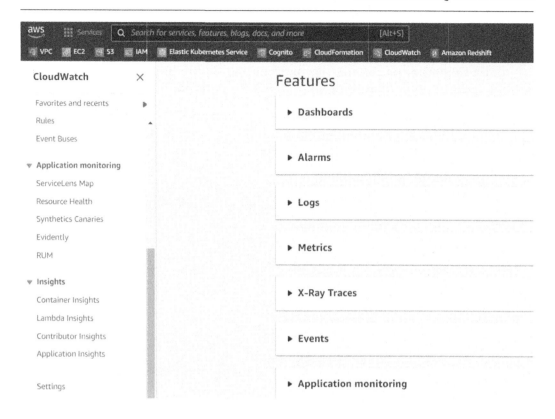

Figure 7.2 – Features

One useful feature for the IT auditor in Amazon CloudWatch is **Events**. In the **Events** tab, you can create a **CloudWatch** event that triggers an event. To create a rule, you need to navigate to **Events**, and click on the **Rules** tab, which will take you to EventBridge (formerly known as AWS CloudWatch Events), as seen in *Figure 7.3*:

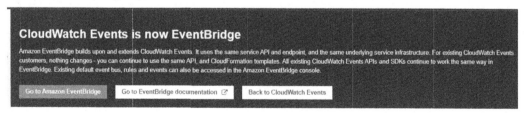

Figure 7.3 – EventBridge main page

An event indicates a change in the AWS environment. An IT auditor can create an event that is triggered when a certain state changes. I will provide examples of two rules an IT auditor can create. For detailed instructions on creating a rule that triggers an event from an AWS resource, go to `https://docs.aws.amazon.com/eventbridge/latest/userguide/eb-get-started.html`.

To create a rule, you have to define the rule detail, as seen in *Figure 7.4*:

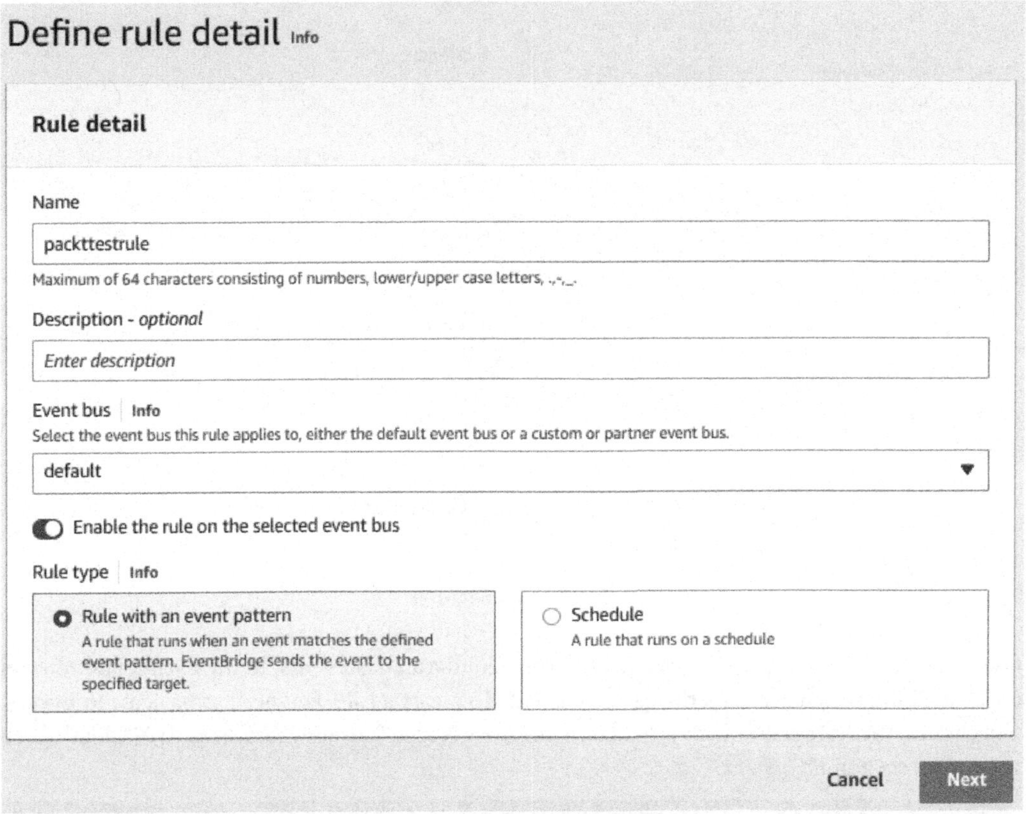

Define rule detail Info

Rule detail

Name

    packttestrule

Maximum of 64 characters consisting of numbers, lower/upper case letters, .,-,_.

Description - *optional*

    Enter description

Event bus | Info

Select the event bus this rule applies to, either the default event bus or a custom or partner event bus.

    default   ▼

🔘 Enable the rule on the selected event bus

Rule type | Info

⦿ **Rule with an event pattern**
A rule that runs when an event matches the defined event pattern. EventBridge sends the event to the specified target.

○ Schedule
A rule that runs on a schedule

                                                                          Cancel   Next

Figure 7.4 – Define rule detail

Next, we have to define the AWS event. We will also need to define an output to where events will be sent to. In our first example, we will select an event that triggers when an AWS **Elastic Compute Cloud** (**EC2**) instance state changes. Abnormal changes to EC2 instances may indicate malicious activity.

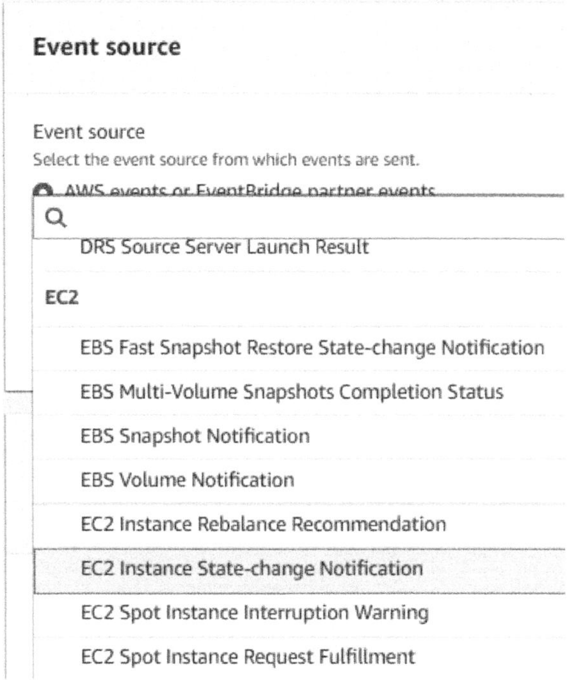

Event source

Event source
Select the event source from which events are sent.

○ AWS events or EventBridge partner events

Q

DRS Source Server Launch Result

EC2

EBS Fast Snapshot Restore State-change Notification

EBS Multi-Volume Snapshots Completion Status

EBS Snapshot Notification

EBS Volume Notification

EC2 Instance Rebalance Recommendation

EC2 Instance State-change Notification

EC2 Spot Instance Interruption Warning

EC2 Spot Instance Request Fulfillment

Figure 7.5 – Event source

In our second example, we will select an event that triggers when an AWS **Simple Storage Service** (**S3**) object **Access Control List** (**ACL**) is updated. We could use this rule to monitor objects whose access changes in S3 buckets. An IT auditor could use this rule to look for misconfigured S3 buckets allowing public access. This is one of the most common security misconfiguration risks within AWS.

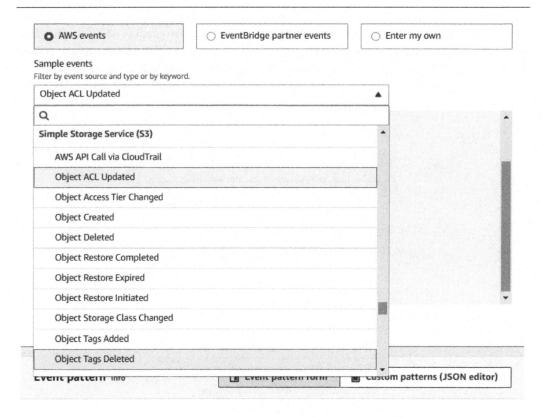

Figure 7.6 – Object ACL Updated

Another useful feature in Amazon CloudWatch is **Alarms**. The **Alarms** feature allows you to watch Amazon CloudWatch metrics and to receive notifications when the metrics fall outside of the thresholds defined. To create an alarm, go to the **Alarms** tab, as seen in *Figure 7.7*:

Figure 7.7 – The Alarms tab

You can create alarms using thousands of predefined metrics, as seen in *Figure 7.8*:

Select metric

| | 20:15 | 20:30 | 20:45 | 21:00 | 21:15 | 21:30 | 21:45 | 22:00 | 22:15 | 22:30 | 22:45 | 23:00 |

| Browse | Query | Graphed metrics | Options | Source | | | Add math ▼ | Add query ▼ |

Metrics (2,610)   Graph with SQL   Graph search

🔍 *Search for any metric, dimension or resource id*

| ApiGateway | 38 | ApplicationELB | 12 | Billing | 26 | CertificateManager | 1 |
| DynamoDB | 25 | EBS | 108 | EC2 | 431 | ECS | 4 |

Cancel   Select a single metric to continue

Figure 7.8 – Metrics

Once you create your alarms, you will get a dashboard like the one seen in *Figure 7.9*:

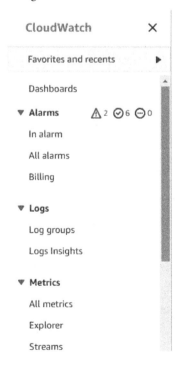

Figure 7.9 – Dashboards

In our example, we have received two alarms for metrics outside their thresholds, as seen in *Figure 7.10:*

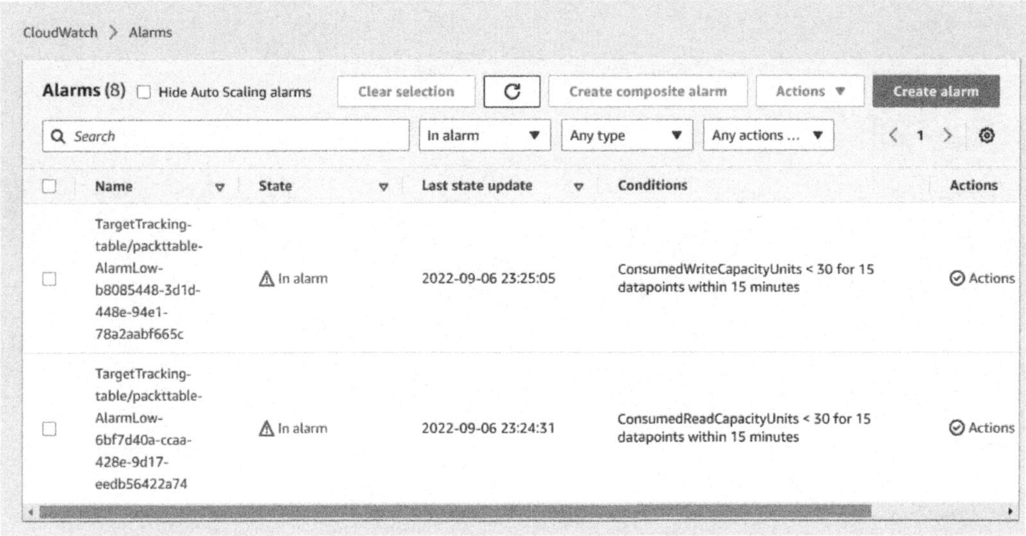

Figure 7.10 – Example alarms

This can give you an idea of the flexibility of the **Alarms** functionality in Amazon CloudWatch.

Next, we will look at another AWS tool called Amazon Inspector.

Amazon Inspector

Another tool an IT auditor can leverage in AWS is Amazon Inspector. Amazon Inspector is an automated vulnerability management service that continually scans AWS resources for software vulnerabilities and inadvertent network exposure.

Amazon Inspector collects events from various vulnerability intelligence sources, including **Common Vulnerabilities and Exposures (CVE)**, the **National Vulnerability Database (NVD)**, and **MITRE**. To get to Amazon Inspector, you can search for it on a browser or the AWS console, as seen in *Figure 7.11:*

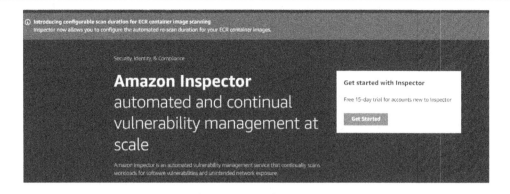

Figure 7.11 – Amazon Inspector

You need to enable Amazon Inspector to facilitate the discovery of data, as seen in *Figure 7.12*:

Figure 7.12 – Enabling Amazon Inspector

Navigate to the **Dashboard** tab on Amazon Inspector and you will find information such as **Critical findings** and **Risk based remediations**:

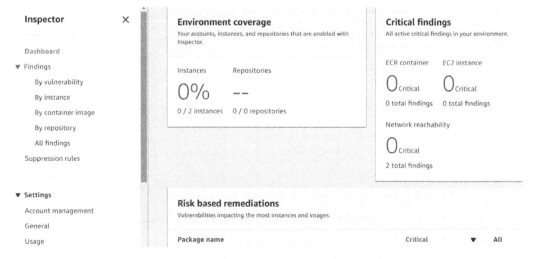

Figure 7.13 – The Amazon Inspector dashboard

One useful tab in Inspector is **Findings**. In our example, there are two findings noted: ports 22 and 3389 are reachable from an internet gateway. Ports 22 and 3389 are **Secure Shell (SSH)** and **Remote Desktop (RDP)**, respectively. If you can recall from *Chapter 4, Network, Infrastructure, and Security Controls*, we noted that Azure CIS Benchmarks recommends that clouds should not allow unrestricted access to remote server administration ports, such as SSH to port 22 and RDP to port 3389. Exposing SSH and RDP to the internet can increase opportunities for malicious activities, such as brute-force attacks.

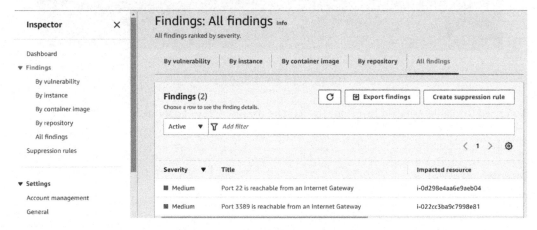

Figure 7.14 – The Amazon Inspector findings

In addition, Amazon Inspector has integration with Amazon EventBridge and AWS Security Hub. You can see this integration with AWS Security Hub in *Figure 7.15*:

Figure 7.15 – Integration with AWS Security Hub

Next, we will look at tools in the Azure cloud environment.

Azure

Now, we will review cloud auditing tools that can be leveraged in the Azure cloud platform.

Azure Monitor

One tool an IT auditor can leverage in the Azure environment is Azure Monitor. As per the Azure documentation, Azure Monitor *"helps you maximize performance and availability of your applications and proactively identify problems in seconds."*

To launch Azure Monitor, you can easily search for it in a browser or on the Azure console, as seen in *Figure 7.16*:

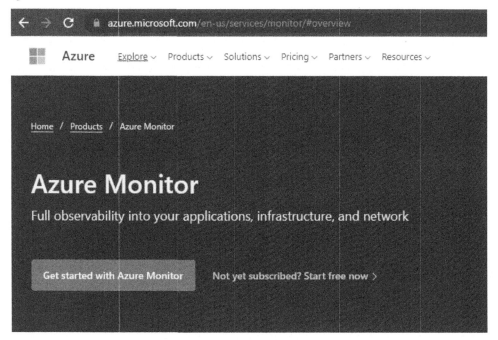

Figure 7.16 – Azure Monitor

Overview presents the different options that an IT auditor can utilize from **Application Insights**, **Container Insights**, **VM Insights**, and **Network Insights**, as seen in *Figure 7.17*:

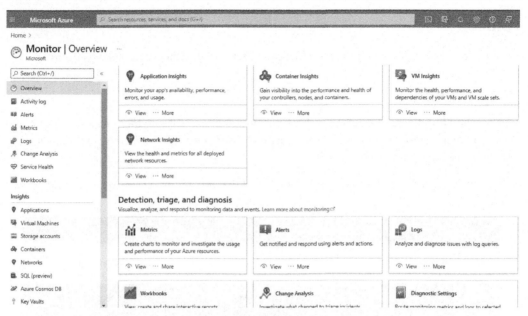

Figure 7.17 – Azure Monitor Overview

A useful feature of Azure Monitor is **Activity Log**, which displays the last transactions executed in the Azure cloud and who initiated the transaction, as seen in *Figure 7.18*:

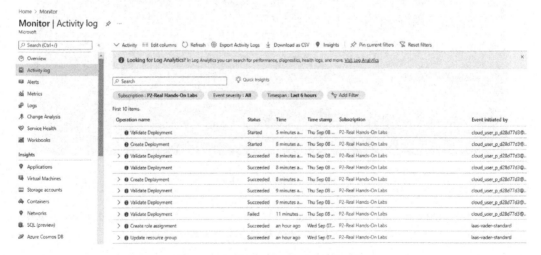

Figure 7.18 – Azure Monitor Activity log

This can be useful to an IT auditor who needs to document who performed a certain transaction.

Another feature that can be useful to an IT auditor is **Alerts**. You can set up alerts for various conditions. In this example, we are setting up alerts for **All Administrative operations** over the last week, as seen in *Figure 7.19*. This type of rule can be useful to an IT auditor when monitoring administrative operations and ensuring they are authorized.

Figure 7.19 – Creating an alert rule

Next, we will look at another Azure tool, referred to as Azure Network Watcher.

Azure Network Watcher

Another tool an IT auditor can leverage is **Azure Network Watcher**. Azure Network Watcher is designed to monitor and repair the network health of **infrastructure as a service (IaaS)** products, which include virtual machines, virtual networks, application gateways, load balancers, and so on. To launch Azure Network Watcher, you can easily search for it in a browser or on the Azure console, as seen in *Figure 7.20*:

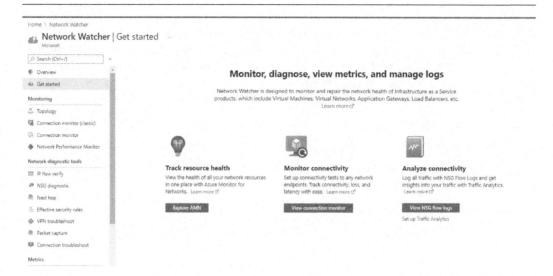

Figure 7.20 – Azure Network Watcher

One feature of interest to an IT auditor is the **Effective security rules** tab. For our example, let us navigate to the **Effective security rules** tab as shown in *Figure 7.21*:

Figure 7.21 – Effective security rules

We will then click on the **packttest2-nsg** rule to expand it and review the individual rules, as seen in *Figure 7.22*. As we can see, we have two exclamation marks on two inbound rules that would be of extreme interest to an IT auditor. Examining these rules closely, we will find that **SSH** and **RDP** access is not restricted inbound from the internet. If you can recall from *Chapter 4, Network, Infrastructure, and Security Controls*, we noted that the Azure CIS Benchmarks recommend that any **Network Security Groups** (**NSG**) should not allow unrestricted inbound access to remote server administration ports, such as **SSH** to port **22** and **RDP** to port **3389**. This is because attackers can use various brute-force techniques to gain access to Azure Virtual Machines using remote server administration ports, such as **22** and **3389**.

Figure 7.22 – packttest2-nsg

Next, we will look at tools in GCP.

GCP

Lastly, we will look at cloud auditing tools that can be leveraged within GCP.

Google Cloud Monitoring

IT auditors can leverage Google Cloud Monitoring to gain real-time visibility into GCP. We can get to Cloud Monitoring by simply searching for it on the Google Cloud console, as shown in *Figure 7.23*:

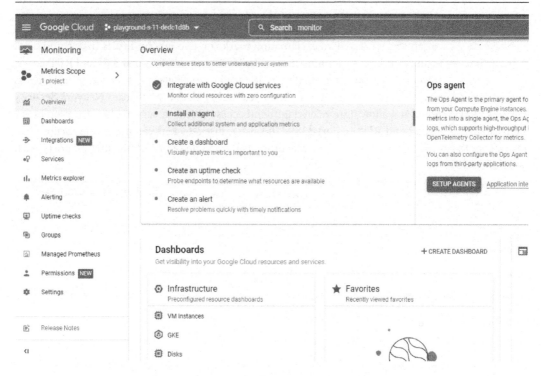

Figure 7.23 – Google Cloud Monitoring Overview

A useful feature for an IT auditor is **Dashboards**. This provides us with dashboards for **Disks**, **Firewalls**, **Infrastructure Summary**, and **VM Instances**:

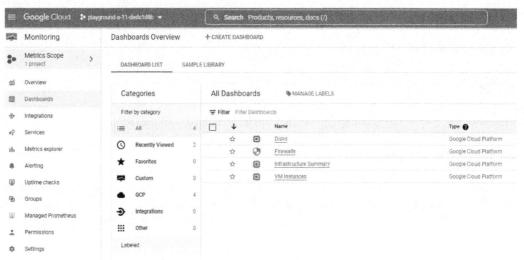

Figure 7.24 – Dashboards Overview

One valuable dashboard to review is **Firewalls**. Let us go to the **Firewalls** dashboard, as seen in *Figure 7.25*:

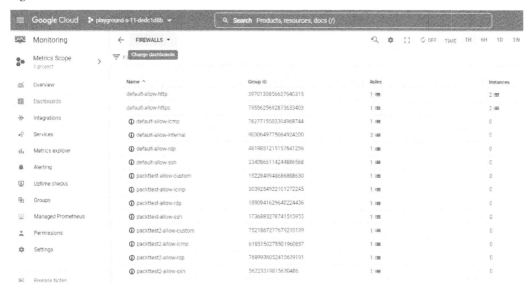

Figure 7.25 – The Firewalls dashboard

If we dig deeper, we note that there is an ingress/inbound rule that allows traffic from the internet **(0.0.0.0/0)**. This particular rule should pique an IT auditor's interest as port 22 (SSH) is a network protocol that has system administrator capabilities.

Figure 7.26 – Security Rules

Another useful feature of Google Cloud Monitoring is **Alerting**. The **Alerting** feature can allow you to trigger an alert based on a predefined metric. The **Alerting** dashboard can be seen in *Figure 7.27*:

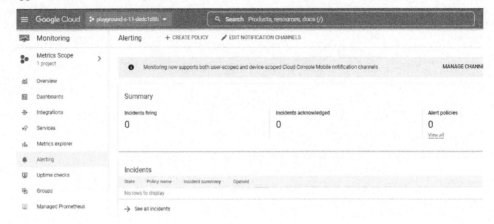

Figure 7.27 – Alerts

As an example, we can add a metric such as **Audited Resource**, as seen in *Figure 7.28*:

Figure 7.28 – Selecting a metric

Next, we will look at another tool in GCP referred to as Network Intelligence Center.

Network Intelligence Center

Another tool an IT auditor can leverage for visibility in GCP is Network Intelligence Center. As per Google's documentation, "*Network Intelligence Center provides a single console for Google Cloud network observability, monitoring, and troubleshooting.*"

Network Intelligence Center has five modules:

- **Network Topology**
- **Connectivity Tests**
- **Performance Dashboard**
- **Firewall Insights**
- **Network Analyzer**

Firewall Insights and **Network Analyzer** provide very valuable information for an IT auditor. You can get to **Network Intelligence** by searching for it on the Google console, as seen in *Figure 7.29*:

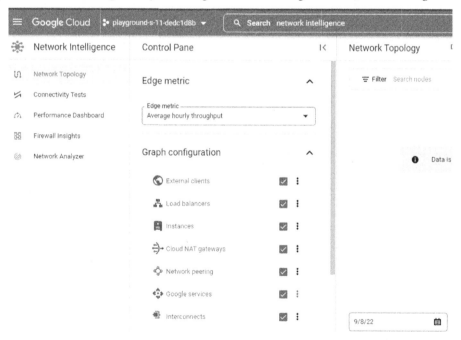

Figure 7.29 – Network Intelligence

Let us start with **Firewall Insights**. As per Google's documentation, "*Firewall Insights helps in optimizing firewall rules. Firewall Insights provides data about how firewall rules are being used, exposes misconfigurations, and identifies rules that could be made stricter.*" When you launch **Firewall Insights**, you will see a dashboard with different categories of rules, as seen in *Figure 7.30*:

Figure 7.30 – Firewall Insights

Let us click on the **Allow rules with overly permissive IP address or port ranges** tab. In our example, the IT auditor should note there are default rules present, including allowing inbound network traffic to SSH and RDP. In *Chapter 4, Network, Infrastructure, and Security Controls*, we stated that default firewall rules are over-permissive and insecure; therefore, the IT auditor needs to examine these default rules closely to ensure they match the organization's risk posture. The default rules can be seen in *Figure 7.31*:

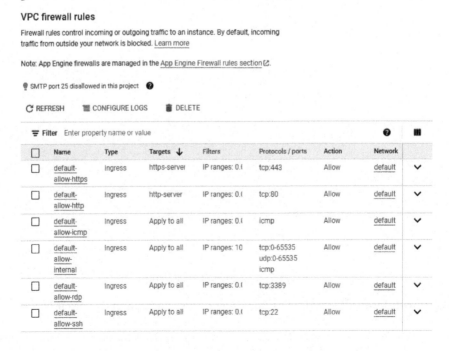

Figure 7.31 – VPC firewalls rules

Another module the IT auditor should leverage is **Network Analyzer**. As per Google's documentation, *"Network Analyzer automatically monitors your VPC network configurations and detects misconfigurations and suboptimal configurations."* **Network Analyzer** can provide very useful information to an IT auditor, such as VPC Network and Network Services, as seen in *Figure 7.32*:

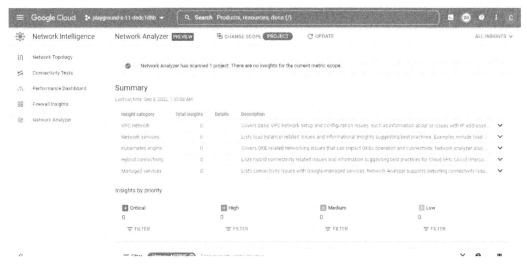

Figure 7.32 – Network Analyzer

Summary

In this chapter, we looked at the tools for monitoring the performance, availability, and security of infrastructure and applications for AWS, Azure, and GCP environments. We covered standard tools and options that exist within each cloud environment, and how an IT auditor can leverage them to monitor and assess the respective clouds.

In our next chapter, we will perform a walk-through demonstrating how to assess **identity and access management (IAM)** controls.

8

Walk-Through – Assessing IAM Controls

From *Chapter 1, Cloud Architecture and Navigation*, to *Chapter 6, Tips and Techniques for Advanced Auditing*, we built foundational knowledge of cloud structure, navigation, and security controls, and in *Chapter 7, Tools for Monitoring and Assessing*, we learned about tools available for auditing. Now, it's time to put our learning into practice by performing some example audit walk-throughs of basic controls within the major cloud providers.

In this chapter, we'll cover the following main topics:

- Preparing to assess cloud IAM controls

- Assessing authentication and authorization

- Assessing access assignment controls

- Assessing privileged access controls

- Assessing device controls

We will pose an assessment question for each of the topic areas and execute a basic test procedure. By the end of this chapter, you will be able to perform a basic audit walk-through of a few IAM controls across the three major cloud environments.

Preparing to assess cloud IAM controls

As we covered in *Chapter 2, Effective Techniques for Preparing to Audit Cloud Environments*, developing a good audit plan requires a thorough understanding of how the enterprise environment is architected and connected. When it comes to IAM controls, knowing that the cloud environment is federated with another identity store versus using a localized identity store only, for example, will change the test procedures that should be used and the evidence that you would expect to gather. It may also influence the points of contact within the organization you would need to work with to obtain evidence details. In addition to understanding the architecture and integration design of the environment, like other audits, it's essential to understand the risk and control objectives the organization is trying to address as part of the cloud audit process. As we've uncovered throughout *Chapter 1, Cloud Architecture and Navigation,* to *Chapter 6, Tips and Techniques for Advanced Auditing,* there is a myriad of options for configuring security controls within your enterprise cloud environments, and the configuration options an organization chooses should be reflective of their risk tolerance and control objectives.

In the sections that follow, as a prerequisite, you will require a minimum level of view or read access to obtain the test evidence independently. Depending upon your specific organization's configuration and any additional customizations, you may require additional access rights or group memberships to directly access specific content, or you may be required to work with an administrative point of contact for your organization as you observe them pulling control evidence. For reference, any screenshots in the following sections are based on a user with administrative privileges to the cloud environment.

Another thing to keep in mind as you prepare to assess cloud IAM controls is that although some basic tenants are the same across the cloud providers, the nomenclature and structure vary. Please review *Chapter 3, Identity and Access Management Controls,* as a refresher on the IAM components across the three cloud providers.

Now that we have touched on a few points of preparation let's perform our first walk-through challenge to assess authentication and authorization.

Assessing authentication and authorization

In the case of user authentication and authorization, it's important to understand the source of identities and where they are managed. Cloud providers offer the ability to consume, share, and/or sync identity information within hybrid environments, across cloud providers, and with on-premise identity stores. As a brief reminder, authentication is the process of verifying an identity claim, and authorization is the process of verifying that the identity has the proper permissions to access content or resources. Both processes should be inclusive of human and non-human (service accounts, workload identities, and automation accounts) identities.

For our walk-through in this section, our control testing will determine whether the organization's cloud environment adheres to a control policy that requires accounts that are inactive for 180 days to be disabled. In our example, we will walk through simple methods to obtain this information within AWS and Azure cloud environments; however, please keep in mind that there are often many other methods for pulling this information. Leveraging the established frameworks that we referenced in *Chapter 2, Effective Techniques for Preparing to Audit Cloud Environments,* may assist you in utilizing some of these other methods.

AWS IAM

In AWS, a convenient way to identify that users inactive for 180 days are disabled, is to execute the following test steps:

1. Navigate and log in to the AWS console.

2. Select the **Identity and Access Management (IAM)** service.

3. Select **Credential report**.

4. As shown in *Figure 8.1*, you will have the option to download this report locally. The downloaded report will provide you with a list of all users associated with the AWS instance and the status of their credentials, including the creation date and last login information:

Figure 8.1 – AWS IAM Credential Report

Once you've downloaded and opened the report, depending on the scope of the audit and the size of the user population, you may need to extract a sample from the list. However, within the report, as shown in *Figure 8.2*, you will be able to see two pertinent columns for the control – **user_creation_time** and **password_last_used**. This will give you an indication of the age of the account and the period for which it has or hasn't been active. Based on the accounts here, our testing shows this control passes for the AWS environment:

C	D	E	F	G	H
user_creation_time	password_enabled	password_last_used	password_last_changed	password	mfa_activ
2020-09-14T11:17:53+00:00	not_supported	2022-09-11T22:03:35+00:00	not_supported	not_supp(	TRUE
2022-09-11T22:05:13+00:00	TRUE	no_information	2022-09-11T22:05:13+00:00	N/A	FALSE

Figure 8.2 – AWS credential report download

Now that we've performed the control assessment within AWS IAM, let's look at performing the same control assessment in Microsoft Azure.

Microsoft Azure

To validate the control requiring that users inactive for 180 days be disabled, you can execute the following test steps to get an initial sample:

1. Navigate to the Microsoft Azure portal.

2.   Select **Azure Active Directory**.

3.   Navigate to the **Users | All users** blade.

Either select the option to filter users created within the last 360 days or edit the columns to include the **Creation time** field, as shown in *Figure 8.3*. If this is the first audit being conducted, you may want to go back further than 360 days for the user population:

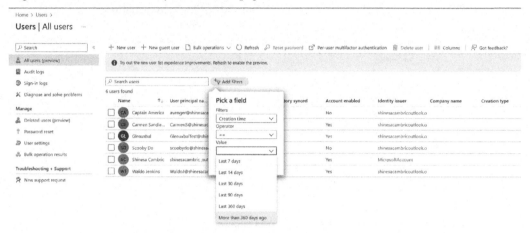

Figure 8.3 – Microsoft Azure user list

After identifying your sample population, you will want to compare this with sign-in details for those accounts. In this example, we have found that Carmen Sandiego, as shown in *Figure 8.4*, meets our sample selection criteria, so now let's see if our inactivity control passes for these users:

Figure 8.4 – Microsoft Azure filtered user list

To review the sign-in details for the selected users, you can execute the following test steps:

1.   Navigate and log in to the Microsoft Azure portal.

2.   Navigate to **Azure Active Directory**.

3.   Navigate to the **Users** blade.

4.   Perform a search for one of the selected users by entering the display name in the search and then selecting that user by clicking on the hyperlinked display name. Here you will be able to view sign-in details or directly access the sign-in logs for the user, as shown in *Figure 8.5*:

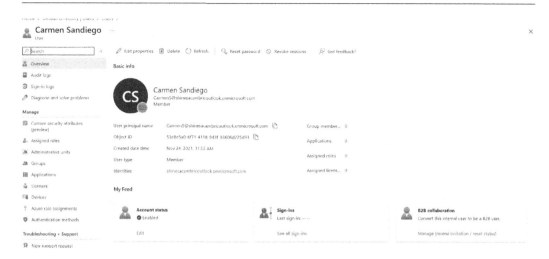

Figure 8.5 – Microsoft Azure selected user with sign-in details

Note that in our sample scenario, this control has failed. As shown in *Figure 8.6*, this user has no recent sign-ins, and based on the user creation date, it is clear that the user has been inactive for greater than 180 days:

Figure 8.6 – Microsoft Azure user sign-in history

Based on the previous steps, we can say that there are easy methods for gathering evidence for some basic IT general computing controls within cloud environments. We've also demonstrated the importance of assessing the control in multiple cloud environments if the organization is using more than one cloud provider for operations.

Now that we have performed a walk-through of a typical authentication and authorization control, let's look at assessing access assignment controls.

Assessing access assignment controls

Beyond establishing who can access an environment and what they can do, another important area to assess is who can configure or modify access assignments for identities. In some environments, the assignment of access may be a completely automated procedure through account life cycle workflows. However, even with this automation, it's important to establish who can modify it and influence the access being granted. It's also important to clarify whether there are any exception processes in place that could potentially bypass that automation.

In this walk-through, we will assess which identities can perform user and access administration. For our control, we will look at testing Azure and GCP cloud environments to validate that all user access is provisioned through the organization's entitlement life cycle process. For our example control, we need to verify that there is no evidence of access being manually assigned.

Microsoft Azure

To validate the control that access for the cloud environment is only assigned through an enterprise lifecycle tool, we will execute the following test steps to verify which accounts have provisioned access within our desired testing time frame:

1. Navigate and log in to the Microsoft Azure portal.
2. Navigate to **Azure Active Directory**.
3. Navigate to the **Roles and administrators** blade.
4. Select the **Audit logs** blade.

As shown in *Figure 8.7*, when accessing **Audit logs** from this navigational path, the results are automatically filtered on the **RoleManagement** category. You can do additional filtering as needed to get events for the desired date range and even filter on a more granular set of activities:

Figure 8.7 – Microsoft Azure role management audit logs

Within the list of audit log results, you can select each entry to get more details about the activity and what may have been modified. It's important to note that in some cases, your report results will include default system maintenance activities, such as in *Figure 8.8*. These can be distinguished based on the **Initiated by (actor)** details:

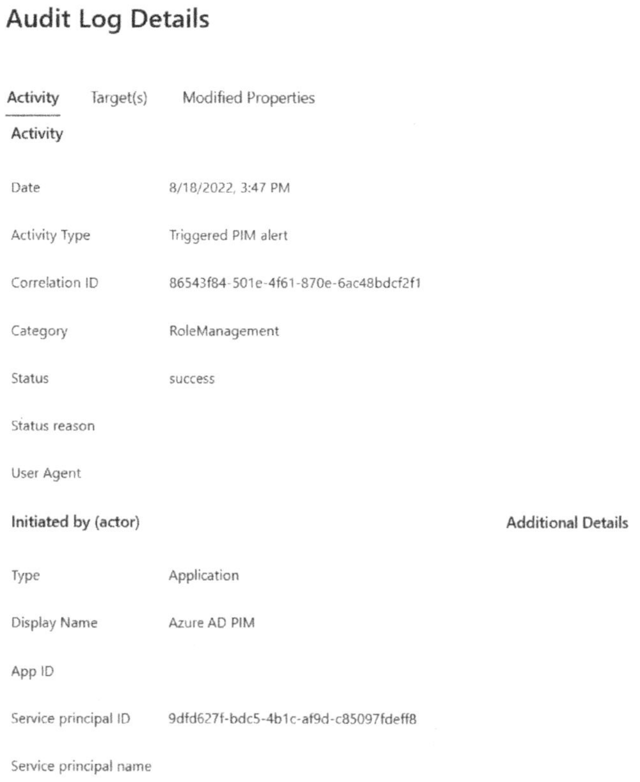

Audit Log Details

Activity   Target(s)   Modified Properties

Activity

Date   8/18/2022, 3:47 PM

Activity Type   Triggered PIM alert

Correlation ID   86543f84-501e-4f61-870e-6ac48bdcf2f1

Category   RoleManagement

Status   success

Status reason

User Agent

Initiated by (actor)   **Additional Details**

Type   Application

Display Name   Azure AD PIM

App ID

Service principal ID   9dfd627f-bdc5-4b1c-af9d-c85097fdeff8

Service principal name

Figure 8.8 – Microsoft Azure audit log entry performed by a default service

Now that we've determined a method for testing access assignment controls within Microsoft Azure, let's look at testing this control in GCP.

GCP

Within the GCP environment, Google has provided resources that allow for the dynamic querying of policies and policy settings. As shown in *Figure 8.9*, you can develop your own custom query from scratch or use another query template to get started:

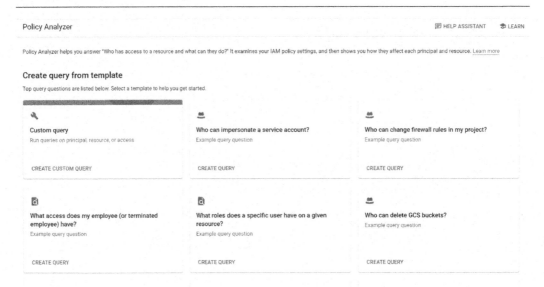

Figure 8.9 – GCP Policy Analyzer custom query

To effectively leverage this querying ability, you will need to understand the roles, permissions, and/ or properties you want to assess. As shown in *Figure 8.10*, the query builder allows you to filter and select based on different options. In *Chapter 3, Identity and Access Management Controls*, we covered the resources available to help familiarize yourself with the roles and permissions within GCP.

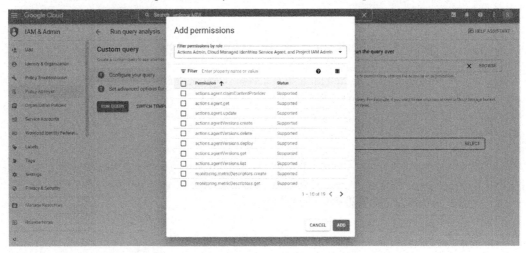

Figure 8.10 – GCP Policy Analyzer custom query filter

After creating a query with a list of the permissions and/or roles that you want to validate, as shown in *Figure 8.11*, you will get some additional options to query based on options related to inheritance. Remember that inheritance is one of the constructs that GCP uses and that you will need to be aware of it as you perform control testing assessments. Once you have a list of users with permission to perform access assignments, you can then query activity logs to determine whether that access has been used:

Figure 8.11 – GCP Policy Analyzer custom query and inheritance options

Now that we've covered some ways to assess a basic control related to understanding who can perform access and assignments and when that ability may have been used outside of the control process, let's look at performing an assessment of privileged access controls in AWS and Azure.

Assessing privileged access controls

As an auditor, it's important to understand who has been granted privileged access within an environment. Knowing who has been granted privileged access and whether that level of access is appropriate given the individual's job responsibilities is often a foundational step before assessing other IT general computing controls.

AWS IAM

One primary way of identifying users in AWS that have privileged access is by reviewing which users have access keys and when those access keys were last used. To pull this evidence, you can perform the following steps:

1. Navigate and log on to the AWS console.

2. Select the **Identity and Access Management (IAM)** service.

3. Select **Users** within the **Access management** option.

4. Within the **Users** report, you can review and filter users by a given set of criteria. To ensure all relevant options are visible in the report, you will need to open **Preferences** and ensure the options related to privileged access are part of your visible column list; as shown in *Figure 8.12*, you will have the following options:

Figure 8.12 – AWS EC2 Users report column selection

Once we have this list of users with privileged access, we can compare this with the expected list of users. Keep in mind this gives us one method to view users with privileged access; however, this is not the only method. Depending upon the configuration of the enterprise cloud environment, additional steps may need to be taken to obtain all users with privileges with access to cloud services.

Now that we've seen one method for pulling a list of privileged users with AWS IAM, let's look at an option for pulling a list within Microsoft Azure.

Microsoft Azure

To validate a list of privileged users within an Azure environment, we need to execute the following test steps to verify the assignment of privileged access:

1. Navigate and log in to the Microsoft Azure portal.
2. Navigate to **Azure Active Directory**.
3. Navigate to the **Roles and administrators** blade.

As shown in *Figure 8.13*, when accessing the **Roles and administrators** blade, we have the option to select **Download assignments**. This will give us a comprehensive list of users with **Azure Active Directory** role assignments, from which we can validate the actual versus the expected list of users:

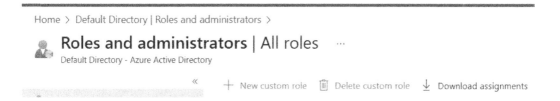

Figure 8.13 – The Microsoft Azure Roles and administrators blade

After selecting the **Download assignments** option, you then need to navigate to the **Bulk operation results** blade, as shown in *Figure 8.14*, to view and extract the report. A list of downloads that have been requested will be visible. To open the report, click on the entry under the **Type** column for the report that you wish to open:

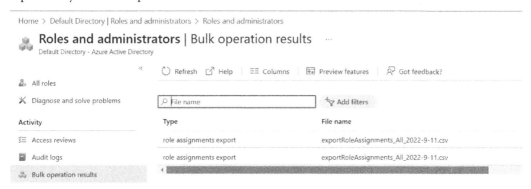

Figure 8.14 – Microsoft Azure Roles and administrators bulk operation reports

Upon opening the report, as shown in *Figure 8.15*, you will find the role assignments (**roleDisplayName**) and users (**displayName**) to which they are assigned. You can also distinguish between built-in privileged roles (**isBuiltIn**) and the user type (**objectType**). Within this report, you can easily sort the specific privileged role assignments and see a list of users with this access. If you are unfamiliar with which built-in roles have privileged access, you can refer to the information shared in *Chapter 3, Identity and Access Management Controls*, on where to go for additional details.

roleDisplayName	isBuiltIn	principal(	userPrincipalName	displayNa	objectType
Application Administrator	TRUE	d965573e-	scoobydo@shinesac	Scooby Dc	user
Conditional Access Administrator	TRUE	a0b2c84e-	avenger@shinesaca	Captain A	user
Directory Readers	TRUE	9ae2fe0d-	00000014-0000-0000	Microsoft.	servicePrincipal
Global Administrator	TRUE	8aa2ca2b-	shinesacambric_out	Shinesa C	user
Global Administrator	TRUE	811ec4a9-	WaldoJ@shinesacar	Waldo Jer	user
Groups Administrator	TRUE	a0b2c84e-	avenger@shinesaca	Captain A	user

Figure 8.15 – The AWS EC2 Users report column selection

Now that we've done a walk-through of identifying privileged users, let's take a look at assessing device controls within a couple of cloud environments.

Assessing device controls

In our last walk-through session for IAM controls, let's look at assessing a common control related to devices – the configuration of **multi-factor authentication** (**MFA**). In our sample walk-through, we will validate whether MFA is being enforced for all users and their devices in our AWS and Microsoft Azure cloud environments.

AWS IAM

In the previous section on assessing privileged access controls, we saw that AWS provides a **Users** report within the **Identity and Access Management (IAM)** service. As shown in *Figure 8.16*, we can see that MFA requirements for individual users can be found here. In the screenshot, we can see that the user is not enrolled in or required to use MFA, which would mean the control test fails in this instance:

Figure 8.16 – The AWS IAM Users report column selection

Another way to see the same information is within the credential report, which we reviewed in the section on assessing authentication and authorization controls. As shown in *Figure 8.17*, the report includes a field that indicates whether MFA is active for each user, providing an easy way to sort and determine whether the control objective is met:

C	D	E	F	G	H
user_creation_time	password_enabled	password_last_used	password_last_changed	password	mfa_active
2020-09-14T11:17:53+00:00	not_supported	2022-09-11T22:03:35+00:00	not_supported	not_suppo	TRUE
2022-09-11T22:05:13+00:00	TRUE	no_information	2022-09-11T22:05:13+00:00	N/A	FALSE

Figure 8.17 – The AWS IAM Users report column selection

Now that we've seen how some of the previous testing procedures in AWS can also help in assessing device controls such as MFA, let's take a look at reviewing MFA controls within Microsoft Azure.

Microsoft Azure

As we've covered throughout this book, there are often many paths within cloud environments to get to the same information, and reviewing device controls and compliance within Microsoft Azure is no different. One way that we can test that there are no exceptions to device control policies such as MFA would be to take the following steps:

1. Navigate and log in to the Microsoft Azure portal.

2. Navigate to **Azure Active Directory**.

3. Navigate to the **Devices** blade.

As shown in *Figure 8.18*, the overview shows that there are no devices that are uncompliant with the device policy. However, we should investigate this a little further:

Figure 8.18 – Microsoft Azure Devices | Overview

Prior to accepting the content of **Devices | Overview** as evidence that there are no exceptions to the policy, let's check what the policy is by looking at the **Device settings** blade. Here, as shown in *Figure 8.19*, we can now see that there may be exceptions that allow MFA to not be enforced upon certain behaviors. This highlights why it is important for you as an auditor to understand not only what is being provided as test evidence but also how the specific cloud environment is configured to align with that test evidence.

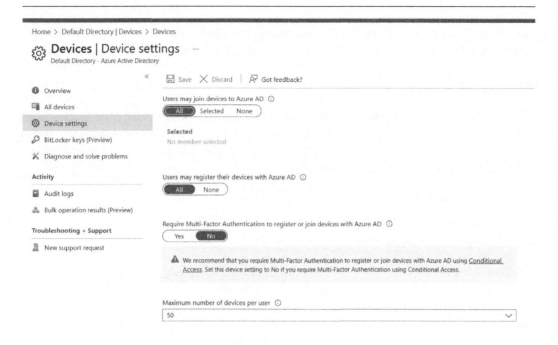

Figure 8.19 – Microsoft Azure Device settings

In this section, we've performed a simple walk-through of device MFA enforcement settings, and we are now aware that in addition to overview reports showing compliance, we need to dig deeper and assess what is in the compliance policies to confirm whether control objectives are being met.

Summary

In this chapter, we performed a walk-through of common and practical IT general computing controls that may be performed when auditing cloud environments. We covered steps to assess authentication and authorization and reviewed that in a multi-cloud environment, these controls should be tested in all clouds. We also performed an assessment of access assignment controls and executed steps to determine who has privileged access.

We finished this chapter by performing a walk-through of a device-related control (MFA) and saw the importance of understanding how relying on overview details as test results could prevent the detection of configuration that does not align with the control objectives.

In the next section, we'll continue with our walk-throughs – this time assessing policy settings and resource controls.

Walk-Through – Assessing Policy Settings and Resource Controls

In the previous chapter, we put our learnings of cloud IAM control settings to the test. Now, we will perform some practice with identifying and assessing policy and resource control settings.

In this chapter, we'll cover the following main topics:

- Preparing to assess network, infrastructure, and resource controls
- Assessing network and firewall settings
- Assessing resource management policies
- Assessing data security policies

We will pose a sample assessment question for each of the topic areas and execute a basic test procedure. By the end of this chapter, we will have a deeper understanding of assessing network, resource, and data security policies as part of an enterprise cloud audit.

Preparing to assess network, infrastructure, and resource controls

From *Chapter 4, Network, Infrastructure, and Security Controls*, to *Chapter 6, Tips and Techniques for Advanced Auditing*, we learned about some of the network, infrastructure, and resource controls available to enterprises across the three major cloud providers. As a reminder, we've only covered a subset of the various options that are available in order to provide some foundational knowledge. As we covered in *Chapter 2, Effective Techniques for Preparing to Audit Cloud Environments*, obtaining a thorough understanding of how the enterprise environment is architected and connected is critical to determining which areas within a cloud environment should be scoped for audit.

Having architectural diagrams that indicate areas of integration will highlight whether there are hybrid and/or multi-cloud controls that should be assessed. As we identified in our control walk-through in *Chapter 8, Walk-Through – Assessing IAM Controls*, based on integration and architecture, a control may need to be assessed for effectiveness across more than one enterprise cloud platform to determine whether the control objective is being met for the enterprise. Architectural diagrams showing the flow of data and resources will help to highlight that need. These diagrams should indicate environment tiering (for example, production versus test environments), data flows and sensitivity of the data, encryption, destinations, ports, protocols, and connectivity to external environments not managed by the enterprise.

Another critical component, especially for network, infrastructure, and resource controls within hybrid environments, is determining roles and responsibilities for the management of these components. It is very common that the individuals responsible for managing on-premise network architecture are not the same individuals who are managing this within cloud environments. Walking through the integration diagram with both sets of responsible/accountable individuals will help to provide a more holistic view of the strength of integrated controls from either side.

In the sections that follow, as a prerequisite, you will require a minimum level of view or read access to obtain the test evidence independently. Depending upon your specific organization's configuration and any additional customizations, you may require additional access rights or group memberships to directly access specific content, or you may be required to work with an administrative point of contact for your organization as you observe them pulling control evidence. For reference, any screenshots in the following sections are based on a user with administrative privileges to the cloud environment.

Now that we have touched on a few points of preparation, let's perform our first walk-through challenge to assess network and firewall settings within an enterprise cloud environment.

Assessing network and firewall settings

With network and firewall settings, it's important to have clarity of environment isolation requirements, which resources are deployed in an environment, network traffic requirements, and governance over routing tables and defining subnets.

For our walk-through in this section, our control testing will determine whether traffic logging and alerting have been enabled to detect anomalies with connectivity and network traffic. Please review the compliance frameworks that we referenced in *Chapter 2, Effective Techniques for Preparing to Audit Cloud Environments*, as these may guide you to additional methods for gathering test evidence. In our example, we will walk through one simple method to obtain this information within the Azure cloud environment; however, please keep in mind that there are often many other ways of collecting the same information. Let's review one option to do this within Microsoft Azure.

Microsoft Azure

To validate the control requiring that network flow logs and alerting are enabled, take the following steps:

1. Navigate to the Microsoft Azure portal.
2. Select **Monitor | Networks**.
3. Navigate to the **Traffic**.

Compare the list of items that are shown with any architecture and network diagrams to determine whether logs and alerting have been enabled for the network resource. As shown in *Figure 9.1*, **Australia East(1) NSG** does not have flow logs configured, which means this portion of compliance testing has failed:

Figure 9.1 – Microsoft Azure network traffic logging

Within the same screen, you can also see on the right that **0 Total alert rules** have been configured, as shown in *Figure 9.2*, indicating that the portion of the control requiring configured alerts has also failed:

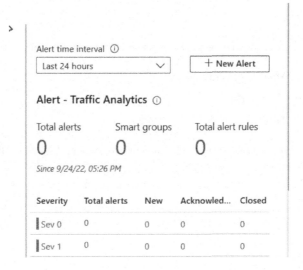

Figure 9.2 – Microsoft Azure network traffic alerts

Now that we have performed a walk-through of basic network traffic logging control, let's look at assessing resource management policies.

Assessing resource management policies

Within cloud environments, there are several different types of resource controls. One type, the ability to manage billing and cost controls, not only has a financial impact but also has technical implications as well. In many cases, these controls may define a hierarchy of who can add additional compute resources, how those resources are provided, and the scale of those resources being allocated. Not managing this properly could lead to environmental sprawl and architecture that is not fully documented or vetted and to significant charges for resource consumption if effective controls are not in place. Additionally, in some cases, being defined as a billing administrator also provides a level of privileged technical access within the enterprise cloud environment, making this ability especially sensitive. Another type of resource control that we covered in *Chapter 5, Financial Resources and Change Management*, was the use of enabling policies, labels, and tags to control the management of resources.

In this walk-through, we will step through pulling resource adherence to compliance policies. In Azure, we will validate that all resources are compliant with the enabled policies, and in GCP, we will confirm the asset count of resources and that each is appropriately tagged and labeled to indicate use and sensitivity.

Microsoft Azure

To validate that our resources adhere to all enabled controls, we can execute the following test steps to confirm the automated controls that are applied and which our resources are compliant with:

1. Navigate and log in to the Microsoft Azure portal.

2. Navigate to **Policy | Compliance**.

3. In the filters, select the relevant **Scope**.

As shown in *Figure 9.3*, there are some scopes for which the compliance checks have failed. The count of policies that did not pass can also be seen in the following figure:

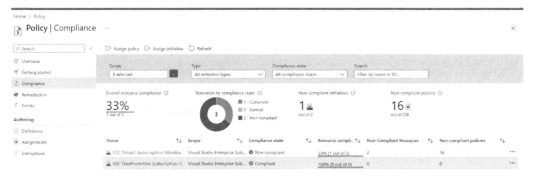

Figure 9.3 – Microsoft Azure compliance policies

When reviewing compliance policy adherence, note the second item in the list for which it shows 100% compliance, but the number of resources is **0**. When we look at this further, as shown in *Figure 9.4*, we can see that in this instance, the scope does not contain any resources for which the assigned policies are relevant, and this may warrant further investigation regarding policies that have been applied:

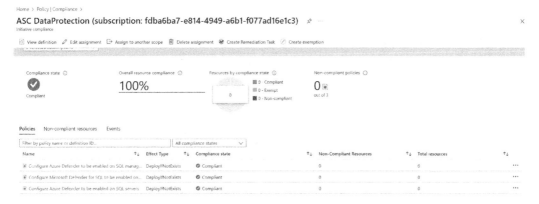

Figure 9.4 – Microsoft Azure compliance, no policies applied

Now that we've determined a method for verifying adherence to enabled policies within Microsoft Azure, let's look at testing the resource asset inventory in GCP.

GCP

Within the GCP environment, to get a list of assets and confirm that labeling and tags have been applied, we can execute the following test steps:

1. Navigate and log in to the **Google Cloud** console.

2. Navigate to **IAM & Admin | Asset Inventory**.

As shown in *Figure 9.5*, you can see a list of assets associated with the GCP project. This list can be filtered to show only those that are enabled:

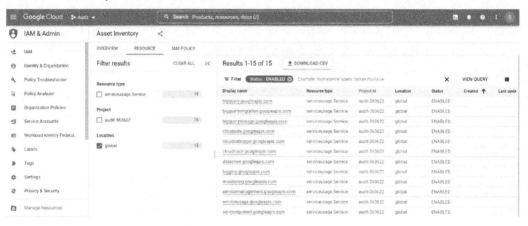

Figure 9.5 – GCP Asset Inventory

From this list, we can then determine a sample against which we can review whether labels and tags have been applied according to our enterprise control. To review the labels and tag information for our samples, we can filter our results and then download them to CSV format to see this information, as shown in *Figure 9.6*, or we can click on each entry within the GCP portal to see additional details:

L	M	N	O	P
Location	Labels	Network tags	Additional attributes	
global				
global				
global				
global				
global				
global				
global				

Figure 9.6 – GCP Asset Inventory labels and network tags

Now that we've covered some ways to assess basic controls related to resource management through policy applications (Azure) or tagging and labels (GCP), let's look at performing an assessment of data security policy controls in AWS and Azure.

Assessing data security policies

Data within an enterprise may be one of the most essential assets that an organization owns, and ensuring that any sensitive data is properly protected through means such as encryption, data masking, and logging of changes to data are likely to be critical controls. In this walk-through, we'll look at assessing adherence to data security policies in AWS and Azure by checking to see that logging and appropriate levels of encryption have been enabled.

AWS

One primary way to check adherence to data security policies within AWS is by reviewing findings in the AWS **Security Hub**. To review these findings, we will need to perform the following steps:

1. Navigate and log on to the AWS Console.
2. Select the **Security, Identity, & Compliance** service.
3. Select **Security Hub**.

Within the **Security Hub** report, we can review a list of findings that relate to some of the standards and frameworks that were referenced in *Chapter 2, Effective Techniques for Preparing to Audit Cloud Environments*. In *Figure 9.7*, we can see that one of our S3 buckets does not have logging or an alarm for changes to the policies of the S3 bucket:

Figure 9.7 – AWS EC2 data security findings

An additional review of our S3 buckets to confirm encryption and logging can be done by navigating to the S3 service and selecting a specific S3 bucket and reviewing the bucket properties, as shown in *Figure 9.8*. Here, we see that encryption and server access logging have been disabled:

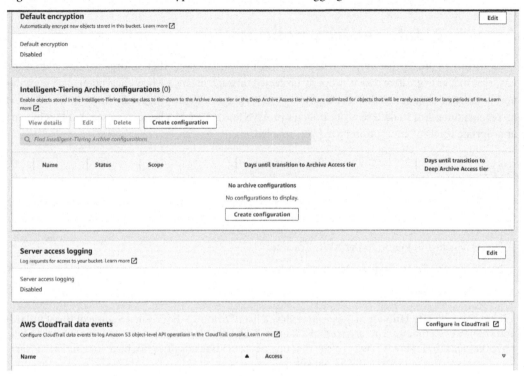

Figure 9.8 – AWS S3 bucket properties

Now that we've assessed some data security settings in AWS, let's look at an option for pulling this within Microsoft Azure.

Microsoft Azure

To validate data security settings for logging and encryption controls on our resources, we'll need to perform the following steps:

1. Navigate and log in to the Microsoft Azure portal.

2. Navigate to **All resources**.

3. Select the relevant resources; in this case, we've selected **tsecstorage Storage account**.

As shown in *Figure 9.9*, after selecting the resource, we can see the properties of the resource as part of **Overview**:

Figure 9.9 – Microsoft Azure Storage account overview

Here, we can see information regarding data security, such as **Version 1.2** has been assigned to **Minimum TLS version**, but **Infrastructure encryption** is listed as **Disabled** (note that most cloud providers store data as encrypted at rest; however, refer back to the concept of shared responsibility covered in *Chapter 1, Cloud Architecture and Navigation*).

To see additional information on data security for this resource, we can use some of the navigation options on the left side of the portal, as shown in *Figure 9.10*. Here, we see options for checking additional details on **Encryption** as well as **Data protection**:

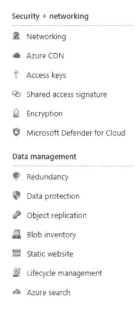

Figure 9.10 – Azure data security

Upon opening the **Encryption** blade, we can see that in addition to encryption being disabled, there are no scopes to which it would be applied, as shown in *Figure 9.11*:

Figure 9.11 – Azure encryption settings and scopes

We've now completed our walk-through of data security controls, as well as other policy settings and resource controls.

Summary

In this chapter, we performed a walk-through of basic testing and evidence gathering that can be used for enterprise cloud policy settings and resource controls. We covered preparing to assess network, infrastructure, and resource controls and did some general walk-throughs of the various cloud environments.

In our final chapter, we'll wrap up our walk-throughs by assessing logs, change management, and monitoring and alerting controls across the cloud providers.

10

Walk-Through – Assessing Change Management, Logging, and Monitoring Policies

In the previous chapter, we put our knowledge of network, infrastructure, and resource controls to the test. Now, we will practice identifying and assessing change management, logging, and monitoring policies.

In this chapter, we'll cover the following main topics:

- Preparing to assess change management controls
- Assessing audit and logging configurations
- Assessing change management and configuration policies
- Assessing monitoring and alerting policies

We will pose sample assessment questions and execute a basic test procedure for each of the topic areas. By the end of this chapter, we will have a deeper understanding of assessing change management, logging, and monitoring policies as part of an enterprise cloud audit.

Preparing to assess change management controls

As we covered in *Chapter 5*, *Financial Resource and Change Management Controls*, obtaining a thorough understanding of where logging and history can be found for changes performed is critical to determining which areas within a cloud environment should be scoped for audit. *Chapter 5*, *Financial Resource and Change Management Controls*, was where we learned about the use of enabling policies, labels, and tags to control the management of resources.

Change management is a systematic approach to managing changes. The primary objective of the change management process is to facilitate changes to the cloud while minimizing risks to cloud environments.

Cloud environments are designed for agility. In addition, cloud environments facilitate the use of a variety of automation, integration, and deployment tools that allow an organization to make rapid changes. Therefore, in a cloud environment, the visibility of changes is the main control for managing changes. In the cloud, organizations should leverage automation to manage changes. By using automation, many of the manual approval steps can be fully automated with a higher degree of confidence.

Change management performed in the cloud introduces additional benefits in comparison to traditional change management processes. The cloud allows for ease of deployment with built-in automation and deployment tools removing manual processes associated with the planning and implementation of traditional changes. In a traditional change management process, manual rollbacks would have to be performed in case of any issues with the changes. However, in the cloud, due to automation, the risk is minimized as most cloud services allow for instant rollbacks in case of any issues.

Tools utilized for change management in the cloud provide workflows and pre-approved change tasks that can reduce the delay in the approval process while retaining flexibility in the change process. Lastly, these change management tools can track and record all changes made in the cloud and have the ability to generate reports for tracking and reviewing trends for further action.

Cloud service providers provide various monitoring tools that are used to track changes. IT auditors should leverage these monitoring tools to gain visibility into the changes performed.

These are the key questions that IT auditors should ask with regard to the change management process:

- What is the process for requesting or approving changes?
- What is the process for moving the changes into production?
- Is there any notification when changes drift from the established baseline?
- Is there a process to roll back changes in case of security concerns?
- Is there a process to facilitate emergency changes?

It is important for the IT auditor to ensure there is adequate segregation of duties within the change management process. For example, an individual who develops a change should not be the same individual moving the change into production.

In the sections that follow, as a prerequisite, you will require a minimum level of view or read access to obtain the test evidence independently. Depending upon your specific organization's configuration and any additional customizations, you may require additional access rights or group memberships to directly access specific content, or you may be required to work with an administrative point of contact for your organization as you observe them pulling control evidence. For reference, any screenshots in the sections that follow are based on a user with administrative privileges to the cloud environment.

Now that we have touched on a few points of preparation, let's perform our first walk-through challenge to assess network and firewall settings within an enterprise cloud environment.

Assessing audit and logging configurations

Logs are files that detail all the events that occur within the cloud. Logs can show deviations from expected activity, giving visibility of potential security issues. Different log types include application, server, access, network logs, and so on. Logging is a practice that enables you to collect and correlate log data from cloud applications, services, and infrastructure. It is performed to help identify issues, measure performance, and optimize configurations. Logging is a valuable tool for security analysis, as it can help an organization maintain an audit trail of transactions performed in the cloud.

The three cloud providers; AWS, Azure, and **Google Cloud Platform** (**GCP**) provide native tools for logging. AWS provides AWS CloudTrail and Amazon CloudWatch Logs, Azure provides Azure Monitor Logs while GCP offers Cloud Logging. This is not an exhaustive list, but some of the key tools that are used for audit and logging. Let's look at the three cloud providers in detail.

AWS

Two services that can be leveraged in tandem by the IT auditor are Amazon CloudWatch Logs and AWS CloudTrail. Amazon CloudWatch Logs furnishes logs in a unified flow of events ordered by time. On the other hand, AWS CloudTrail is a service that logs actions performed in an AWS environment.

Amazon CloudWatch Logs

To launch Amazon CloudWatch Logs, perform the following steps:

1. Navigate to the AWS portal.

2. Search for `CloudWatch`.

3. Navigate to **CloudWatch | Logs | Logs Insights | History**.

As shown in *Figure 10.1*, you can interactively query and analyze your log data in Amazon CloudWatch Logs:

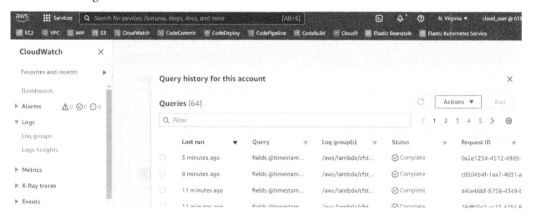

Figure 10.1 – Amazon CloudWatch Logs | Logs Insights

AWS CloudTrail

To launch AWS CloudTrail, take the following steps:

1. Navigate to the AWS portal.

2. Search for CloudTrail.

3. Navigate to **CloudTrail** | **Event history**.

    As shown in *Figure 10.2*, you can see a user named **cloud_user** has created and modified attributes of a **virtual private cloud** (**VPC**). This might be useful information for an IT auditor:

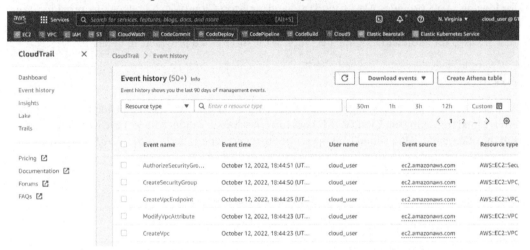

Figure 10.2 – AWS CloudWatch Logs | Event history

Now that we have looked at logging and auditing tools in AWS, let us look at the tools an IT auditor can leverage in Microsoft Azure.

Microsoft Azure

Within Microsoft Azure, we'll be looking at Azure Monitor. Azure Monitor aggregates and correlates data across Azure cloud resources.

Azure Monitor

Within Azure Monitor, there is an Activity Log feature that provides insight into cloud events. The activity log includes information such as when a resource is created or modified.

To launch Activity Log within Azure Monitor, take the following steps:

1. Navigate to the Microsoft Azure portal.

2. Select **Monitor** | **Activity log**.

As shown in *Figure 10.3*, the IT auditor can review what operations have been performed. We can see a virtual machine was created. During an assessment, an IT auditor could inquire whether **cloud_user_p_58a8eb** is authorized to create or make changes to infrastructure:

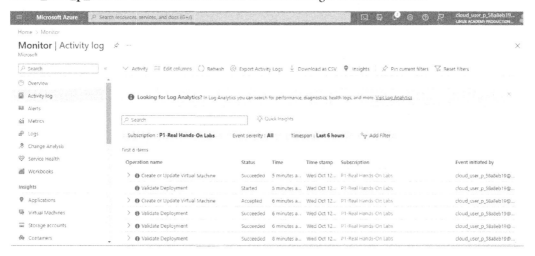

Figure 10.3 – Azure Monitor | Activity log

Another useful feature in Azure Monitor is **Change Analysis**. **Change Analysis** detects various types of changes, from the infrastructure layer through application deployment, as seen in *Figure 10.4*:

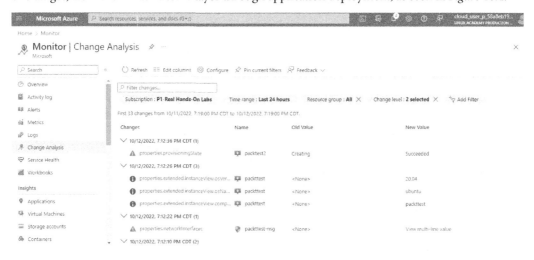

Figure 10.4 – Azure Monitor | Change Analysis

Now that we have looked at logging and auditing tools in Azure, let us look at tools an IT auditor can leverage in GCP.

GCP

Under GCP, we'll be looking at Cloud Logging. Google Cloud Logging provides log data that you can use to gain insights into GCP.

Cloud Logging

Logs Explorer is a feature in Google Cloud Logging that can be used to retrieve, view, and analyze log data.

To launch Logs Explorer within Cloud Logging, take the following steps:

- Navigate to the Google Cloud portal.

- Select **Logging | Logs Explorer**.

As shown in *Figure 10.5*, the **Logs Explorer** interface lets you query resource log data using resource types such as **VM Instance**, **GCE Firewall Rule**, and **GCE Network**:

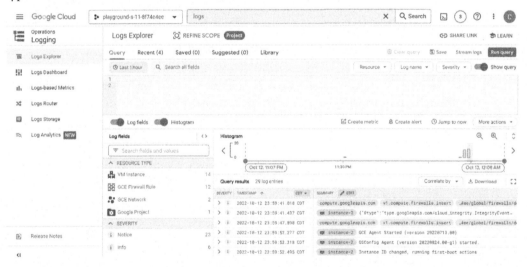

Figure 10.5 – GCP Logs Explorer

Now that we have performed a walk-through of basic audit and logging configurations let's look at assessing change management and configuration policies.

Assessing change management and configuration policies

As we covered in *Chapter 5, Financial Resource and Change Management Controls*, in the cloud, automation is embedded into change management processes. Leveraging automation reduces the opportunity for manual IT control failures. Organizations need to ensure that there are safeguards within the automated process that enforce separation of duties, that the automation workflows are regularly reviewed to ensure they adhere to change controls requirements, and that there is clear visibility and approval for those individuals with access to change the automation workflows or perform approvals as part of the workflows.

Each of the cloud providers has its own set of capabilities that can be used to manage changes. We will look at one capability provided by AWS named AWS Systems Manager | Change Manager.

Change Manager is a tool that can be utilized for managing changes to AWS resources.

To launch Change Manager within AWS Systems Manager, take the following steps:

1. Navigate to the AWS cloud portal.

2. Select **AWS Systems Manager | Change Management | Change Manager**.

    As you can see on the **Change Manager | Overview** tab, an organization can create custom templates or change requests, as seen in *Figure 10.6*:

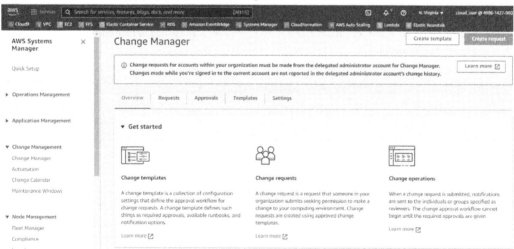

Figure 10.6 – AWS Systems Manager | Change Manager

3. When you launch **Change templates**, under the **Overview** tab, the organization can define required approvals, as seen in *Figure 10.7*. During an assessment, an IT auditor may want to verify that the approvers are actually authorized by the organization:

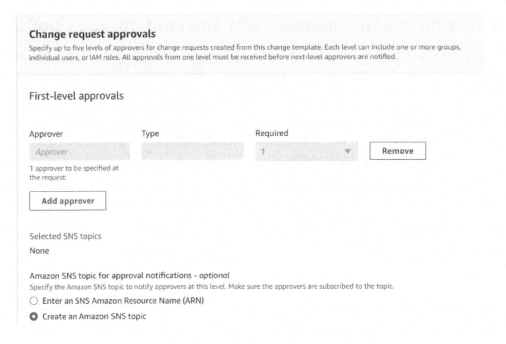

Change request approvals

Specify up to five levels of approvers for change requests created from this change template. Each level can include one or more groups, individual users, or IAM roles. All approvals from one level must be received before next-level approvers are notified.

First-level approvals

Approver	Type	Required	
Approver	-	1 ▼	Remove

1 approver to be specified at the request.

Add approver

Selected SNS topics
None

Amazon SNS topic for approval notifications - *optional*
Specify the Amazon SNS topic to notify approvers at this level. Make sure the approvers are subscribed to the topic.
○ Enter an SNS Amazon Resource Name (ARN)
◉ Create an Amazon SNS topic

Figure 10.7 – Change Manager | Change request approvals

4. On the **Change Manager | Requests** tab, an IT auditor can review approved or rejected requests, as seen in *Figure 10.8*:

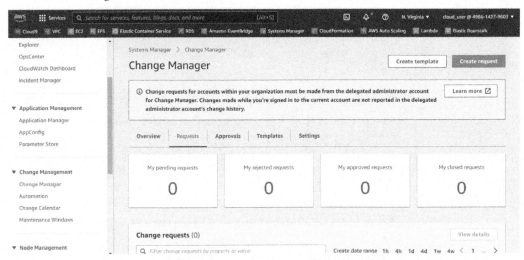

Figure 10.8 – Change Manager | Requests

Another key feature within AWS Systems Manager | Change Management, is **Automation**.

With **Automation**, an organization can define the actions that Systems Manager performs on its AWS resources when an automation runs. An automation template needs to be selected. The automation template defines the automation steps to be performed for a given workflow. In the following screenshot, we have selected **Patching workflows** to be automated. As you can see, there is an option to automate patches with a rollback in case of any issues:

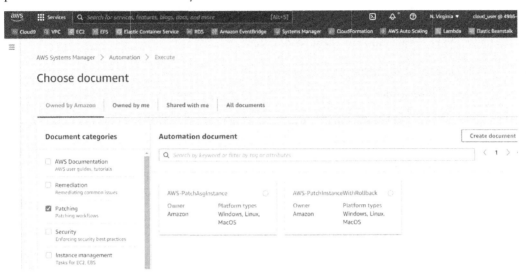

Figure 10.9 – AWS Systems Manager | Automation

AWS Systems Manager | Change Management, also offers a **Change Calendar** calendar with which an organization can schedule its changes, as seen in *Figure 10.10*:

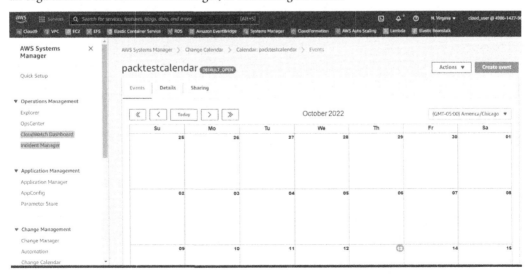

Figure 10.10 – AWS Systems Manager | Change Calendar

Azure Automation

Another tool that organizations use for change and configuration management is **Azure Automation**. Azure Automation allows an organization to automate changes in the Azure environment and across external systems.

You first need to create an Automation account before using Azure Automation.

To launch Azure Automation, use the following steps:

1. Navigate to the Microsoft Azure portal.

2. Select **Automation**.

A useful feature for an IT auditor under **Configuration Management** is **Change tracking**. **Change tracking** allows you to track infrastructure changes. The **Overview** tab can also provide a summary of the status of changes, as seen in *Figure 10.11*:

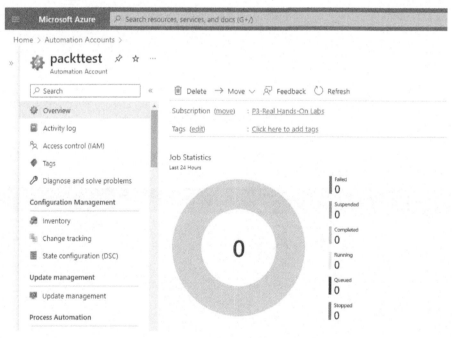

Figure 10.11 – Azure Automation Configuration Management | Change tracking

Another useful feature in Azure Automation is **Activity log**, as seen in *Figure 10.12*. **Activity log** displays the status of operations performed, as well as who initiated the event. This is very useful information for an IT auditor:

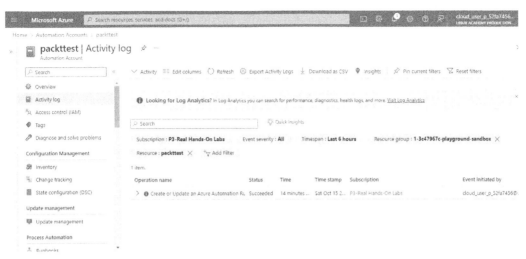

Figure 10.12 – Azure Automation | Activity log

Another tool that can be used to manage changes in the cloud is Terraform.

Terraform

Terraform is an open source, **infrastructure as code** (**IaC**) software created by HashiCorp. Many organizations utilize Terraform **open source software** (**OSS**) to help provision and configure infrastructure in the cloud. To be familiar with how an organization can use Terraform OSS to provision resources in AWS, we will provide an example. We first need to install various components, including Terraform OSS.

The first step in the Terraform workflow is to write your Terraform configuration. Here is a snippet of our sample code:

```
# Generating Access Key and Secret Key
provider "aws" {
 region     = "us-east-1"
 access_key = "AKIAWWE6G4DQY7JAARQE"
 secret_key = "xRG37djD/WIsjsOQ90RmwT5e/tkgNHqXvU25eqKO"
}

terraform {
  required_providers {
    aws = {
      source = "hashicorp/aws"
    }
  }
}

resource "aws_instance" "i-0e117de41c0ee94bd" {
  ami           = var.ami
  instance_type = var.instance_type
```

Figure 10.13 – Terraform configuration

The second step is to prepare the code for download by running the `terraform init` command.

```
PS C:\users\antagonist\documents\aws> terraform init

Initializing the backend...

Initializing provider plugins...
- Finding latest version of hashicorp/aws...
- Installing hashicorp/aws v4.35.0...
- Installed hashicorp/aws v4.35.0 (signed by HashiCorp)

Terraform has created a lock file .terraform.lock.hcl to record the provider
selections it made above. Include this file in your version control repository
so that Terraform can guarantee to make the same selections by default when
you run "terraform init" in the future.

Terraform has been successfully initialized!

You may now begin working with Terraform. Try running "terraform plan" to see
any changes that are required for your infrastructure. All Terraform commands
should now work.

If you ever set or change modules or backend configuration for Terraform,
rerun this command to reinitialize your working directory. If you forget, other
commands will detect it and remind you to do so if necessary.
PS C:\users\antagonist\documents\aws>
```

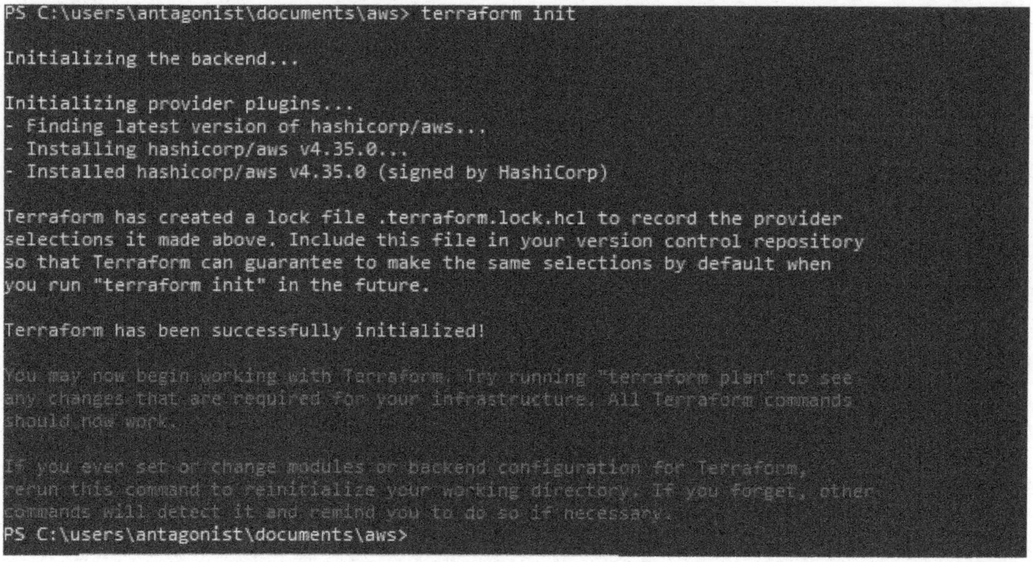

Figure 10.14 – The terraform init command

This command initializes the environment and downloads the AWS provider. The AWS provider is a plugin that Terraform relies on to interact with remote systems.

The third step is to review the changes using the `terraform plan` command, as seen in *Figure 10.15*. This command creates an execution plan for the environment and confirms no bugs are found.

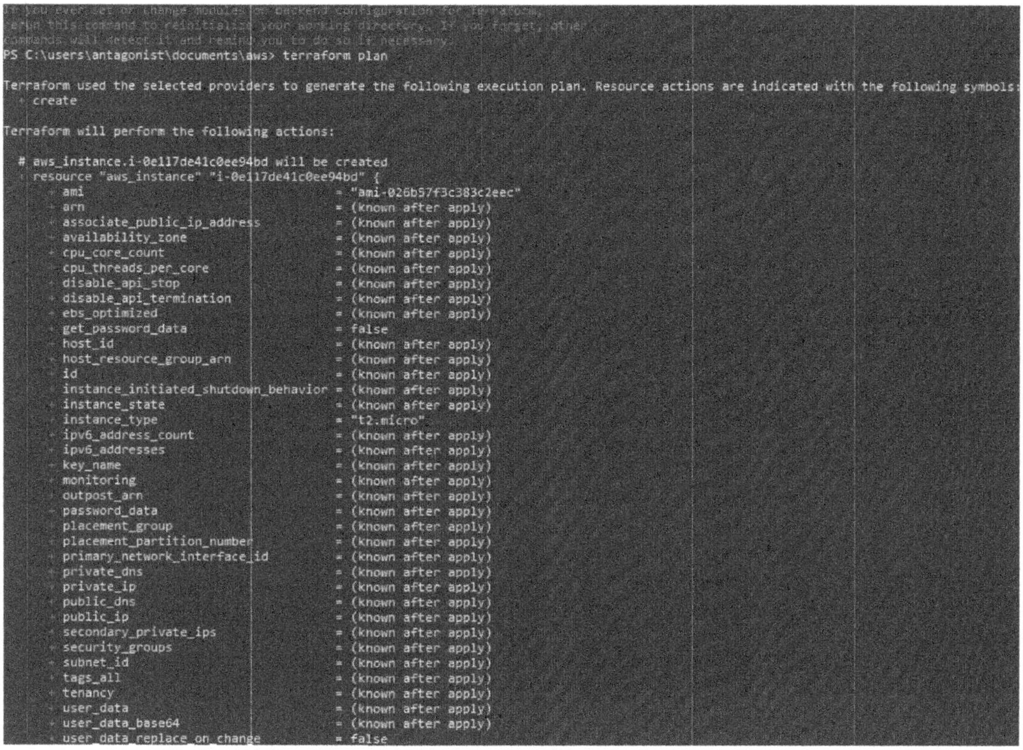

Figure 10.15 – The terraform plan command

The last step is to accept the changes and apply them against the organization's infrastructure using the `terraform apply` command, as seen in *Figure 10.16*:

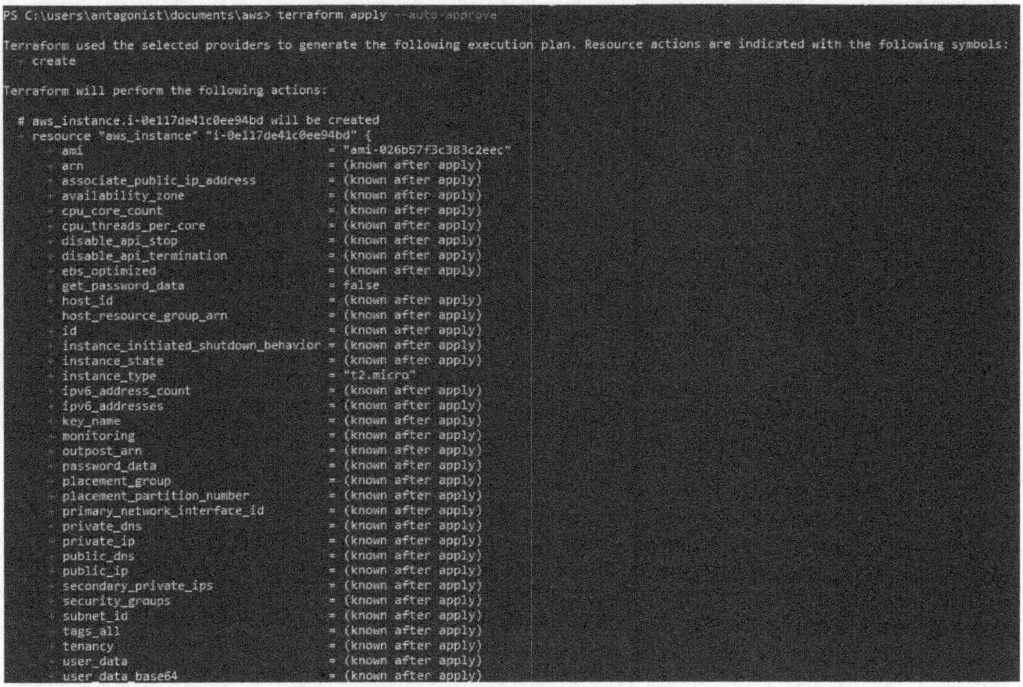

Figure 10.16 – The terraform apply command

One thing you should have noticed is that our Terraform code contains hardcoded credentials. Software developers with poor security practices often embed credentials into their code to save time during the code development process. This poses a security risk to the organization, as code containing credentials may then be inadvertently uploaded into a public repository service. In a real-life scenario, an IT auditor should document the hardcoded credentials as a finding.

An IT auditor can utilize Terraform Enterprise to monitor changes in an organization's cloud. Once we have installed Terraform Enterprise, we will need to log in with an API token, as seen in *Figure 10.17*:

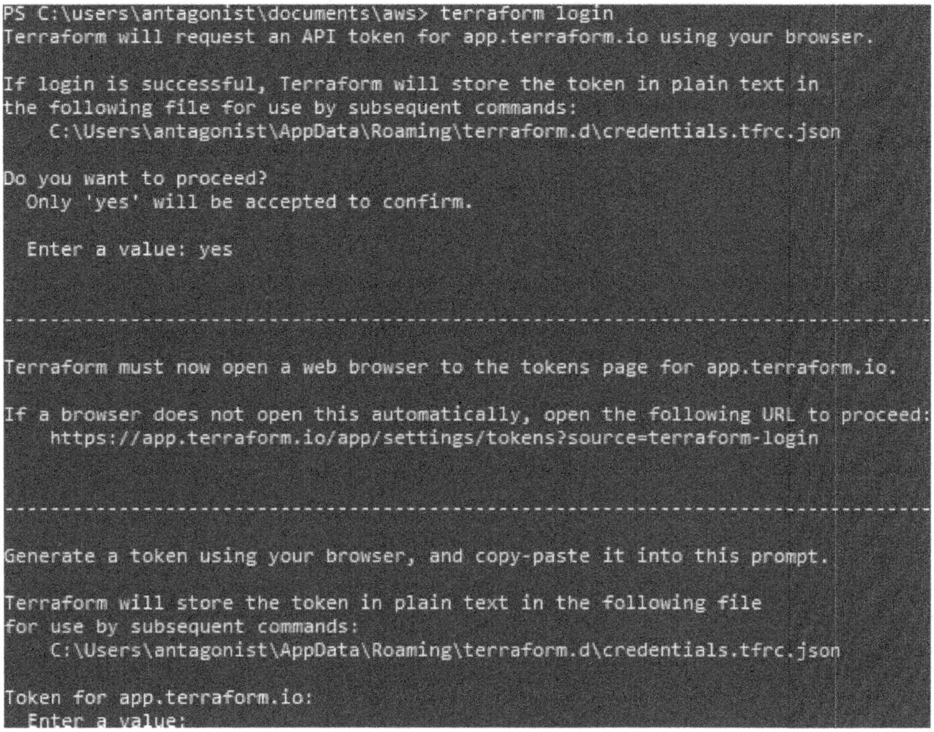

```
PS C:\users\antagonist\documents\aws> terraform login
Terraform will request an API token for app.terraform.io using your browser.

If login is successful, Terraform will store the token in plain text in
the following file for use by subsequent commands:
    C:\Users\antagonist\AppData\Roaming\terraform.d\credentials.tfrc.json

Do you want to proceed?
  Only 'yes' will be accepted to confirm.

  Enter a value: yes

----------------------------------------------------------------------------

Terraform must now open a web browser to the tokens page for app.terraform.io.

If a browser does not open this automatically, open the following URL to proceed:
    https://app.terraform.io/app/settings/tokens?source=terraform-login

----------------------------------------------------------------------------

Generate a token using your browser, and copy-paste it into this prompt.

Terraform will store the token in plain text in the following file
for use by subsequent commands:
    C:\Users\antagonist\AppData\Roaming\terraform.d\credentials.tfrc.json

Token for app.terraform.io:
  Enter a value:
```

Figure 10.17 – Terraform Enterprise login with API token

Once logged in, the IT auditor can run some commands. One useful command is the following:

```
terraform graph
```

The terraform graph command is used to generate a visual representation of infrastructure defined in Terraform code in a diagram, as seen in *Figure 10.18*:

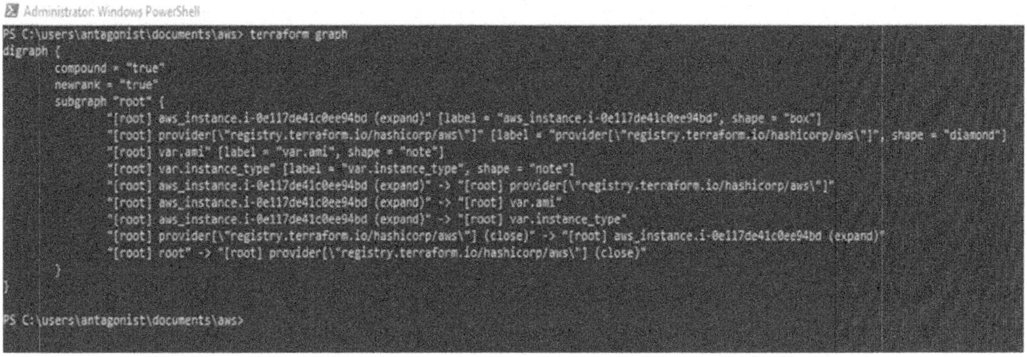

```
Administrator: Windows PowerShell
PS C:\users\antagonist\documents\aws> terraform graph
digraph {
    compound = "true"
    newrank = "true"
    subgraph "root" {
        "[root] aws_instance.i-0e117de41c0ee94bd (expand)" [label = "aws_instance.i-0e117de41c0ee94bd", shape = "box"]
        "[root] provider[\"registry.terraform.io/hashicorp/aws\"]" [label = "provider[\"registry.terraform.io/hashicorp/aws\"]", shape = "diamond"]
        "[root] var.ami" [label = "var.ami", shape = "note"]
        "[root] var.instance_type" [label = "var.instance_type", shape = "note"]
        "[root] aws_instance.i-0e117de41c0ee94bd (expand)" -> "[root] provider[\"registry.terraform.io/hashicorp/aws\"]"
        "[root] aws_instance.i-0e117de41c0ee94bd (expand)" -> "[root] var.ami"
        "[root] aws_instance.i-0e117de41c0ee94bd (expand)" -> "[root] var.instance_type"
        "[root] provider[\"registry.terraform.io/hashicorp/aws\"] (close)" -> "[root] aws_instance.i-0e117de41c0ee94bd (expand)"
        "[root] root" -> "[root] provider[\"registry.terraform.io/hashicorp/aws\"] (close)"
    }
}
PS C:\users\antagonist\documents\aws>
```

Figure 10.18 – The terraform graph command

You can use various utilities, such as `graphviz`, to output the graph. An example of a graph copied from the HashiCorp website can be seen in *Figure 10.19*. The graph is very useful to an IT auditor as it gives a representation of what the infrastructure environment looks like:

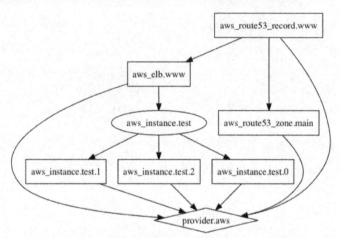

Figure 10.19 – Example of a Terraform graph output

In addition, Terraform Enterprise has another product named **Sentinel**. Sentinel contains the functionality to ensure an organization's code against infrastructure aligns with specific policies. This idea is called **Compliance as Code** or **Policy as Code**.

Compliance as code refers to using software code for automating the implementation, validation, and management of the required compliance standards that an organization needs to be compliant with.

With compliance as code, controls and policies are agreed to and defined in a tool such as Sentinel. Sentinel constantly monitors the applications for changes. Any change is evaluated and checked according to the compliance rules. If Sentinel detects an application violating a compliance rule, it triggers another action or modifies the application back to a compliant state.

As an example of compliance as code, imagine a company that is subject to **Payment Card Industry** (**PCI**) regulations. One of the PCI regulations, Requirement 4, mandates an organization to *protect cardholder data with strong cryptography during transmission over open, public networks*. The organization has a standard to implement **Transport Layer Security** (**TLS**) 1.2 protocol or newer for data in transit, which is a strong cryptographic standard.

The organization can then write a policy in Sentinel that evaluates whether there are any protocols older than TLS 1.2 running on the organization's systems. If a violation is found, Sentinel triggers an alert allowing for manual or automated remediation to occur. Next, let's look at an open-source tool an IT auditor can leverage to assess identity changes.

Policy Sentry

Another tool that an IT auditor can use to monitor changes in **Identity and Access Management (IAM)** is an open source solution named **Policy Sentry**. Policy Sentry is a great tool to manage IAM entities. Policy Sentry also has functionality as an audit and analysis database. It compiles database tables based on AWS IAM documentation. Policy Sentry relies on a JSON file that contains all of the data from the actions, resources, and condition keys documentation hosted by AWS. Policy Sentry supports querying that database through the **Command Line Interface (CLI)**.

To get started with Policy Sentry, take the following steps:

1. Download and install Python: `https://pypi.org/project/policy-sentry/`.

2. Install Policy Sentry using the following command, as seen in *Figure 10.20*:

```
pip3 install --user policy_sentry
```

Figure 10.20 – Policy Sentry installation on the command line

3. Next, we connect to the AWS CLI through the `aws configure` command, as seen in *Figure 10.21*:

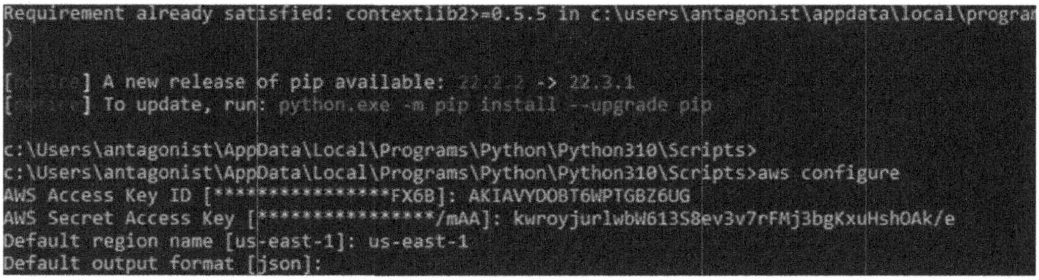

Figure 10.21 – Connecting to AWS through the CLI

I will demonstrate a couple of commands an IT auditor can execute to query the AWS IAM database. The first command is the following:

```
policy_sentry query action-table --service all --access-level
permissions-management
```

This command gets a list of all IAM actions across all services that have permissions-management access, as seen in *Figure 10.22*:

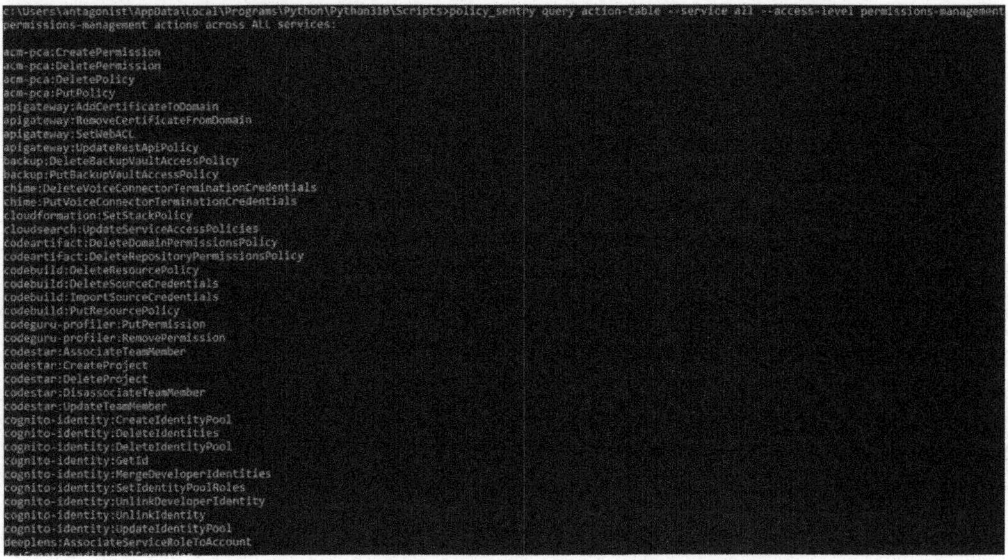

Figure 10.22 – The policy_sentry query command, example one

Now let's use the following command:

```
policy_sentry query action-table --service ram --access-level
permissions-management
```

This gets a list of all IAM actions under the RAM service that have the `permissions-management` access level, as seen in *Figure 10.23*:

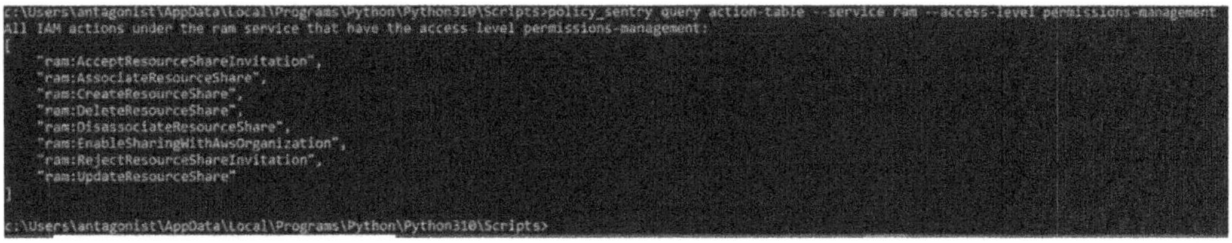

Figure 10.23 – The policy_sentry query command, example two

Next, we will look at tools that an IT auditor can leverage for monitoring in the cloud.

Assessing monitoring and alerting policies

As we covered in *Chapter 7*, *Tools for Monitoring and Assessing*, cloud monitoring is a method of reviewing, observing, and managing the health and security of a cloud. Using monitoring tools, organizations can proactively monitor their cloud environments to identify issues before they become security risks. AWS, Azure, and GCP offer native solutions that an IT auditor can leverage to monitor and assess cloud environments. Let us start by looking at AWS.

AWS

The first monitoring tool an IT auditor can leverage in AWS is Amazon CloudWatch.

Amazon CloudWatch

Amazon CloudWatch is an AWS native monitoring and management service that is designed for the purpose of monitoring the services and resources that are used. Amazon CloudWatch can be used to collect and track metrics, monitor log files, and set alarms, among many other functions. To review these findings, we will need to perform the following steps to launch Amazon CloudWatch, as seen in *Figure 10.24*:

1. Navigate to the AWS Management Console.
2. Select **CloudWatch | Dashboards**.

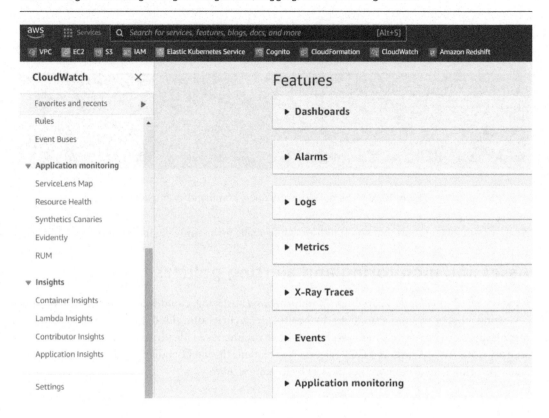

Figure 10.24 – Amazon CloudWatch

Under **Dashboards**, an IT auditor can create custom dashboards. Under **Automatic dashboards**, you can pick further options. In this scenario, we have picked **Billing** and **CloudWatch Logs** to add to our custom **packtestdashboard** dashboard, as seen in *Figure 10.25*:

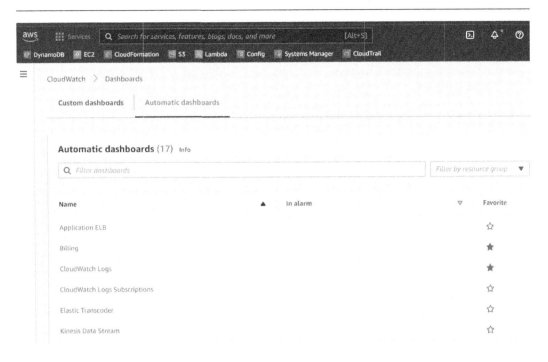

Figure 10.25 – CloudWatch | Dashboards

You can see the dashboard displays billing information for different services as well as CloudWatch logs, as seen in *Figure 10.26*:

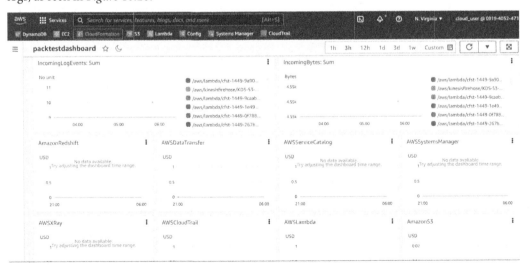

Figure 10.26 – CloudWatch | packtestdashboard

Amazon CloudWatch also has a feature named CloudWatch Alarms that an IT auditor can leverage. CloudWatch Alarms has the functionality to monitor defined metric changes that have crossed a specified threshold. To launch **Alarms** within Amazon CloudWatch, as seen in *Figure 10.27*, perform the following steps:

1. Navigate to the AWS Management Console.

2. Select **CloudWatch | Alarms**.

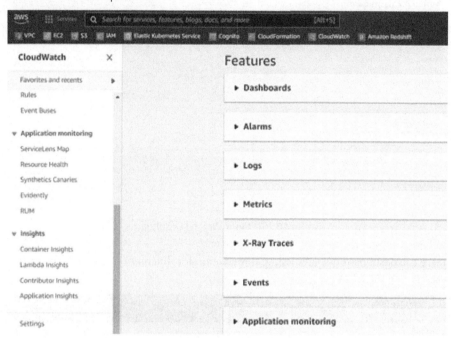

Figure 10.27 – CloudWatch | Alarms

An IT auditor can create an alarm that triggers when a certain metric changes. I will provide examples of two rules an IT auditor can create.

> **Note**
>
> For detailed instructions on creating CloudWatch alarms, go to:
>
> - `https://docs.aws.amazon.com/eventbridge/latest/userguide/eb-get-started.html`.
>
> - `https://docs.aws.amazon.com/AmazonCloudWatch/latest/monitoring/AlarmThatSendsEmail.html`.

In our first example, we select a metric that triggers an alarm when an AWS **Simple Storage Service (S3) bucket permission** changes, as seen in *Figure 10.28*. An IT auditor could use this rule to monitor changes in S3 buckets. They could also use this rule to look for misconfigured S3 buckets that allow public access. This is one of the most common security misconfiguration risks within AWS.

Figure 10.28 – Amazon S3 Bucket Permissions metric

In our second example, we can select the **Large Number of EC2 Security Group Rules Applied to an Instance** metric to trigger an alarm, as seen in *Figure 10.29*:

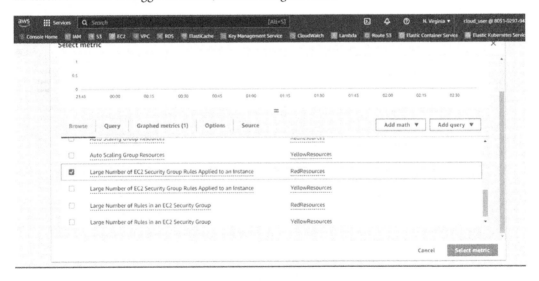

Figure 10.29 – The Large Number of EC2 Security Group Rules Applied to an Instance metric

An IT auditor could use this rule to monitor for malicious activity or insider threat activity where a user would add security groups to an EC2 instance, bypassing the regular process.

Now that we have looked at monitoring tools in AWS, let us look at tools we can leverage in Azure.

Azure

One of the tools an IT auditor can leverage for monitoring in Azure is Azure Monitor.

Azure Monitor

As we mentioned earlier, Azure Monitor aggregates and correlates data across Azure cloud resources. Within Azure Monitor, there is a useful feature named **Change Analysis**. Change Analysis detects and helps monitor various types of changes, from the infrastructure layer through application deployment, as seen in *Figure 10.30*:

To launch Change Analysis within Azure Monitor, perform the following steps:

1.   Navigate to the Microsoft Azure portal.

2.   Select **Monitor | Change Analysis**.

Figure 10.30 – Azure Monitor | Change Analysis

Azure Monitor also has the ability to trigger alerts. This can be done through the configuration of alert rules. Perform the following steps to launch **Alerts** within Azure Monitor, as seen in *Figure 10.31*:

1.   Navigate to the Microsoft Azure portal.

2.   Select **Monitor | Alerts**.

An IT auditor can set up alerts for various conditions. In this example, we are setting up alerts for **All Administrative Operations** over the last week, as seen in *Figure 10.31*:

Figure 10.31 – Azure Monitor | Alert rules

This type of rule can be useful to an IT auditor to monitor administrative operations and ensure they are authorized.

For illustration, we went ahead and performed some administrative operations. The alerts were triggered, as seen in *Figure 10.32*. The IT auditor can perform further investigations on the alerts:

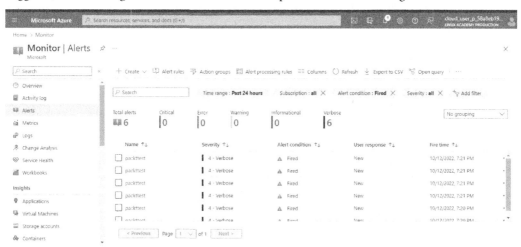

Figure 10.32 – Azure Monitor | Alerts

In addition, an IT auditor can create an activity log alert rule from the **Activity log** plane. The **Activity log** plane contains information about Azure resource changes. Use the following steps to launch **Activity log** within Azure Monitor, as seen in *Figure 10.33*:

1. Navigate to the Microsoft Azure portal.

2.   Select **Monitor** | **Activity log**.

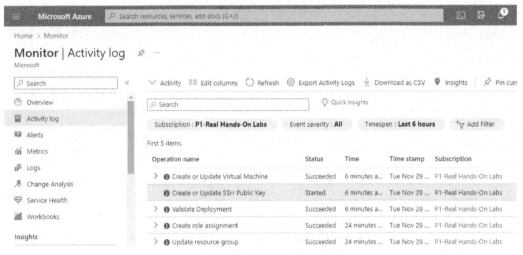

Figure 10.33 – Azure Monitor | Activity log

To create an alert, select any activity within **Activity log**. In this example, I selected one of the events, **Create or Update Network Security Group**, as seen in *Figure 10.34*:

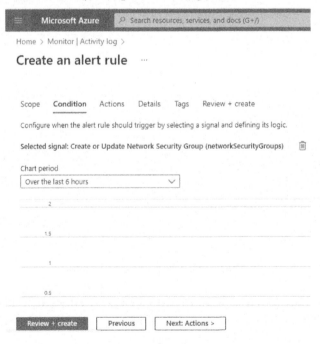

Figure 10.34 – Alert Rule: Create or Update Network Security Group

Now that we have looked at monitoring tools in Azure, let us look at tools we can leverage in GCP.

GCP

One of the tools an IT auditor can leverage to perform monitoring in GCP is **Google Cloud Monitoring**.

Google Cloud Monitoring

Google Cloud Monitoring collects metrics of Google Cloud resources. IT auditors can leverage Google Cloud Monitoring to gain real-time visibility into GCP, as seen in *Figure 10.35*. To launch the **Monitoring** explorer, take the following steps:

1. Navigate to GCP.
2. Select **Monitoring | Dashboards**.

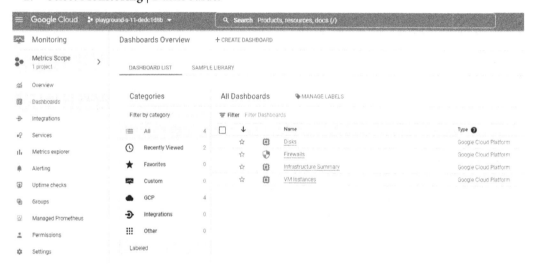

Figure 10.35 – Google Cloud Monitoring

The **Dashboards** feature within Google Cloud Monitoring provides dashboards of various resources, such as **Disks**, **Firewalls**, **Infrastructure Summary**, and **VM instances**. As an example of an assessment, let us review the **FIREWALLS** dashboard, as seen in *Figure 10.36*:

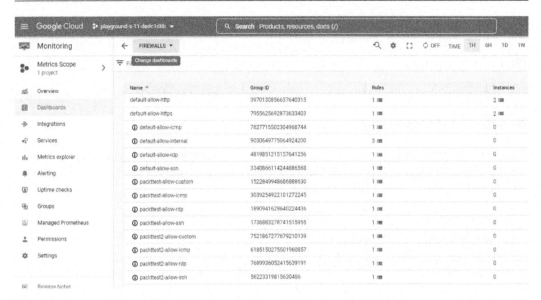

Figure 10.36 – Google Cloud Monitoring | Dashboards

If we dig deeper, we can note that there is an ingress/inbound rule that allows traffic from any IP address on the internet (0.0.0.0/0) to port TCP 22 (SSH), as seen in *Figure 10.37*:

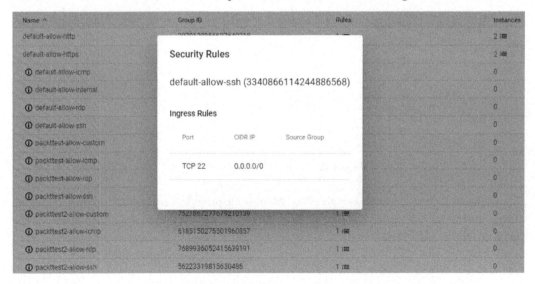

Figure 10.37 – Security Rules

This particular rule should pique an IT auditor's interest as port 22 is a network protocol that has system administrator capability. Attackers can use various brute force techniques to gain access to GCP resources using remote server administration ports, such as 22; therefore the IT auditor should inquire about the business need to have port 22 open to anyone on the internet.

Another useful feature of Google Cloud Monitoring is **Alerting**. The **Alerting** feature allows you to trigger an alert based on a predefined metric, as seen in *Figure 10.38*. An IT auditor can create an alerting policy so that they are notified when the performance of a resource doesn't meet the criteria defined. To launch the **Cloud Monitoring** explorer, take the following steps:

1.   Navigate to the Google Cloud portal.

2.   Select **Monitoring | Alerting**.

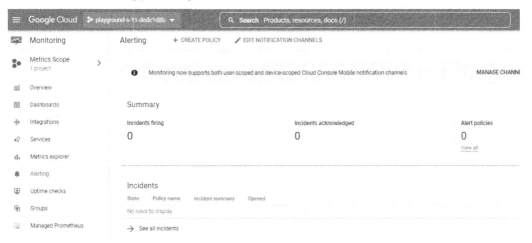

Figure 10.38 – Google Cloud Monitoring | Alerting

As an example, we can add a metric, such as **Audited Resource**, as seen in *Figure 10.39*:

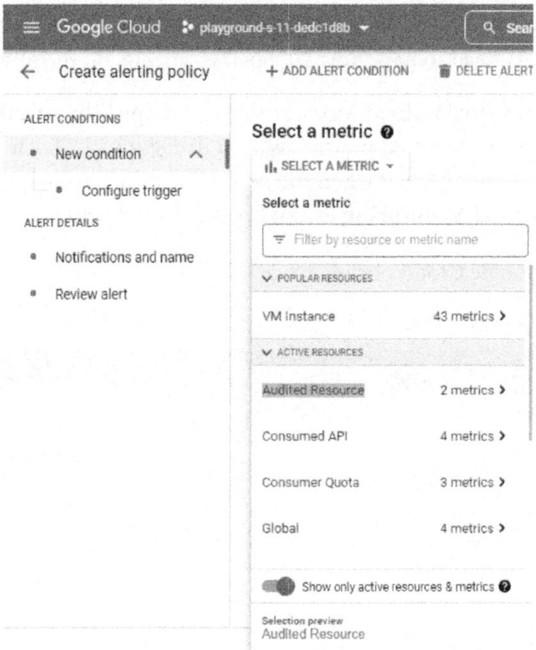

Figure 10.39 – Create alerting policy | Audited Resource metric

We've now completed our walk-through of monitoring and alerting policies within AWS, Azure, and GCP. IT auditors should now have a repertoire of toolsets they can use to effectively perform their audits in the cloud.

Summary

In this chapter, we performed a walk-through of change management, logging, and monitoring policies for the AWS, Azure, and GCP platforms. We specifically covered how to assess change management controls; audit and logging configurations, and change management and configuration policies. Finally, we reviewed how an IT auditor can leverage monitoring and alerting policies.

We have reached the end of the book. Well done! I want to thank you for sharing this journey with us. The book has provided a roadmap for how to build and execute effective cloud auditing plans for AWS, Azure, and GCP. We hope this will be a valuable resource that you can utilize, and that it enables you to secure and add real value to the organizations that you audit.

Index

V

W

Packt.com

Subscribe to our online digital library for full access to over 7,000 books and videos, as well as industry leading tools to help you plan your personal development and advance your career. For more information, please visit our website.

Why subscribe?

- Spend less time learning and more time coding with practical eBooks and Videos from over 4,000 industry professionals

- Improve your learning with Skill Plans built especially for you

- Get a free eBook or video every month

- Fully searchable for easy access to vital information

- Copy and paste, print, and bookmark content

Did you know that Packt offers eBook versions of every book published, with PDF and ePub files available? You can upgrade to the eBook version at packt.com and as a print book customer, you are entitled to a discount on the eBook copy. Get in touch with us at customercare@packtpub.com for more details.

At www.packt.com, you can also read a collection of free technical articles, sign up for a range of free newsletters, and receive exclusive discounts and offers on Packt books and eBooks.

Other Books You May Enjoy

If you enjoyed this book, you may be interested in these other books by Packt:

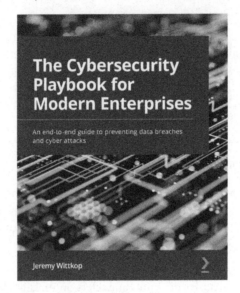

The Cybersecurity Playbook for Modern Enterprises

Jeremy Wittkop

ISBN: 9781803248639

- Understand the macro-implications of cyber attacks
- Identify malicious users and prevent harm to your organization
- Find out how ransomware attacks take place
- Work with emerging techniques for improving security profiles
- Explore identity and access management and endpoint security
- Get to grips with building advanced automation models
- Build effective training programs to protect against hacking techniques
- Discover best practices to help you and your family stay safe online

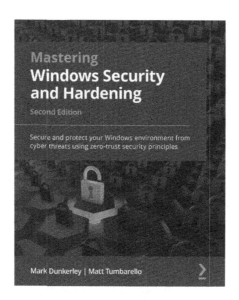

Mastering Windows Security and Hardening - Second Edition

Mark Dunkerley, Matt Tumbarello

ISBN: 9781803236544

- Build a multi-layered security approach using zero-trust concepts
- Explore best practices to implement security baselines successfully
- Get to grips with virtualization and networking to harden your devices
- Discover the importance of identity and access management
- Explore Windows device administration and remote management
- Become an expert in hardening your Windows infrastructure
- Audit, assess, and test to ensure controls are successfully applied and enforced
- Monitor and report activities to stay on top of vulnerabilities

Packt is searching for authors like you

If you're interested in becoming an author for Packt, please visit `authors.packtpub.com` and apply today. We have worked with thousands of developers and tech professionals, just like you, to help them share their insight with the global tech community. You can make a general application, apply for a specific hot topic that we are recruiting an author for, or submit your own idea.

Share your thoughts

Now you've finished *Cloud Auditing Best Practices*, we'd love to hear your thoughts! Scan the QR code below to go straight to the Amazon review page for this book and share your feedback or leave a review on the site that you purchased it from.

`https://packt.link/r/1803243775`

Your review is important to us and the tech community and will help us make sure we're delivering excellent quality content.

Download a free PDF copy of this book

Thanks for purchasing this book!

Do you like to read on the go but are unable to carry your print books everywhere? Is your eBook purchase not compatible with the device of your choice?

Don't worry, now with every Packt book you get a DRM-free PDF version of that book at no cost.

Read anywhere, any place, on any device. Search, copy, and paste code from your favorite technical books directly into your application.

The perks don't stop there, you can get exclusive access to discounts, newsletters, and great free content in your inbox daily

Follow these simple steps to get the benefits:

1. Scan the QR code or visit the link below

https://packt.link/free-ebook/9781803243771

2. Submit your proof of purchase
3. That's it! We'll send your free PDF and other benefits to your email directly

11507657R00149